THE SOUND OF LIBERATING TRUTH

Buddhist-Christian Dialogues

in Honor of Frederick J. Streng

CURZON CRITICAL STUDIES IN BUDDHISM

General Editors:
Charles S. Prebish and Damien Keown

The Curzon Critical Studies in Buddhism Series is a comprehensive study of the Buddhist tradition. The series explores this complex and extensive tradition from a variety of perspectives, using a range of different methodologies.

The Series is diverse in its focus, including historical studies, textual translations and commentaries, sociological investigations, bibliographic studies, and considerations of religious practice as an expression of Buddhism's integral religiosity. It also presents materials on modern intellectual historical studies, including the role of Buddhist thought and scholarship in a contemporary, critical context and in the light of current social issues. The series is expansive and imaginative in scope, spanning more than two and a half millennia of Buddhist history. It is receptive to all research works that inform and advance our knowledge and understanding of the Buddhist tradition. The series maintains the highest standards of scholarship and promotes the application of innovative methodologies and research methods.

THE REFLEXIVE NATURE OF AWARENESS
A Tibetan Madhyamaka Defence
Paul Williams

BUDDHISM AND HUMAN RIGHTS
Edited by Damien Keown, Charles Prebish, Wayne Husted

ALTRUISM AND REALITY
Studies in the Philosophy of the Bodhicaryāvatāra
Paul Williams

WOMEN IN THE FOOTSTEPS OF THE BUDDHA
Kathryn R. Blackstone

THE RESONANCE OF EMPTINESS
A Buddhist Inspiration for Contemporary Psychotherapy
Gay Watson

IMAGING WISDOM
Seeing and Knowing in the Art of Indian Buddhism
Jacob N. Kinnard

AMERICAN BUDDHISM
Methods and Findings in Recent Scholarship
Edited by Duncan Ryuken Williams and Christopher Queen

PAIN AND ITS ENDING
The Four Noble Truths in the Theravāda Buddhist Canon
Carol S. Anderson

THE SOUND OF LIBERATING TRUTH
Buddhist-Christian Dialogues in Honor of Frederick J. Streng
Edited by Sallie B. King and Paul O. Ingram

THE SOUND OF LIBERATING TRUTH

Buddhist-Christian Dialogues

in Honor of Frederick J. Streng

edited by

Sallie B. King
and
Paul O. Ingram

CURZON

First Published in 1999
by Curzon Press
15 The Quadrant, Richmond
Surrey, TW9 1BP

Editorial Matter © 1999 Paul O. Ingram and Sallie B. King

Typeset in Sabon by LaserScript Ltd, Mitcham
Printed and bound in Great Britain by
TJ International, Padstow, Cornwall

British Library Cataloguing in Publication Data
A catalogue record of this book is available from the British Library

Library of Congress in Publication Data
A catalogue record for this book has been requested

ISBN 0–7007–1121–X

CONTENTS

Contributors   viii

Introduction: What is the Sound of Liberating Truth?
Remembering Fred Streng (1933–1993)   xi
Paul O. Ingram

Prologue   xvii
Paul O. Ingram and Sallie B. King

PART ONE: Interreligious Dialogue   1

Chapter 1: Buddhist Interreligious Dialogue: To Build a
            Global Community   3
            David W. Chappell

Chapter 2: Response to David Chappell   36
            Winston L. King

Chapter 3: Interreligious Dialogue   41
            Winston L. King

Chapter 4: Response to Winston King   57
            David Chappell

PART TWO: Ultimate Reality 63

Chapter 5: 'In the Beginning ... God': A Christian's View of
Ultimate Reality 65
Bonnie Thurston

Chapter 6: Response to Bonnie Thurston's '"In the Beginning ...
God": A Christian's View of Ultimate Reality' 78
Malcolm David Eckel

Chapter 7: The Concept of the Ultimate in Madhyamaka
Thought: In Memory of Frederick Streng 84
Malcolm David Eckel

Chapter 8: Response to: 'The Concept of the Ultimate in
Madhyamaka Thought' 101
Bonnie Thurston

PART THREE: Nature and Ecology 105

Chapter 9: The Buddhist Conception of an Ecological Self 107
Alan Sponberg

Chapter 10: Response to Alan Sponberg's 'The Buddhist
Conception of an Ecological Self' 128
Paula M. Cooey

Chapter 11: Creation, Redemption, and the Realization of the
Material Order 133
Paula M. Cooey

Chapter 12: Creation, Redemption, and the Realization of the
Material Order: A Buddhist Response 149
Alan Sponberg

PART FOUR: Social and Political Issues of Liberation 157

Chapter 13: Buddhism and Social Engagement 159
Sallie B. King

Chapter 14: Some Questions About the World 181
John P. Keenan

Contents

Chapter 15: The Mind of Wisdom and Justice in the
Letter of James 186
John P. Keenan

Chapter 16: Response to John Keenan 200
Sallie B. King

PART FIVE: Ultimate Transformation or Liberation 205

Chapter 17: Under the Bodhi Tree: An Idealized Paradigm
of Buddhist Transformation and Liberation 207 ,
Thomas P. Kasulis

Chapter 18: Nailed to a Tree: An Idealized Paradigm of
Buddhist Transformation and Liberation 220
Ruben L. F. Habito

Chapter 19: The Resurrection of the Dead, and Life Everlasting:
From a Futuristic to a Realized Christianity 223
Ruben L. F. Habito

Chapter 20: The Momentous and the Momentary 239
Thomas P. Kasulis

PART SIX: Epilogues 245

Chapter 21: A Buddhist Epilogue 247
Taitetsu Unno

Chapter 22: A Christian Epilogue 265
John B. Cobb, Jr.

Index 272

CONTRIBUTORS

David W. Chappell, Professor of Religion at the University of Hawaii, was the founding editor of the annual journal *Buddhist-Christian Studies* and past President of the Society for Buddhist-Christian Studies. He is author of *T'ien-t'ai Buddhism: An Outline of the Fourfold Teachings* and editor of *Buddhist and Taoist Practice in Medieval Chinese Society.* He is now working on the relationship of Buddhism to contemporary society.

John B. Cobb, Jr. was born in Japan of Methodist missionary parents. His education was chiefly at the University of Chicago Divinity School. Most of his teaching career was spent in Claremont at the School of Theology and the Graduate School. He retired in 1990. As a Christian theologian he has been involved in Buddhist-Christian dialogue, working especially with Masao Abe in the organization of a theological encounter group and subsequently in the Society for Buddhist-Christian Studies. His book, *Beyond Dialogue: Toward a Mutual Transformation of Christianity and Buddhism*, contributes to the discussion.

Paula Cooey is Professor of Religion at Trinity University, San Antonio, Texas. She is the author of numerous books and articles. Her most recent books are *Family, Freedom & Faith: Building Community Today* (Westminster-John Knox Press, 1988) and *Religious Imagination and the Body: A Feminist Perspective* (Oxford University Press, 1996).

Malcolm David Eckel is Associate Professor of Religion and Associate Director of the Division of Religious and Theological Studies at Boston University. His most recent book is *To See the Buddha: A Philosopher's Quest for the Meaning of Emptiness.*

Ruben L. F. Habito is Professor of World Religions and Spirituality at Perkins School of Theology at Southern Methodist University. He taught at Sophia University for twelve years prior to his coming to SMU. His publications include: *Original Enlightenment: Tendai Hongaku Doctrine and Japanese Buddhism* (International Institute for Buddhist Studies), *Healing Breath: Zen Spirituality for a Wounded Earth* (Orbis Books), *Total Libertion: Zen Spirituality and the Social Dimension* (Orbis Books), as well as more than ten books in Japanese.

Paul O. Ingram is Professor of Religion at Pacific Lutheran University, Tacoma, Washington. He is the author of *The Modern Buddhist-Christian Dialogue* (Edwin Mellon) and *Wrestling With the Ox: A Theology of Religious Experience* (Continuum). He co-edited *Buddhist-Christian Dialogue: Essays in Mutual Transformation* with Frederick J. Streng (University of Hawaii).

Thomas P. Kasulis is Professor of Comparative Studies at Ohio State University. He is the author of *Zen Action/ Zen Person* (University of Hawaii) as well as numerous other publications on Japanese philosophy and religion.

John P. Keenan is an Episcopal Priest, a former Resident Scholar at the Nanzan Institute for Religion and Culture in Japan, and Professor of Religion at Middlebury College. He is the author of *The Meaning of Christ: A Mahayana Theology* (SUNY Press).

Sallie B. King is Professor in the Department of Philosophy and Religion at James Madison University, Harrisonburg, Virginia. She is the author of *Buddha Nature* and *Journey in Search of the Way*, both published by SUNY Press, and, with Christopher S. Queen, the co-editor of *Engaged Buddhism: Buddhist Liberation Movements in Asia*, also published by SUNY Press.

Winston L. King is Emeritus Professor of Religion at Vanderbilt University. He also taught with distinction at Grinnell College and Colorado State University. He is the author of nine books, the most recent of which are *Death Was His Koan* (1986) and *Zen and the Way of the Sword* (1993), well as numerous essays and articles.

Alan Sponberg taught Buddhist studies at Princeton and Stanford universities for eleven years before moving to the University of Montana where he is Professor of Asian Religion and Philosophy. His research interests focus on cross-cultural transformations of Buddhism, both historical and contemporary, and his publications include *Maitreya, the Future Buddha*.

Bonnie Thurston holds a BA from Bethany College, and MA and PhD degrees from the University of Virginia. She has done post-doctoral work in New Testament at Harvard Divinity School, Eberhard Karls Universitat (Tuebingen, Germany), and the Ecole Biblique (Jerusalem) and currently teaches New Testament at Pittsburgh Theological Seminary. She is the author of six books and over sixty articles.

Taitetsu Unno retired in 1998 from his position as the Jill Ker Conway Professor of Religion and East Asian Studies at Smith College in Northampton, Massachusetts He is a leading scholar of Shin Buddhism. His revised second edition of *Tannisho: A Shin Buddhist Classic* appeared in 1996, and his *River of Fire, River of Water* was published by Doubleday in 1998.

What is the Sound of Liberating Truth? Remembering Fred Streng (1933–1993)[1]

Paul O. Ingram

> Friends have eyes and ears, but their flashes of insight are not equal. Some are like ponds that reach only to the mouth or shoulder; others are like ponds that one could bathe in. – *Rig Veda* 10.7[2]

Death is usually 'untimely' for those who die and for persons who love those who have died. Frederick J. Streng's death from cancer at age sixty stunned many of us to silence. There are all kinds of silences; each means different things to different people. There is the silence that comes with morning in a rain forest, and this is different from the silence of a sleeping city. There is the silence before a rainstorm and after a rainstorm, and these are not the same. There is the silence of emptiness, of fullness, of fear, of death. There is a certain silence that can emanate from a lifeless object, as from a chair lately used, or from a piano with old dust upon its keys, or from anything that has answered the needs of human beings for pleasure or for work. The voice of silence may whisper melancholy, but not always so. The chair may have been left by a laughing child or the last notes on the piano may have been raucous or joyful. Whatever the mood or circumstances, the quality of silence may linger in what follows, like a soundless echo.

The lifeless object from which silence seems to emanate every time I look at it is a photograph of Fred and me taken on an isolated beach near Honolulu in the summer of 1990. I was on my way home to Tacoma, Washington, from a sabbatical trip to Japan, and I stopped over in Honolulu for two weeks to attend the Sixth East-West Philosophers Conference. My karma was indeed running on positive overload, because, as I was checking into the hotel, Fred snuck up behind me and wrapped a hug around my shoulders with his long, powerful arms. It was a wonderful surprise. Going to this conference was a last-minute decision, so I did not know Fred was going to be in attendance and was giving one of the principal addresses.

A week later, on a warm Sunday afternoon, we went to a quiet beach, did a little skin diving, chased some fish, and later, in the light of a sun hanging on the horizon like an orange mask, asked a passerby to take our picture. Then we sat quietly, perhaps even meditatively, focused on the sun disappearing on the horizon, the sound of the waves cracking on the beach, the coolness of the breeze. But Fred seemed to be listening to the end of the day rather than seeing it with me, for while his eyes did not move about, there was an air of attentiveness in him I had never seen before. Then, after a long silence, he told me about his life's koan.

'You mean you've been practicing Zen meditation,' I remember quipping.

'I haven't been doing zazen,' he said, 'but a koan has grabbed my attention and I can't shake it. It seems to sum up all the questions I've been thinking and writing about for thirty years.'

'Tell me,' I said.

'What's the sound of liberating truth?'

'Any solutions?'

'Something seems to be emerging. I only know for certain that it's become my life's koan.'

We spent the rest of the night talking about his life's koan, which he first publicly shared two years later in his presidential address to the Society for Buddhist-Christian Studies during its fourth Buddhist-Christian Dialogue Conference in Boston from July 22–August 3 – his last words to the Society.[3]

In his address, Fred granted that his life's koan was capable of many solutions, but that he had found the sound of liberating truth in 'ultimate transformation.' Any solution, he felt, must transform a person's life in mutual transformative interaction with other persons in community – not simply by describing reality, the way things really are, but also by asserting a stance or commitment through which self and community may be healed, be made whole, become enlightened, eliminate bondage to illusion – that is, become 'ultimately transformed.' Fred spoke about three interrelated areas of ultimate transformation: (1) the 'internal' and 'external' pluralism found in interreligious dialogue, especially Buddhist-Christian dialogue; (2) the dialogue of religiously engaged persons with the objectivity of academic-scientific studies of religion; (3) the encounter with the religious Ways of humanity with the plurality of economic, gender, social, political, and racial oppressions that affect human beings globally.

The solution to his koan that Fred offered to us was, in fact, one that gradually evolved through the course of his earlier training and subsequent scholarship as a historian of religions always involved in the practice of interreligious dialogue. Like many of us practicing Buddhist-Christian dialogue through the lenses of history of religions, Fred was convinced that no particular form of liberating truth could be sufficient or satisfying for him. Creative transformation was thus a theme that first emerged during his graduate study at the University of Chicago, where he worked with Mircea Eliade, Joseph Kitagawa, and Bernard Meland, from 1956–1963. But the first hint of Fred's koan can be found in his doctoral dissertation on the Buddhist logician Nāgārjuna, which was later published as his first book, *Emptiness: A Study in Religious Meaning*, in 1967.[4]

The thesis of *Emptiness* is that religious knowledge is not merely a special kind of information or a collection of concepts, but an awareness of reality, the way things really are. He illustrated his thesis by Nāgārjuna's intention, which, he wrote, was soteriological, not speculative. Thus, even though Nāgārjuna taught that the knowledge of Emptiness was a transforming knowledge that lacked an object to be known in distinction from the knower, it was still saving knowledge because it removed ignorance and attachment, and was therefore a means to ultimate transformation. Fred's insightful interpretation of the religious import of Nāgārjuna's teaching of emptiness has become required reading for leading philosophers and theologians in America. In fact there is perhaps no liberal theologian today who is not conversant with the Buddhist teaching on emptiness, mostly because Fred's book is the single most important Western interpretation of this Mahayana Buddhist teaching.

Early in his career, then, Fred was committed to helping us see transformative power at work in the plurality of religious traditions, from both outside and inside, both objectively and empathetically. His father was a Lutheran pastor, but he once told me he always felt confined by just one religious identity. That is why later in his life he became an active member of the Unitarian Universalist Church.

In 1969 Fred inaugurated the Religious Life of Man Series with Dickenson Publishing Company, a series that included volumes from different authors on Islam, Japanese Religion, Chinese Religion,

Buddhism, Hinduism. Judaism, Christianity, and Native American traditions. Additional volumes were also published that included original source materials from the various traditions. These volumes have become one of the standard series of texts used during the past twenty years to introduce these traditions to beginning students.

My favorite volume in the Dickenson series is the introduction Fred wrote entitled *Understanding Religious Man*, later retitled in the second and third editions in 1976 and 1985 as *Understanding Religious Life*. The preface to the 1976 edition noted that 'religious life is a complex process through which people are being transformed.' This view – that religious experience is not best understood in terms of structures of belief systems, but as interdependent processes of transformation – was further supported in two books Fred coedited: (1) with Charles L. Llyod and Jay T. Allan, *Ways of Being Religious: Readings for a New Approach to Religion;* (2) with Paul O. Ingram, *Buddhist-Christian Dialogue: Mutual Renewal and Transformation*[5]

In *Emptiness: A Study in Religious Meaning*, Fred divided Indian thought into three forms of religious apprehension: the mystical, the intuitive, and the dialectical. In *Understanding Religious Life*, he changed this triad to a fourfold typology: personal encounter with the Sacred, ritual, living harmoniously through conformity with cosmic law, and attaining freedom through spiritual discipline.[6] It was this typology that allowed Fred to affirm that *any* reasonably specific means that *any* person adopts with the serious hope or intention of moving toward ultimate transformation should be considered religious. Later chapters of *Understanding Religious Life* also listed methods of self-integration, political activity to achieve human rights, new life through technocracy, and living a fully sensuous and aesthetic life as means of ultimate transformation.

Consequently, Fred's definition of religion as 'a means toward ultimate transformation' emphasized a process within two interdependent contexts: a transcendent, cosmic dimension interpenetrating human experience and action within the structures of human society and the natural order.

By the third edition of *Understanding Religious Life*, Fred's emphasis on religious experience and faith as a means of ultimate transformation was shifted a bit in a chapter entitled 'Understanding Through Interreligious Dialogue.' By this time he was convinced that religious knowledge and authentic living at their deepest level are dependent upon seeking out alternative forms of religious experience,

comparing them, and entering into dialogue with them. Interreligious
dialogue, he believed, may involve: (1) a mystical sense of unity
underlying the diversity of humanity's ways of being religious; (2) the
perception that the religious Ways of humanity are alternative or
complementary means of ultimate transformation; (3) a focus on
enriching one's personal faith and participation in one's own religious
tradition; or (4) a combination of all three of the above. Fred also
developed these themes further in an essay (included in an anthology
by the two of us) entitled 'Selfhood Without Selfishness: Buddhist and
Christian Approaches to Authentic Living.'[7]

Fred's search for the solution of his life's koan was not confined to
the scholarly discipline of history of religions or the practice of
interreligious dialogue. Nor was it expressed solely in his scholarly
research and publications. His search also energized his excellence as
an undergraduate and graduate teacher at Southern Methodist
University and Perkins School of Theology and his presidential
leadership of four academic societies: the Society for Asian and
Comparative Philosophy (1979–72); the American Oriental Society,
Southwest Branch (1982–83); the American Society for the Study of
Religion (1987–90); and the Society for Buddhist-Christian Studies
(1991–93).

Fred had so many friends, and all have special memories unique to
themselves. David Chappell remembers asking Fred whether his
definition of religion as 'a means to ultimate transformation' included
being run over by a steamroller. Fred laughed his usual belly laugh and
said that, for him, the adjective 'ultimate' always implied something
positive. I remember Fred's encouragement of my work and the work of
other friends and colleagues – including the contributors to this volume
– with his humor and always dependable and generous support. A few
days before he died, I am told, his wife Susan mentioned some local
political obstacles to bringing relief to needy children in the Dallas-Fort
Worth area. Fred supported her concern, but also gently told her that he
only had room for positive thoughts, not complaints. That was always
Fred's way, and his family and friends treasure him for his ready
laughter, clear intelligence, and compassionate concern and inclusive
care for others.

For me, therefore, the special silence emanating from that
photograph of Fred and me standing in fading sunlight on an almost
empty beach in Hawaii reminds me of how the occasions of our lives
imperceptibly change, like the light, at a constant rate. At any given
glance we may see that the dog has rolled over in his sleep, or that the

trees have lost their leaves, or that a friend has gone before we could say good-bye. Morning drains imperceptibly into lunch time, or Christmas time. From the window of my study I see Canada geese migrating overhead, just as they did last time I looked. We wash the dishes, turn around, and it's summer again, or some other time, or time to go. Fred knew and enjoyed the trickster character of reality. If he were here, in my study, listening to the silence of our photograph with me, my guess is that he would laugh and say, 'Yes, isn't reality a wonderful koan? It's the way it should be because that's the way it is.'

We may be sad that Fred has left us, but we should never complain, because it is wonderful to remember and be grateful for how he touched and changed us as he moved imperceptibly through the occasions of our lives.

Frederick J. Streng is survived by his wife Susan, and his children Elizabeth Ann Devoll, Mark Andrew Streng, Steven Deane Streng, Lesa Evans, and by us.

Notes

1 This memorial first appeared in *Buddhist-Christian Studies* 14 (1994): 2–7. A revision is reprinted here with the permission of the editors of *Buddhist-Christian Studies*.
2 Wendy Doniger O' Flaherty, trans., *The Rig Veda: An Anthology* (New York: Penguin Books, 1981), 61–62.
3 Frederick J. Streng, 'Mutual Transformation: An Answer to a Religious Question,' *Buddhist-Christian Studies* 13 (1993): 121–26.
4 Frederick J. Streng, *Emptiness: a Study of Religious Meaning* (Nashville: Abingdon Press, 1967).
5 Englewood Cliffs, NJ: Prentice Hall, 1973, and Honolulu: University of Hawaii Press, 1986, respectively.
6 Frederick J. Streng, *Understanding Religious Life* (Belmont, CA: Dickenson Press, 1976), 22.
7 Paul O. Ingram and Frederick J. Streng, eds., *Buddhist-Christian Dialogue: Mutual Renewal and Transformation* (Honolulu: University of Hawaii Press, 1986), 177–94.

PROLOGUE

Paul O. Ingram and
Sallie B. King

This book has been written and compiled in honor of the late Frederick J. Streng. Among the many leadership roles that Fred Streng superlatively filled was his presidency of the Society for Buddhist-Christian Studies, in which he was incumbent at the time of his death. To celebrate Fred Streng's scholarship and leadership, the Society asked us to edit a *festschrift* in his honor. Upon reflection, we decided the most appropriate volume would be one which would carry forward the Buddhist-Christian dialogue that was so important to Fred Streng, incorporating the finest scholarship available.

This volume contains a collection of dialogues written for the occasion in 1995–96. We invited a group of outstanding scholars and dialoguers to submit statements from a Buddhist or a Christian point of view on a topic in which they were established scholars. We determined the topics to be covered by considering both their importance for the present stage of Buddhist-Christian dialogue and their importance in the work of Fred Streng and the world of his active social concerns. The topics included are: interreligious dialogue, ultimate reality, nature and ecology, social engagement, and ultimate transformation or soteriology. We wished the volume to reflect real dialogue and not simply side-by-side presentations from two points of view, so we invited each author to respond to the statements of his or her dialogical partner. We further strengthened the dialogical aspect of the book by inviting two senior scholars, one Buddhist and one Christian, to each reflect upon the entire volume from his own scholarly and religious perspective.

The topics of these essays are so interdependent that each must be read in light of all the others. Fred Streng's scholarship in religious studies and his practice of Buddhist-Christian dialogue showed the interdependence of serious reflection on such apparently 'separate' topics as ultimate reality, our experience of nature, our involvement in social engagement against the forces of oppression, and our sense of the possibilities for humanity's and all of life's ultimate transformation. This interdependence is quite apparent in the present essays. For example, metaphysical and cosmological beliefs can be seen to very much affect the manner of interaction with nature and with social issues; each faith's present historical situatedness profoundly affects its priorities in, and beliefs about, interreligious dialogue. Moreover, the reader will notice many instances in which a given issue (for example, the question of whether ultimate reality has a personal dimension) turns up again and again throughout the essays.

Another kind of interdependence is at play here as well. Of course, all the authors draw upon the core teachings and paradigms of the tradition they represent. Still, the reader will notice many instances in which authors demonstrate their openness to the core teachings, paradigms, and insights of their dialogical partners, even to the point of appropriating insights from them, which they bring 'home' to their own religious perspective. While remaining faithful to their own respective core teachings, they are able to recognize both differences between themselves and their dialogue partners as well as experiences of convergence and complementarity.

This leads to another kind of interdependence that needs to be mentioned. It has been a 'given' in interreligious dialogue for some years that in order to have dialogue, it is necessary to have a Christian speak for Christianity and a Buddhist speak for Buddhism. The editors were well aware, when they began organizing this volume, that matters are not so simple, so black and white. Not everyone can say simply, 'I am a Buddhist' (as opposed to Christian) or 'I am a Christian' (as opposed to Buddhist). However, we were surprised to discover how far this blurring of the lines of religious identity has progressed. Many of those who have been involved in the dialogue for several years find themselves having to say something like, 'my own religious identity is worked out at the boundary of these two traditions,' or 'I speak as a Buddhist to Buddhist groups and as a Christian to Christian groups,' or simply, 'I am a Buddhist and a Christian.' This kind of 'betwixt and between' or 'both-and' position in religious identity is more common (though not universal) among our scholars speaking from the Buddhist perspective, but it is by no means limited to them. On both the 'Buddhist' and the 'Christian' sides of our volume there are both those who claim a religious identity exclusively affiliated with one religion and others who observe varying degrees of influence from both religions that have been incorporated into their personal perspectives and religious identities.

Interreligious Dialogue

Winston King is one of the most experienced Buddhist-Christian dialoguers living today. Drawing from his years of personal encounter with Buddhists in Asia, as well as his years of participation in informal dialogue, King first clarifies, from his perspective, what genuine interreligious dialogue is. It is not 'dialogical action,' or humanistic cooperation among faiths, necessary as this is for suffering humanity. Nor is it the sharing of spiritual techniques, important as this is for the spiritual practice for many persons of faith. While it is clear that King esteems these forms of religious encounter and wishes them to go forward, they miss an essential ingredient for real dialogue. Genuine dialogue, for King, must address the 'sticking points' of views and doctrines.

For King, the ideal of interreligious dialogue requires that participants, while being committed to their own religion, be open to the possibility of conversion to the best in the other religion. Thus dialogue is more than a friendly and tolerant exchange between persons who have no intention to change their faith stance. It requires openness to real change, perhaps deep change, which implies a willingness on each dialoguer's part to face his or her own incompleteness. In King's view, this necessarily entails that few people will ever seriously engage in interreligious dialogue.

Believing that doctrinal issues are at the heart of interreligious dialogue, King briefly considers three important areas of doctrinal matters at the center of Buddhist-Christian dialogue, asking whether there are 'non-negotiables,' doctrinal commitments so necessary to the religion that they are not open to change. Dialogue on ultimate reality, he observes, has focused on the concepts of God and emptiness. King remarks that Masao Abe's attempt to link the two by emphasizing the self-emptying God (Philippians 2:58) has met with some interest among dialoguers, but he doubts that this view of God will ever mean much to the great body of Christian faithful. He further notes that at least some Buddhists find the Christian symbol of the cross repugnant. On the other hand, he finds the apparent gulf between Christian worship and Buddhist meditation readily breachable from each side. The reader may note that David Eckel and Taitetsu Unno also have something of interest to say on this matter in their essays.

Second, King indicates that the deeply divergent views of Buddhists and Christians on the concept of human being have not received the attention they deserve. He finds these two views quite incompatible, except when Zen Buddhists, for their own reasons, drop references to rebirth.

Third, on the matter of religiously inspired social action, King points out that while traditional Christianity is generally much more engaged in struggling against the wrongs of this world than is traditional Buddhism, today Buddhists are much more socially engaged and, moreover, they still have not begun to tap the potential for social engagement in the traditional idea of the Bodhisattva. Thus on this issue no fundamental incompatibility seems to exist.

David Chappell, former president of the Society for Buddhist-Christian Studies, presents a survey of the history of Buddhist-Christian dialogue, emphasizing Buddhist contributions. His essay, 'Buddhist Interreligious Dialogue: to Build a Global Community,' organizes this history into three categories. The first category focuses on verbal exchange and emphasizes doctrinal and philosophical exploration across religious boundaries, especially on the 'perception and understanding of reality.' Second, Chappell brings forward the important Buddhist-Christian encounters that have emphasized experience, particularly shared contemplative experience. Finally, Chappell points to 'dialogue on social engagement,' that is, interreligious dialogue which takes place in the context of efforts to heal the suffering of the world. Among these, Buddhists have been most interested in the third kind of dialogue as a moral commitment to build a global community of peace through interreligious collaboration.

In his introductory and concluding remarks, Chappell emphasizes the importance of the situatedness of Buddhism for its attitudes towards other religions. Looking back, Buddhism's situatedness in religiously plural cultures was decisive in framing its attitudes towards co-existence with other religions. In modern times, the presence or absence of such factors as government control and/or oppression, war, colonial domination and exile has been decisive in shaping the degree and form of Buddhist outreach and openness to other faiths.

Three forms of dialogue are mentioned in their initial statements by both King and Chappell: intellectual doctrinal discussion, the sharing of religious practices, and joint social action. However, while King clearly gives priority to intellectual doctrinal exchange, and regards only this as dialogue, Chappell endorses all three forms of dialogue. Thus the perspectives of King and Chappell on dialogue are virtually opposite.

In his response to King, Chappell defends his view that all three forms of dialogue are both valid and vital. True dialogue, in his view, is comprehensive of a 'multi-dimensional range of experience, including social responsibility and joint meditation.' He endorses a dialogue that can encompass the 'heart, head, and hands,' while acknowledging that certain aspects of dialogue (e.g., the intellectual) will be fruitful for some, while other aspects (e.g., shared religious practice) will be more fruitful for others. Winston King, for his part, acknowledges the truth of Chappell's claim that (with the notable exception of Masao Abe) 'Christian theology has failed to spark any serious interest, challenge, or growth in the Buddhist community.' He further comments that if much of the future of this dialogue is to be concentrated in the arena of joint social action, Buddhists and Christians will still need to face their profound doctrinal differences regarding ideas of justice and moral responsibility.

Ultimate Reality

Bonnie Thurston's essay, '"In the Beginning . . . . God:" A Christian View of Ultimate Reality,' is not only a fine discussion of the Christian concept of God, but a fine short introduction to Christianity as well. She emphasizes throughout her essay that for Christians, God is a person; for Christians, the universe in which we live is personal at its roots.

Furthermore, God's personal existence is relational. Jesus called God 'Abba,' a term translated as 'father,' but implying both authority and tender nurture. God as Trinity also manifests God's relational nature, since the Trinity is God as three 'persons' in relation. Thus, 'the inner life of God is a life of relationship, a community of love.' God's relational nature is characterized by love.

Since God's fundamental nature is love, and love is personal, God had to be manifested as a person, Jesus. 'God loved human beings enough . . . to die for them.' Christian love thus is not a feeling but a 'choice to act for the benefit of the other.' Christians are called to share in the essence of God by living a life of such love.

Frederick Streng first leapt into academic fame with his book, *Emptiness: a Study in Religious Meaning*. Appropriately, David Eckel begins his essay, 'The Concept of the Ultimate in Madhyamaka Thought: In Memory of Frederick Streng,' with an account of 'ultimate reality' in the Madhyamaka School of Buddhism by reminding us of the way in which Streng profoundly altered Western scholarly understanding of emptiness by showing that emptiness is 'a spiritual and intellectual discipline aimed ... at a goal of "ultimate transformation"' rather than a concept representing the Buddhist 'Absolute.'

As an inheritor of this tradition (who once asked Streng how he could carry forward his work on emptiness), Eckel indeed carries forward both Streng's careful analysis of Madhyamaka texts and his interest in the living function of emptiness in Buddhist religious practice. Eckel focuses upon three such functions, aligned with three metaphors. First, emptiness is represented as a journey, a dialectical negation that religiously is the course of practice itself, a journey in which the practitioner is profoundly transformed. Second, emptiness is represented as an empty place. This is the anti-foundationalist commitment of the Madhyamaka, the crucial point that when the process of dialectical negation has done its work, there is no foundation or remainder left behind; emptiness itself is emptiness. Religiously, this is expressed in pilgrimages to places where the Buddha is not, and in a nirvana that is not located in any place. Freed from any fixation on or 'in' nirvana, the Bodhisattva is freed for compassionate action.

Perhaps more than any other contributors to this volume, Thurston and Eckel each clearly (and independently) make a conscious effort to search for common ground to build bridges between their views. Perhaps they wanted to do this because their initial statements seemed, on the face of them, to be so diametrically opposed. For her part, Thurston pointed out that Buddhism and Christianity begin from very different premises. Christianity asserts an ultimate reality, God. For her, as a Christian, these are first principles: God is ultimate reality and God exists. This view obviously stands in complete contrast to the anti-foundationalism of Buddhist emptiness.

Despite this fundamental difference, Thurston finds a good deal in Eckel's account that she, as a Christian, can embrace: the transformative nature of religious practice, the recognition that central concepts may have functional dimensions, the idea of following a path which involves leaving behind limiting ideas, the notion of spirituality as a process of gaining insight. Nonetheless, while for Thurston the Christian, like the Buddhist, is 'transformed by a form of practice that never quite stands still,' for the Christian, finally, there is a foundation in Christ, wherein the Christian finds real identity. This, it seems, is, in Winston King's terms, a non-negotiable for Thurston.

Eckel begins by acknowledging that Buddhism has a long tradition of actively refuting the idea of a personal-creator God. Despite this, he reaches out from the strict negation of emptiness toward Thurston's perspective by pointing out that in Buddhism 'there is no fundamental barrier between the emptiness of the philosophers and the "person" who constitutes the Buddha of popular devotion.' Not only Buddhas, but bodhisattvas, teachers, and even the mind of the practitioner are all 'persons' in whom emptiness is known and made present. The reader might compare Winston King's account of the devotional role of the Buddha, in the Theravada context, another officially apophatic Buddhist path.

Eckel ends by challenging Thurston, and through her, Christianity, on what he rightly calls 'one of the great issues in the Buddhist-Christian dialogue.' 'Christians seem committed to the notion that their tradition knows best what it means to love.' This, Eckel points out, seems very odd if one accepts Thurston's definition of (Christian) love as 'a conscious choice to act for the benefit of others in spite of the consequences for oneself.' Clearly, this definition could serve for a Buddhist Bodhisattva as well as for a Christian saint. Perhaps, Eckel suggests, the difference lies elsewhere, perhaps in their respective views on human existence and the meaning thereof: was it loving of God to start life and/or loving of the Buddha to 'allow some of it to stop'?

Nature and Ecology

In 'Self, Nature, and Ecology in Buddhism,' Alan Sponberg notes that traditional Buddhist sources have little to say about nature in the abstract and still less about ecology as understood in contemporary scientific thought. While Sponberg's essay is not a summary of traditional Buddhist attitudes towards nature, he does focus on a cluster of key 'axiomatic' concepts and attitudes that shape Buddhist perceptions of nature 'at the most fundamental level:' (1) the concept of non-self (*anātman*) as an on-going process rather than an underlying, substantial reality; (2) the cosmological context of Buddhist teachings of dependent co-arising and impermanence, especially as this cosmology is interpreted through the concepts of emptiness and karma; and (3) traditional Buddhist forms of meditative practice centering on the quest for freedom from suffering through overcoming the mechanisms by which persons cling to permanence in an impermanent universe. His thesis is that these core axioms of Buddhist tradition have led Buddhists to see no need to develop a 'special and separate position on nature and ecology' since such a position cannot be put into practice without completely transforming one's response to nature and the environment.

Paula Cooey's response to Sponberg notes that both Buddhist and Christian traditions see egocentricity as the root of suffering – an egocentricity that can be transformed, though the conditions of this transformation rest on very different assumptions. For example, in contrast to Buddhist thought, Christian thought focuses on origins as well as ends, although this focus arises less out of metaphysical speculation than on soteriological and eschatological concerns. The God who redeems is the God who creates, which in turn ensures the intrinsic goodness of all creatures as well as the material reality of the earth. Accordingly, the inherent goodness of divine creation grants all creaturely existence the same initial status as 'very good.' The shared goodness that interconnects all creatures to each other as well as the creation itself to its creator, Cooey notes, represents an absolute contrast to the 'transhuman karmic trajectory' Sponberg thinks is central to Buddhist thought and experience. Accordingly, it is not clear to Cooey that human beings necessarily need a karmic connection to other sentient beings in order to promote their well-being. Thus, as a Reformed Protestant Christian steeped in the doctrine of the incarnation, Cooey describes her ethical difficulties with the Buddhist notion of liberation, difficulties that she more fully discusses in her essay, 'Creation, Redemption, and the Realization of the Material Order.' Here, while acknowledging parallels in Christian theology with the Buddhist notion of emptiness, she argues that 'until Christians realize the full implications of materiality, most of us will continue to ignore, to abet, or to address only superficially the ecological destruction we commit.'

In his response to Cooey, Sponberg writes about what he sees as a fundamental asymmetry between Christian and Buddhist traditions that arises from the different relationship each tradition has to modernity, which in turn engenders and supports distinctively Buddhist and Christian responses to nature and the human caused ecological crisis. Both Buddhism and Christianity have pre-modern origins and both are struggling to come to terms with the challenges of modernity. Yet the nature of this struggle is different for each tradition. For example, Christianity is well embedded in the cultural context of modernity even as its values are challenged by modern notions of secularism and materialism. The task for Christianity is thus to adapt its theology and worldview to fit a more complex and multicultural world in order to secure its position as the spiritual underpinning of modernism.

But Sponberg thinks Buddhism has a different challenge and task, namely, to maintain its basic identity in the context of the modernity it did not help create. If Buddhism clings to its non-Western origins and fails to address the challenge of modernity, it runs the danger of becoming an anachronistic artifact 'of little but antiquarian interest in a world increasingly influenced if not dominated by modern ideas and institutions of largely Judeo-Christian and Greek origin.' Given this basic asymmetry, then, Sponberg asks how might a Buddhist proceed in dialogue? He suggests that the first and most crucial task is to rigorously question any assumption of common ground between Buddhism and Christianity, 'especially if the assumption seems so obvious that it is not even explicitly addressed.'

Social Engagement

One of the themes of Sallie King's essay, 'Buddhism and Social Engagement,' is 'the mutual influence of spiritual social activism between Buddhism and Christianity.' While her use of the term 'spiritual social activism' excludes those who use their participation in a religious traditions to justify, hatred, aggression, or violence – which she thinks are forms of secularism whether engaged in by Buddhists or Christians – her essay is a survey of contemporary representative examples of Buddhist spiritual social activism/engagement. Her list is distinguished: Dr. B. Ambedkar, who led millions of ex-untouchable Hindus to Buddhism; Dr. Ariyaratne, the founder of the Sarvodaya Sramadana movement in Sri Lanka; the Dalai Lama's non-violent Tibetan Liberation Movement; Sulak Sivaraksa's 'gadfly' attempts to lead the government of Thailand toward democratic and humanistic reform based on traditional Buddhist teachings; the Won Buddhist movement of Korea; the Fo Kuang Shan movement in Taiwan; and the Nichiren movements of Risshō Kōseikai and Soka Gakkai in Japan.

While these Buddhist movements of social engagement should be understood as unique contemporary responses to particular conditions of oppression, the social activism of each is motivated and guided by distinctively Buddhist teachings and practices. All are non-violent. Each movement understands itself to be an expression of core Buddhist values such as benevolence, compassion, and selflessness. All are grounded in foundational Buddhist texts, doctrines, and practices. All are reform movements seeking to identify and apply Buddhist principles and practices to the political, economic, and military challenges and crises of contemporary existence.

Yet King also notes that while Buddhist movements of social engagement have much to offer global communities, there are also three points on which Buddhists might benefit from dialogue with Christianity. First, Buddhists have yet to seriously confront the tension between structures of spiritual and institutional hierarchy and egalitarian notions and political principles. She argues that Christianity will eventually challenge Buddhists to grapple with the institutionalized injustice of its own power structures. Second, because Buddhists need to rethink the role and meaning of karma and its relation to institutionalized forms of social injustice, encounter with Western and Christian social theory will have much to contribute to this process of re-thinking. Finally, Buddhist spiritual social activism has come of age in the modern world, which means most forms of Buddhist social engagement have come into being in the throes of contemporary crises. This means that Buddhists have had little time to articulate the theoretical foundations of their activism. This too will be an important part of future Buddhist-Christian dialogue.

In his response to Sallie King, 'Some Questions About the World,' John Keenan wonders how, given the Buddhist teaching of dependent co-arising and the Mahayana notion of emptiness, Buddhism can develop a historical narrative about the world sufficient to help Buddhists engage in struggle against institutional forms of oppression and for justice in the world. This problem is exacerbated for Keenan by the traditional Buddhist ahistorical worldview that 'glories in the lack of theological presuppositions.' Keenan then offers a 'Mahayana reading' of selected texts from the Letter of James in 'The Mind of Wisdom and Justice in the Letter of James' that he thinks might be mutually helpful to both Buddhists and Christians in dialogical reflection on the meaning of social engagement as they struggle in common against forces of injustice and oppression here-and-now. What is the organic relation between 'wisdom' and 'compassion,' Keenan asks, as 'aspects of discriminating mind freed from its religious pretensions and committed to the service of the poor'?

King's 'Response to John Keenan' is sympathetic to his Mahayana reading of the Letter to James, while noting that while it is often said that Buddhism has the seeds of a social ethic in its emphasis on selfless compassion, it is entirely lacking in a concept of social justice. Of course, much depends on how one defines 'justice.' Still, she thinks Keenan's essay provides positive suggestions for formulating a concept of justice suitable to Buddhist faith and experience. Keenan's focus on the wise person who is without partiality provides a practical door for Buddhist-Christian discussion on the issue of justice. Both she and Keenan agree that impartiality is an essential goal of Mahayana Buddhist practice and a mark of an enlightened mind, as it apparently is in James' description of the wise person as well. Thus, the impartiality of the wise, enlightened-compassionate mind can be taken as a Buddhist foundation for the creation of a principle of distributive justice.

Ultimate Liberation

With the essays and responses of Thomas P. Kasulis and Ruben Habito, we come to the topic that, when all is said and done, Buddhism and Christianity are about: ultimate liberation, or what in Christian theology is called 'soteriology.' In 'Under the Bodhi Tree: An Idealized Paradigm of Buddhist Transformation and Liberation,' Kasulis describes the story of Gautama the Buddha's enlightenment under the Bo tree as *the* idealized paradigm through which Buddhists hope, experience, and reflect on the experience of final liberation. Kasulis's thesis is that the Buddha's enlightenment is an *idealized* paradigm because most Buddhists do not try to emulate it, since only a tiny minority of Buddhists in the world identify with the rigors and sacrifices that the Buddha's single-minded quest for enlightenment through meditation demands.

Even so, there are elements of the Buddha's story that serve as a defining orientation for most Buddhists. These elements lend focus and meaning to how Buddhists hope to achieve transformation in their lives, whether or not they have abandoned the secular world. One such element of the model presents liberation as an all-or-nothing-affair. One either achieves final enlightened liberation or one doesn't and continues to live in the world through lifetimes of delusion. Thus if we were to literally apply this criterion to the lives of most practicing Buddhists, Buddhism would look like a religion of failure. However, matters are usually not so simple. For practicing Buddhists generally, there seems to be something transformative in their Buddhist experience that continues to be a meaningful source of 'psychospiritual liberation,' even 'without the all-or-nothing, once-and-for-all of insight' that constitutes enlightenment. That is, for most Buddhists, the Buddhist paradigm of the Buddha's enlightenment is not a *'modus operandi* but a spiritual heuristic.' Kasulis' essay is devoted to spelling out what this 'spiritual heuristic' is and what it means for the vast majority of Buddhists.

Ruben Habito's response, 'Nailed to a Tree: Idealized Paradigm, Realized Context,' poses this question: '.... how may one present an idealized paradigm of Christian transformation and liberation that would cut through the different systems of metapraxis and metaphysics among different traditions so that all who identify themselves as Christian could be seen through the same paradigm?' That is, what is the core of Christian identity analogous to how Buddhists perceive 'the man sitting under the bodhi tree?' Of course, what immediately comes to mind is 'the man nailed to a tree.' For Christians, the Crucified One is the paradigmatic image that sums up Christian self-identity. Since it is also a fundamental axiom of the Christian community that the Crucified One is also the Risen One, 'theology of the cross' is central to Christian self-identity. Accordingly, Habito's response offers his own heuristic device for approaching the Crucified One that follows the schema of traditional Indian medicine: symptomatology, eitology. prognosis, and therapy, also assumed by the doctrine of the Four Noble Truths according to which the Buddha is said to have interpreted his experience under the bodhi tree.

Habito further develops his understanding of the central paradigm of Christian self-identity in his essay, 'The Resurrection of the Dead and the Life Everlasting: From a Futuristic to a Realized Christianity,' by pointing to two articles of the Apostle's Creed: 'I believe in ... the resurrection of the body and the life everlasting,' as these articles relate to the implications of eschatology for Christian *praxis.* Historically, these two articles of Christian faith have engendered what Habito calls a 'futuristic outlook' and a 'realized outlook.' While both outlooks presuppose faith as trust in the promise of future eternal life made manifest in Jesus' life, death, and resurrection, Habito argues that the resurrection of the body and the life everlasting are simultaneously a present reality open to anyone who accepts Christ into one's life, and, moreover, that the realized outlook is biblically and theologically more expressive of Christian experience. The main biblical text to which Habito appeals for support of his thesis is the Last Judgment scene in Matthew 25:31–46, which proclaims that faith in Jesus as the Christ entails a way of life open to the needs of one's neighbors, and that acting accordingly is the gate to eternal life here-and now. In other words, the 'good news' is that eternal life is discovered here and now in our midst as we go about our daily tasks and lay ourselves open in loving response to the needs of our neighbor. A 'realized Christianity' sees that life here-and-now is not merely a 'testing place' for a future destiny in eternity, but is instead 'the very ground in which eternal life manifests itself.'

While Kasulis deeply appreciates Habito's insightful use of possible points of dialogue by the appropriation of terms associated with Buddhism: salvation as 'right now;' 'participation in the here-and-now'; and achieving salvation 'in this very body,' his response – 'The Momentous and the Momentary' – seeks to draw out issues he believes Habito needs to address in his continuing dialogue with Buddhism. 'Whose Christianity?' and 'which salvation?' he asks. Is realized Christianity merely another form of Karl Rahner's 'anonymous Christianity? Furthermore, if salvation derives from how one responds to the needs of others, it would seem that the issue of salvation is primarily ethical and that one need not have faith either in Jesus or in God, nor participate in the Church's sacraments. Again, Kasulis thinks that however much Buddhists might respect Habito's realized Christianity, the Buddhist view of temporality cannot be easily reconciled to either futuristic or realized Christianity since Buddhist teaching rejects the notion of a momentous event that transforms ontology and temporality. 'The Buddha did not change the nature of reality,' he notes, 'he discovered it.' Accordingly, he concludes that without awareness of how Jesus Christ has altered both ontology and temporality – an awareness that can only be achieved through faith – 'the very nature of realized Christianity has no foundation.'

The Buddhist and Christian Epilogues

Taitetsu Unno's epilogue is written from the point of view of a Shin Buddhist. While he is impressed by how far the enterprise of Buddhist-Christian dialogue has progressed since the inception of the Society for Buddhist-Christian Studies in 1980, he points to an on-going issue of this dialogue: while all of the essays and responses are in essential agreement with Cooey's statement that 'both Buddhist and Christian traditions thus see egocentricity as the root of suffering and environmental damage,' what are the different uses of language and the crucial role of religious *praxis* in the religious lives of both Buddhist and Christian people? For example, teachings such as 'emptiness' are often understood by both Buddhist and Christian academics as descriptive terms divorced from Buddhist practice, which in turn distorts dialogue and creates further misunderstandings. Accordingly, Unno argues that the centrality of praxis should be the focal point of dialogical engagement between Buddhists and Christians, since to divorce doctrine from techniques of *practice* deprives dialogue of real substance.

Accordingly, Unno sees the essays and responses of this volume as evidence that contemporary Buddhist-Christian dialogue is entering a new stage in which Christians can offer exegesis on Buddhist texts to help Buddhists plumb the depths of their own tradition, as Buddhists might offer their own reading of Christian texts to help Christians shed new light on Christian faith and practice. Indeed, this would signal a transformative evolution in Buddhist-Christian dialogue. In light of this, Unno proposes some further areas for dialogical comparison. First, as non-discriminative wisdom seems indeed to be common to Buddhism and Christianity, a closer working relationship on social justice issues, environmental issues, and ethnic and racial violence would be welcomed by those so engaged. Second, since both Buddhism and Christianity cope with suffering, regardless of their differing doctrinal views, future dialogue might discuss and formulate a cross-culturally valid ethic that takes into serious consideration the deep-rooted egocentricity in humankind. Third, a dialogue centered on religious *praxis* and transformation might contribute to furthering reflection on the philosophy of language and the sociology of knowledge. Finally, more precise readings of the scriptures and commentaries of Buddhism and Christianity by representatives of the opposite tradition may be fruitful and raise Buddhist-Christian conversation to higher levels of dialogical exchange.

'One thing that those who participate in dialogue learn early,' writes John Cobb in his 'Christian Epilogue,' 'is that generalizations about Buddhism and Christianity, or about Buddhists and Christians, are difficult and dangerous.' There are always exceptions to every generalization, sometimes so many that the generalization turns out to be dead wrong. Still, the need for generalizations about the Buddhist and Christian contributions to this volume are necessary, provided one is aware of exceptions and differences. One such generalization that Cobb note is that the Buddhist essays are more historical and descriptive in their approaches while the Christian essays are more personal statements of belief. Of course, 'both are both. But the difference is noticeable and fairly consistent.' The question is what this generalization expresses about Buddhism and Christianity, or at least the Buddhism and Christianity of contemporary Americans. Cobb offers three suggestions in this regard.

First, because contemporary Christians inherit a long tradition of theological reflection as a way of formulating belief and practice in light of the situation, much energy is expended on studying the strengths and weaknesses of successive formulations in the work of individual Christian thinkers. This means many contemporary Christians locate themselves as heirs of a tradition that has, as a whole, become problematic in both credibility and relevance. The task, then, is to seek theological formulations that respond to these challenges. Cobb's formulation of this is that Christianity is primarily a socio-historical movement in which the unity of Christian tradition does not consist in unchanging teachings but in a common origin that is celebrated in a multiplicity of ways and forms. Thus reflection on the relation of the present to the common origin is essential for the continuation of the Christian movement.

From a Christian perspective, the Buddhist writers in this volume seem different. Being a Buddhist seems not nearly as problematic for thoughtful Buddhists as being a Christian is for thoughtful Christians. That is, Buddhists do not need to engage in 'constructive theology.' However, this does not mean that the Buddhist contributors to the volume are triumphalist. The 'shortcomings' of Buddhism are freely and nondefensively recognized. Moreover criticism of Christianity is gentler that typical Christian self-criticism. Buddhists generally acknowledge the need for fresh reflection in a changing historical context, especially American Buddhists. But this reflection is designed to bring to bear more effectively on the present historical context an understanding and realization that have been present in the tradition for millennia. This means that while Christians often experience Buddhism as a fundamental challenge to Christian self-understanding, even as they might be eager to appropriate Buddhist insights and practices into their own faith, Buddhists do not often experience Christian theology as a major threat to their basic self-understanding. So while Buddhists are genuinely open to learning how Christians have organized their institutions and adapted themselves to the modern world, and while Buddhists are interested in seeing where Christian thought converges with their own, 'none of this requires dialogue in the narrow sense.'

Second, the Christian essays are explicit or implicit calls to action and creativity. As Cooey notes in her essay, if we do not act creatively in the world, God's love may be destroyed. The Buddhist essays are all accounts of 'the way,' and although the Buddhist way includes compassionate ministering to the needs of all sentient beings, it is, in the last analysis, 'a way of cessation,' as illustrated by Sallie King's description of the Cambodian peasants' desire for a cessation of the round of suffering rather than for justice. 'Of course, the Buddhist acts. But the goal of acting is to end the need for such acting.'

This leads Cobb to his third point – the question of justice, which Sallie King raises in her essay. The struggle for justice has not been a major force in Buddhist teaching or history, but is central to Christian self-understanding and teaching. Since in standard Christian teaching, there are greater evils than violence, what is the relation between justice and non-violence? Christians misrepresent their tradition if they do not emphasize the importance of justice. Thus Cobb find himself 'not quite happy' with the non-violent attitudes of the Cambodian peasants mentioned by King, since 'even those Christians 'who emphasize love and forgiveness, also want justice.' While justice is not the same as revenge or retaliation, Christians 'want those who have committed crimes to be legally prosecuted and punished, for it is not good for unjust persons or institutions 'to get away with it.' Consequently, Cobb argues that in future dialogue, Christians should reflect on their passion for retributive justice in light of the Buddhist passion for non -violence as Buddhists might reflect on the need for justice in their practice of non-violence.

The editors wish to express their gratitude to the authors of these essays for their cooperation and patience throughout the process of compiling and editing. Finally, and above all, the editors are grateful to the Society for Buddhist-Christian Studies for allowing us the opportunity to edit this volume of essays in honor of our friend and colleague, Frederick J. Streng.

PART ONE

Interreligious Dialogue

CHAPTER ONE

Buddhist Interreligious Dialogue: To Build a Global Community

David W. Chappell

The Problem

Thich Nhat Hanh begins his book *Living Buddha, Living Christ* by recalling an interreligious meeting in Sri Lanka where participants were assured: 'We are going to hear about the beauties of several traditions, but that does not mean that we are going to make a fruit salad.' When it came time for Nhat Hanh to speak, he commented: 'Fruit salad can be delicious! I have shared the Eucharist with Father Daniel Berrigan, and our worship became possible because of the sufferings we Vietnamese and Americans shared over many years.' Nhat Hanh went on to observe that some of the 'Buddhists present were shocked ... and many Christians seemed truly horrified.'[1]

Obviously the meetings between Daniel Berrigan and Nhat Hanh involved Buddhist-Christian dialogue: both were ordained clergy in their respective traditions; both were living in exile because of the Vietnam war, and were sharing with each other based on their deepest religious life.[2] What brought them together, however, was not an intellectual curiosity, but a gift from those who had died: a sense of compassion and kinship that deepened their spiritual life while transcending institutional boundaries.

Because modern Buddhists and Christians often practice dialogue for different reasons, it is useful to distinguish various kinds of dialogue. Eric Sharpe, writing out of a Hindu-Christian context, has identified four kinds: discursive, human, secular, and interior/spiritual dialogue.[3] *Discursive* dialogue is filled with religious content since it is largely theological, whereas less religious content is expressed in

Sharpe's *human and secular* dialogues which are limited to interchange between individuals as individuals or between religious people about secular problems. On the other hand, *interior/spiritual* dialogue primarily involves religious contemplation, but is more experiential and less verbal than discursive dialogue.

According to his 'Dialogue Decalogue,' the editor of the *Journal of Ecumenical Studies,* Leonard Swidler, proposed that interreligious dialogues must be sincere, trusting, and empathetic dialogues between equals in which the partners are at least minimally self-critical and able to define themselves while engaging in an interchange of mutual learning, changing and growing in their perception and understanding of reality.[4] Swidler's guidelines fully express the methods and goals of discursive dialogue focused on the 'perception and understanding of reality,' and are consistent with the rationalism and individualism of the European enlightenment. Winston King made the observation in 1982 that the motivation for Buddhists to engage in dialogue was often an Asian sense of courtesy as hosts to satisfy the requests of their Christian guests, but that they actually had no interest in learning about Christianity.[5] This situation has not changed much, especially if dialogue is restricted to theology, since Christian theology has failed to spark any serious interest, challenge, or growth in the Buddhist community.

The dialogue between Nhat Hanh and Daniel Berrigan, and Nhat Hanh's endorsement of religious fruit salad, do not fit any of these descriptions of dialogue. Much of Buddhist interreligious dialogue has evolved differently from Western models because of various social factors, including the state control of Buddhism, colonialization, and war, as well as its own religious cultivation of emptiness and meditation. When there is serious interreligious dialogue by modern Buddhists, it often is based not on intellectual curiosity but on moral values in an effort to deepen the spiritual life of society, to remove discrimination and exploitation, and to nurture a sense of global community in a divided world. To achieve a more adequate understanding of contemporary Buddhist interreligious dialogue, some historical background is needed to offer a balanced perspective.

Previous Buddhist Interreligious Dialogue

The attitudes of Buddhists toward other religions have run the gamut from exclusivism, to competition, to acceptance of other religions as inferior but useful for worldly benefits (such as health and prosperity), but only rarely have Buddhists acknowledged that Buddhism was equally conditioned and as fallible as others, or accepted other religions as equally able to save.[6] Buddhism began as a missionary religion since encountering others was advocated 'for the welfare of the people, for the tranquillity of the people, out of love for the people of the world.'[7] Many examples are scattered throughout the Buddhist scriptures showing the Buddha meeting with representatives from different groups and giving a variety of responses, some of them critical. For example, he did not accept some Hindu practices for his own community (animal sacrifices and the caste system), while he accepted but subordinated others (such as honor to the gods),[8] and accepted but redefined others (such as worship to the six directions,[9] being a true brahmin,[10] and meditation). In East Asia, Buddhism always coexisted with Confucianism, Taoism, and Shinto with varying degrees of interaction and accommodation.[11] Even in Southeast Asia where Buddhism became the dominant religious tradition and primary religious identity, worship of the gods and honor to the ancestors has not ceased.[12]

In Buddhist cultures written dialogues often took the form of the host-guest (master-student), and were used to communicate the teaching of Buddhism to the uninitiated, or to demonstrate the superiority of Buddhism in comparison to others. Often these writings were in the form of question-and-answer, such as in catechisms, or were thinly disguised debate or apologetics that focused on doctrinal issues and utilized a rational approach (discursive dialogue). While these discursive dialogues were common throughout Buddhist history, what has attracted Westerners has been the unusual nature of Zen dialogues (*mondō*) characterized by non-rational responses based on enlightened awareness. Some Mahayana scriptures not only advocated visiting other teachers in order to learn, but the *Gaṇḍavyūha Sūtra*[13] even shows the famous pilgrim Sudhana dialoguing with and learning from non-Buddhist teachers.

It must be emphasized, however, that the model of learning from non-Buddhists is the exception, not the rule, and Sudhana only visited non-Buddhists in obedience to instructions from a great bodhisattva. Instead, such famous Buddhist thinkers as Nāgārjuna recommended avoiding non-Buddhists and considered as 'bad friends' those who rely on worldly sciences, those who are eager for worldly goods, and even Hinayana Buddhists who follow the way of the *pratyekabuddha* and *śrāvaka*.[14] Ritually and institutionally, this warning against turning to other religious practitioners is contained in early

Mahayana initiation vows that are still used today.[15] Also, in the eighth and twenty-fourth minor precepts of the foundational ethical text for all East Asian Buddhism, the *Brahma-net Sutra,* we read that Buddhists should not 'receive or uphold any of the rules and prohibitions of the evil views of the Two Vehicles, the *śrāvaka* Buddhists, and those outside the way, or any of the scriptures and precepts based on heretical views.'[16] The usual Buddhist view of other religions was negative. Doctrinally other religions were sometimes depicted as good but usually as inadequate,[17] distracting, distorted, or evil. Ritual initiation into Buddhism through the Taking Refuge ceremony often explicitly meant vowing not to follow other religious teachers and not to study other religious traditions.[18]

The traditional Buddhist form of interreligious dialogue was a competition involving a debate between rivals, or an unequal dialogue in which a master dispensed the truth to a disciple. But, except for a few rare cases, traditional Buddhism was like other religions in not holding the idea of the equality of other religions until this century.

Salvation Outside Of Buddhism

In contrast to the recent discovery of pluralism by Westerners, from its beginning Buddhism has repeatedly flourished in religiously plural cultures. As a consequence, patterns of interreligious competition and mutual exclusion have been less extreme or brutal than in the West, and have often been balanced culturally by many experiences of mutual co-existence, accommodation, and collaboration, and in some instances even of equality. Since the recognition of mutual equality is a necessary basis for interreligious dialogue in the modern sense, it may be useful to explore a number of historical instances, rare though they may be, of Buddhist affirmation of the equal validity of practitioners in other religious traditions. These include the Buddha Gautama, the Chinese Ch'an master Ta-hui Tsung-kao (1089–1163), and the Korean Sŏn master, Hyujŏng (1520–1604).

Gautama Buddha

Perhaps the most important, but little mentioned, instance of affirming that salvation is possible outside of Buddhism (as a religious community and religious identity) was made by Gautama Buddha himself. According to the early texts, he sometimes accepted the idea of multiple religious identity since he advised Upāli, a prominent member of the Jain community, that if Upāli should become his follower he should also not cease being a supporter of the Jain community.[19]

This acknowledgment of other practitioners equally on the path to freedom was given doctrinal status in two forms. One was through the idea that in the past there were other Buddhas before Gautama and in the future there would be others after him. In early texts, there was also a doctrinal recognition of those who were similarly accomplished in spiritual insight and practice but who were not within the Buddhist community (who had not taken refuge in Gautama Buddha) by giving them the name of *pratyekabuddha*. Later texts defined them as differing from the Buddhist monastics (*śrāvaka*) and Mahayana bodhisattvas by being able to achieve enlightenment 'by themselves and for themselves' – they did not need the sangha to attain enlightenment and they did not share their enlightenment with others. Contrary to Mahayana, in the early texts there is a clear kinship between these figures and the Buddhist community. Gautama Buddha and his followers were just one group among many others who were part of a larger ascetic, *śramaṇa* movement that evolved in opposition to the ideas and practices of the established hereditary brahmin priesthood.[20] Questioning the authority of the Vedas, rejecting animal sacrifices, and denying the ultimate sufficiency of the gods, these groups affirmed the spiritual capacities of individuals as not limited to caste birth, while emphasizing the importance of personal ascetic practice and contemplative realization.

In addition, it is reported in the oldest Buddhist text, the *Suttanipāta,* that the Buddha affirmed that there were others besides his own followers who had 'gone beyond birth and ageing:'

> I *do not* say that all religious teachers and brahmins are wrapped in the shroud of birth and ageing', said the Buddha. 'There are some who have let go of world-views, of teaching traditions of thoughts. They have let go of religious practices and rituals, they have left all the different forms behind and they have a total understanding of attachments. For them there are no inner poison drives. These, truly, are the ocean-crossers.[21]

It is important to note that the qualities that are affirmed as necessary for enlightenment and freedom involve fully understanding attachments and going beyond all forms, both intellectual and ritual. What was important was not membership in a group, nor belief in certain doctrines, but following a certain kind of practice that urged non-attachment to the kinds of distinctions that separated religious groups. Similar statements by the Buddha are found in a variety of other early Buddhist scriptures.[22]

Ta-hui Tsung-kao

Although the common ground between early Buddhism and the larger *śramaṇa* movement was soon forgotten as Buddhism became established, centuries later when Buddhism entered China a new common ground was discovered. Although for most of its history Chinese Buddhism lived in competition with other Chinese religious traditions, there is also a recurring affirmation that Confucianism and Taoism shared common goals and values, which became expressed in the popular slogan: 'the three religions return to the one' (*san-chiao kuei-i*).[23] A leading Buddhist advocate for this position was the great Ch'an master Ta-hui Tsung-kao (1089–1163), who affirmed the commonality of the Buddha, Confucius, and Lao Tzu by saying: 'They see with one eye, they hear with one ear, they smell with one nose, they taste with one tongue, they touch with one body, they think with one mind.'[24] Ta-hui affirmed that the three founding figures of Buddhism, Confucianism, and Taoism saw and understood reality in the same way. The problem of explaining how the Three Religions came from the same source yet were so different in their later expressions was resolved by Ta-hui by using the Chinese distinction between substance and function (*t'i* and *yung*).[25] Even though their inner substance or essence was the same, because of different needs of different situations the functions and manifestations of the Three Religions were different.[26]

Ta-hui rejected interreligious rivalry as based on misunderstanding the differences of other religions by not seeing that these arose in response to different needs. If people could see through these differences to the source and their common goal, they could see that there was no conflict, and thereby develop respect and trust toward the other traditions. Robert Gimello has argued that to some degree Ta-hui reflected a cultural movement active during the Northern Sung called *Tao-hsüeh* ('study of the Way') that taught intuitive and immediate insight as the method for reaching the Way, rejecting ponderous learning.[27] Accordingly, Tao-hui downplayed focus on details and emphasized seeing the inner intention, goals, and source. In this way, there was a cultural context that nurtured a flexibility and openness in interpreting the texts and ideas of others[28] that enabled

Ta-hui to pass over conflicting details of other religions and find some common ground.

Ch'ŏnghŏ Hyujŏng

Following the tradition of Ta-hui, the great Sŏn master, Ch'ŏnghŏ Hyujŏng (1520–1604) of Korea, believed that the ways to enlightenment of the Three Religions resonated with each other. To demonstrate this, he compiled a selection of quotations from each of the three traditions and added his own comments.[29] While acknowledging that the Three Religions used many different names and words to match the needs and capacities of practitioners, he also emphasized not getting lost in words, but instead going beyond thoughts to find the universal One that could be called by many names. However, this underlying oneness is not obvious, but has to be divined: hence he titled his writing, 'The Divining Mirror for the Three Religions' (*Samga Kwigam*).

All of these selected, but outstanding, Buddhist leaders – Gautama Buddha, Tahui, and Hyujŏng – taught that salvation was possible in other religious groups outside of Buddhism. While each thinker had his own method of finding common ground with other religions, they were unanimous in moving beyond verbal and doctrinal differences that are the usual focus of discursive dialogue. Not only did they emphasize shared practices, goals, and motivations as more important than conceptual differences, but also they condemned arguments and debates over these conceptual differences as being a mistake.

Collaboration Replaces Competition

Since its beginning, Buddhism has had recurring, if rare, interreligious dialogue with other religions as equals, but what is new during the past century is the promotion of interreligious dialogue as a necessary spiritual task to nurture social harmony and the well being of the global community. Dialogue in this modern sense gained momentum among Buddhist leaders after World War II, not only because of new worldwide communications, but also in view of the horrors of that war and the need to build a global community based on spiritual values. Perhaps the earliest interreligious event based on this goal was the World's Parliament of Religions in Chicago in 1893.

Among the Japanese 'champions of Buddhism' who ventured to the Parliament,[30] only the lay Buddhist, Hirai Kinzō, was able to speak

9

English. He delivered a stirring challenge to the Parliament by recalling the offensive racism and arrogance displayed by Christian missionaries in Japan coupled with the efforts to exploit Japan by the so-called Christian nations. As a foil to his criticism of Christian intolerance, he began by affirming Japan's basic belief in religious harmony as displayed by the co-existence of Buddhism and Shinto within the same shrine area, and within the same home. To cap his claim, he quoted a folk song that is often repeated in Japanese Buddhist dialogue groups in this century: 'Though there are many roads at the foot of the mountain, yet, if the top is reached, the same moon is seen.'[31]

While these delegates returned to Japan reporting on their great success in challenging the West, the delegate who seemed most inspired with a new vision by the World's Parliament was the Rinzai Zen representative, Shaku Sōen, who saw even the most bigoted speaker in terms of their quest to develop a global cooperative human family (*shikai bammin kyōdō kazoku*).[32] Rather than being blindly optimistic, it is more likely that Shaku Sōen chose to emphasize the positive as a device to promote a movement towards a global community.[33] This moral commitment to the value of a global religious community continues to be a feature of modern Buddhist dialogue.

Mutual Appreciation and Cooperation

This global community was advanced even more by Shaku Sōen's translator, D.T. Suzuki. While normally seen as the greatest Zen missionary to the West, he also translated several writings by Swedenborg into Japanese and studied Western mystics. After living twelve years in the West (1897–1909), he returned to Japan for forty years and started a journal called *The Eastern Buddhist* in the spring of 1921. His lead editorial echoed Shaku Sōen, proclaiming: 'The time has come for those who believe in peace and enlightenment and universal brotherhood.' Even though the journal dealt almost exclusively with Mahayana Buddhism, it constantly reflected one of Suzuki's lifelong concerns, namely, the shared depths and mutual illumination of faith and wisdom, of Pure Land and Zen, that was to make him adept at Buddhist-Christian interchange.

In 1957 in the same year of the famous Tillich-Hisasmatsu dialogues at Harvard University, D.T. Suzuki published *Mysticism: Christian and Buddhist. The Eastern and the Western Way* (New

York: Macmillan, 1957). This book sparked responses from several Christian leaders and led to a written dialogue in 1959 with Thomas Merton.[34] In contrast to Hisamatsu and Tillich, who drew on art and philosophy, Suzuki and Merton emphasized contemplation and stories and had a sympathetic understanding in spite of verbal differences. For example, Suzuki noted that for Zen suffering comes from ignorance, whereas for Christians the Fall consisted of partaking of 'the knowledge of good and evil'. While describing a similar process, the words were different: knowledge for Christians, ignorance for Zen. For both Merton and Suzuki, the way to return to a state of innocence, of paradise, was remarkably similar, but again used different words, namely, through emptiness, poverty of heart, and perfect charity, which Suzuki also identified as *anabhoga-cāryā* ('effortless, no striving'): 'Poverty corresponds ontologically to Emptiness and psychologically to selflessness or Innocence.'[35] Although their dialogue was discursive, it was their expression of mutual support and appreciation that was the strongest message of their interchange.

After World War II, many new religious groups arose in Japan, but they were often attacked by traditional institutions. In 1951 a new interreligious coalition was formed called Shinshūren (Federation of New Religious Organizations of Japan) 'to firmly maintain freedom of faith in Japan and, at the same time, to contribute to the peace which everybody hoped for in the chaos of the postwar period. To that end, member organizations promoted interreligious cooperation, transcending their individual, private views and emotions.'[36] A year after its formation, Shinshūren became affiliated with the Japan Religions League, and since that time the chair of the Japan Religions League has rotated among the five affiliated unions: the Japan Buddhist Federation, the Japan Christian Federation, the Association of Shinto Shrines, the Association of Sectarian Shinto, and Shinshūren. In 1965, the year Nikkyo Niwano, leader of the Buddhist New Religion, Risshō Kōseikai, became the head of Shinshūren, it adopted four principles: interreligious cooperation, freedom of faith, separation of religion and politics, and faith for all people.[37] Niwano also became head of the Japan Religions League in 1969 and 1974, and thus was instrumental in having the Japan Religions League be host of the first meeting of the interreligious World Conference on Religion and Peace (WCRP) in 1970. In his welcoming remarks at the first WCRP, Niwano subordinated religious differences to the more important concern of human happiness and world peace:

The time has arrived when religions, instead of antagonizing each other because of what we once thought was a religious conviction, should cooperate with each other in order to contribute to the cause of mankind and world peace, because, in the final analysis, all sectors of religion are and can be bound together by the common aspiration for human happiness and salvation.[38]

Niwano believed that religious differences arose as independent developments of 'tribal' religions with their own guardian deities, but that 'the great, original object of all faiths is one,' and he has earnestly advocated religious union.[39] The WCRP has continued to have worldwide meetings every five years since its second meeting in 1974. Most recently, the sixth worldwide WCRP meeting in November 1994 was held in the Vatican Hall in Riva del Garda; this was the first time the Vatican allowed a non-Christian organization to use one of its facilities. On the dais at center stage sitting side by side on an equal basis were two leaders, one Christian and one Buddhist: Pope John Paul II and Nikkyo Niwano.

Beyond Rationalism: Emptiness and Transformation

After the Meiji modernization reform began in 1868, Westernization was encouraged and European philosophy (that included theology) became an established part of the Japanese university curriculum. In the early twentieth century, beginning from Nishida Kitarō (1870–1945), the Philosophy Department of Kyoto University began discursive dialogue with the West by offering a critical analysis and response based on Buddhist ideas. Disciples of Nishida, such as Tanabe Hajime (1885–1962), Hisamatsu Shin'ichi (1889–1980), Nishitani Keiji (1900–1990), and Abe Masao (1915–) became known collectively as the Kyoto School.[40] While utilizing reason, the Kyoto School also used Buddhist methods to seek truth that was beyond rational limits. For example, following Nishida's advice, Hisamatsu began Zen practice and his experience summed up the meaning of the Kyoto School:

casting off the religion of medieval belief, turning to the philosophy of modern reason, breaking through the extreme limits of rational thought and its objective knowledge, and awakening to the totally unhindered and emancipated True Self.[41]

To interpret this new awareness, Hisamatsu wrote his most important philosophical work, *Tōyō-teki Mu* (Oriental Nothingness) in 1939 to introduce truths that were beyond normal Western rational categories.[42]

Following the war Hisamatsu sent his student, Abe Masao, to Union Theological Seminary in New York for two years (1955–1957) to study Christianity under the leading Protestant theologians, Reinhold Niebuhr and Paul Tillich. Finally in 1957 Hisamatsu Shin'ichi himself went to Harvard for the fall semester and was able to engage in several meetings with Paul Tillich that mark the beginning of modern Buddhist-Christian dialogue. Appropriately, records of these dialogues were later published in *The Eastern Buddhist*, the journal started by D.T. Suzuki.

While Hisamatsu and Tillich both were leading thinkers of their own religious traditions, they both were eager to learn from each other.[43] Hisamatsu expressed to Tillich that 'I should like to learn from you,' especially on topics such as the 'God beyond God', and 'What is it in the nature of the human being that both constitutes the basis and accounts for the necessity of religion?'[44] In this last question, Hisamatsu was referring to the Formless Self based on the experience of Emptiness. Rather than focusing on what was unique in the other tradition, Hisamatsu tried to push beyond both traditions to seek what is common to human existence. This has been a significant feature of Japanese Buddhist discursive dialogue under the influence of the Kyoto School, and it continues in the annual meetings of the Tōzai Shūkyō Kōryū Gakkai (Society for the Mutual Understanding of East-West Religions) that started in 1982.[45]

Whereas Tillich insisted that except for Christ, individuals in space and time could only partially realize the infinite, for Hisamatsu everyone could and should do so, and he rejected all finite distinctions at the level of the formless self.[46] This claim led Hisamatsu (and later his student Abe Masao) to the controversial doctrine of the 'reversibility' of the ultimate and finite, of Buddha and other beings, of past and future. This doctrine of 'reversibility' is a source of disagreement not only with Christians and Jews, but also with most other Buddhists.[47]

The eminent Buddhist leader in Thailand, Bhikkhu Buddhadāsa (1906–1993) provided important refinements for interreligious dialogue by interpreting language in two ways, namely, (1) dharma language and (2) ordinary conventional language. Using this distinction Buddhadasa interpreted the names of different religions as conventional language[48] and not the standpoint of ultimate, enlightened practice. That is to say, differences between religious people are real and it is common to speak this way. However, there is a higher truth that all religions refer to, and it is in this higher truth that all religions are united.[49] Moreover, Buddhadāsa goes on to suggest that there is a further level of religious life in which religion itself disappears. To illustrate his idea of the three levels of religion, Buddhadāsa uses the example of water. First there are many kinds of water: rainwater, ditch water, and sewer water, which ordinary people can and should distinguish. However, at another level, when the pollutants are removed, fundamentally these waters have the same substance. Nevertheless, there is yet a third level of perception in which water itself disappears when we divide it into hydrogen and oxygen. Based on this analogy, there are three levels outlined by Buddhadāsa: conventional distinctions, shared essence, and voidness.

By proposing three levels of understanding, Buddhadāsa offers a tool for distinguishing the approach of the Kyoto School focused on absolute emptiness from the approach of many other Buddhists who are affirming a shared religious practice (insight and non-attachment), or locus of practice (mind), or object of practice (Tao).[50] Like many other Buddhists involved in dialogue, the Dalai Lama also focuses discussion on the middle level by affirming the common goal of religions. 'All of the different religious faiths, despite their philosophical differences, have a similar objective. Every religion emphasizes human improvement, love, respect for others, sharing other peoples' suffering. On these lines every religion has more or less the same viewpoint and the same goal.'[51]

Unfortunately, Buddhadāsa, with this tripartite Buddhist framework for analyzing other religions, never engaged the ideas of the Kyoto School which usually favored a dialectic. Do the 'dazzling darkness' and 'dynamic emptiness' of Masao Abe[52] express only emptiness, or do they embrace the two higher levels of Buddhadāsa, especially his essence of religion? Although Abe also developed a tripartite structure to compare various religions,[53] he most frequently maintained a dialectic since he was most concerned to overcome Western nihilism. In this regard, he reflected the concern of his teacher, Nishitani Keiji,[54] a contemporary of Hisamatsu who took up the Western challenge of the death of the divine order of existence, slain by a mechanistic universe, a Marxian social order, and atheistic philosophy, by arguing that 'The self-presentation of nihility is rather a real presentation of what is actually concealed at the ground of the self and of everything in the world.'[55]

What is this 'self-presentation of nihility' celebrated by Nishitani? In 1963 Abe Masao took this proposal out of his philosophical circles and placed them before Japanese Christians in a two-part article in *Japanese Religions.* Having trained in Christian theology, Abe ingeniously took the Buddhist insights of the Kyoto School into the Christian world by asking what it means to say that the world was created out of nothing (*creatio ex nihilo*).[56] Abe shared Nishitani's concern to respond to the challenge of science, Marxism, and nihilism as a common threat to global religious values, but he also was concerned to awaken Christians to experience emptiness as a Christian truth within themselves. As a result of his unique ability to use Christian sources to ask Buddhist questions, Abe has been the most influential Buddhist dialogue representative in the West. In addition to participating in countless dialogue meetings, he organized with John Cobb The Theological Encounter With Buddhism Group that included the leading Christian theologians in the world,[57] and more recently has initiated a series of dialogues with Jewish partners.[58]

In several ways, Abe is the model for Buddhist interreligious dialogue.[59] Throughout his life, beginning from his thirties, Abe has been exploring Christianity and taking it seriously.[60] During his collaboration with John Cobb, they both came to the conviction that dialogue was not just a matter of discussion and greater under-standing, but of 'mutual transformation.'[61] As evidence, Abe could write in his early seventies about the four major ways in which Christianity had changed his own thinking.[62] It is safe to say that Abe embodies Buddhist interreligious dialogue in the modern sense better than any other Buddhist because (1) he is committed to interreligious collaboration in order to heal negative global forces, (2) he undertook extensive study in order to understand another religion from the inside, (3) he has been tireless and brilliant in strategically engaging important Western thinkers for several decades in their own language and in their own lands, and (4) as a consequence his own religious life has been transformed and made more complete by the process.

Different Religions for Different People

In October 1980 on a visit to Hawaii, the Dalai Lama noted that many religions were needed in the world as a reflection of the various needs of the different kinds of people. Accordingly, he affirmed the pluralism of the world religions and rejected the idea of only one world religion as inadequate, being equivalent to eating rice three times a day, everyday: 'It would be boring.' Instead, the Dalai Lama saw that through their diversity religions could benefit from each other: for example, Buddhists could learn from Christian ways of organizing social-welfare programs. Nevertheless, even though 'affirming what he saw to be differences in religious traditions, he said that fundamentally each of them are concerned with the same goal, to make better human beings.'[63]

While Suzuki and Merton found much common ground, they also agreed that their two traditions differed because Christianity and Zen represent 'two types of mentality which fundamentally differ one from the other: (1) affective, personal and dualistic, and (2) non-affective, non-personal and non-dualistic. Zen belongs to the latter and Christianity naturally to the former.'[64] This view that the Buddhist and Christian traditions represent 'two different types of mentality,' and its corollary that to some degree each tradition also contains the other, as represented in Christianity by the Zen-like mystics and in Buddhism by Christian-like Pure Land devotionalism, is an important way of accounting for and accepting differences among religions.

Recognizing that different religions arise to meet different needs of people with different capacities, and yet affirming that underlying this diversity of religions is a primal unity (the One Vehicle) is a view found most fully in the *Lotus Sutra*. Therefore, it is appropriate that Nikkyo Niwano, the founder of Risshō Kōseikai, a lay Buddhist community based on the *Lotus Sutra*, is one of the foremost contemporary Buddhist leaders in support of interreligious cooperation. As a youth Niwano always respected both Shinto shrines and Buddhist temples, and lived in the midst of fortune-telling, shamanism, and the spirits of his ancestors. He first became impressed by the *Lotus Sutra* when it was effective in healing his daughter,[65] and then discovered in the *Lotus Sutra* 'a rule that could save everyone, a rule that was not mysterious, but was convincingly based on reason.'[66] The *Lotus Sutra* had two teachings that 'suited my personal feelings exactly: the way of compassion of the bodhisattva – helping others and serving everyone in the world – is the true meaning of Buddhism; and the ability of the lay believer both to save and to be saved.'[67]

Zen-Christian Interchange

In 1967 a Zen-Christian Colloquium was begun by Christian Quakers seeking to establish peace after World War II by developing mutual understanding. Their initiative also sought to express Christian enthusiasm resulting from the new Catholic-Protestant dialogues that flowered in the early 1960s.[68] So much enthusiasm was expressed at the first meeting of the Zen-Christian Colloquium that the participants have continued on their own initiative every year since. The two Rinzai Buddhists on the original planning committee, Hisamatsu Shin'ichi and Yamada Mumon, were joined in the early years by Sōtō leaders such as Yamada Reirin, Nara Yasuaki, and Suzuki Kakuzen, as well as by other Rinzai leaders such as Shibayama Zenkei, Abe Masao, Akizuki Ryōmin, Hōzumi Genshō, and Nishimura Eshin. While some members of the Kyoto School were present, the emphasis was not on philosophy and theology. As Irie Yukio recalls, 'As far as possible, we were to try not to refer to what is written in books.' Since the general themes of the first colloquium were (1) my spiritual journey, and (2) a believer's social responsibility today, instead of focusing on written papers, each year the group emphasized personal experience and communication by living together from four to six days.[69]

The joint practice of Zen and Christianity has been a major phenomenon during the last half century,[70] and the small Sanbōkyō-dan Zen lineage centered in Kamakura has played a major role. In 1970, Yamada Kōun became the successor of Yasutani Roshi as head (*kanchō*) of the Sanbōkyōdan. Ruben Habito, a Jesuit who became a student of Yamada Roshi in 1971, recalls that even though several priests and nuns were students of Yamada at that time, still none had been confirmed as having the *kenshō* experience that was seen as the first step of koan practice. A few years later, Habito became perhaps the first Christian to be confirmed as having achieved this opening Zen experience under a Japanese Zen Master.[71] In 1978, another Jesuit, Hugo Makibi Enomiya-Lassalle (1898–1990) was recognized by Yamada as a Zen teacher. Although the recognition of Enomiya-Lassalle was an important turning point in Zen-Christian relations, there had been a long preparation: Enomiya-Lassalle had his first Zen retreat in 1943, and he had begun training under the Sanbōkyōdan lineage in 1956 when Yasutani's teacher, Harada Sōgaku (1879–1961), had accepted him as a Zen student.

Besides Enomiya-Lassalle, there are over a dozen Christian priests and nuns who have been recognized as Zen teachers by Yamada.[72] In addition, other Zen successors[73] of Yamada have also recognized Christian clergy as Zen teachers.[74] Although this consists of a Zen movement in Christianity, it necessarily involves interreligious dialogue for the Zen communities. For example, Bernard Glassman (a successor of Taizan Maezumi who was another successor of Yamada Roshi and who became head of the Los Angeles Zen Center) reports how his own student, Fr. Robert Kennedy, performed the Catholic liturgy in Glassman's New York Zen Center with the result that it led 'the participants to deepen their contemplative life.'[75]

Contemplative Dialogue

Another Buddhist dialogue group based on the religious life was the East-West Spiritual Exchange focused on inter-monastic understanding. Again, the goal was not theoretical but practical: namely, to learn as much as possible about the spiritual life of each other by living in each other's monasteries and following all the observances. Beginning with more than fifty Japanese Buddhist clergy and laity who visited European Christian monasteries in 1979, a second exchange took place in 1983 by a visit of thirteen Christian monks and two nuns from European Catholic monasteries to Buddhist monasteries in Japan.[76] The Third East-West Spiritual Exchange took place from August 23 to September 16, 1987, and consisted of twenty-six monks and three nuns from Japanese Zen monasteries (Sōtō, Rinzai, and Ōbaku) who stayed in Christian monasteries in Europe.[77] The fourth exchange took place in 1990 when fourteen monks and six nuns from European Catholic monasteries visited Japanese monasteries from October 11 to November 9, 1990.[78]

Beyond this series of Japanese-European meetings, there have been many other intermonastic meetings worldwide. Many of these have been reported on, and facilitated by, a networking group called the Monastic Interreligious Dialogue (MID) founded by the Benedictine Confederation in 1978 and centered in America. This Catholic group has often involved meetings with Tibetan Buddhist monastics, but has also included monastics from other Buddhist groups and from different Asian religions, especially inspired by the work of Bede Griffiths among Hindus in India. In July 1996 MID sponsored a Christian/Buddhist Dialogue on Meditation involving the Dalai Lama for a week at Gethsemani Abbey, the former residence of Thomas Merton. The Dalai Lama has emphasized the positive value of dialogue and praying together for generating a 'certain feeling that we can experience that is 'very helpful for inner strength. For a real sense of brotherhood and sisterhood that feeling – that atmosphere and experience – is very useful and helpful. Therefore I particularly appreciate these ecumenical gatherings.'[79] As a consequence, the Dalai Lama encouraged and made arrangements for various interreligious activities, especially intermonastic meetings of Tibetan and Catholic monks.[80]

The small number of monastics involved in the East-West Spiritual Exchange can be contrasted with the thousands who participated in a series of interreligious dialogues focused on meditation organized by the Naropa Institute in Colorado. Like the monastic life, the focus of these annual summer Buddhist and Christian Meditation conferences was the spiritual life of contemplation. When reporting on the seventh conference held July 27–31, 1988, Judith Simmer-Brown, one of the organizers, wrote that 'The purpose of the ongoing dialogue has been the exploration of the common experience of contemplative Christians and Buddhists living in a largely non-contemplative contemporary society.'[81]

Beginning in the early 1990s, another American Buddhist group, the Insight Meditation Society of Barre, Massachusetts, has been annually organizing Buddhist and Christian and Buddhist-Jewish retreats that emphasize contemplative practice.[82]

Socially Engaged Dialogue

Unlike the individual focus of the shared contemplative practices and dialogue by members of the Kyoto School, various Buddhist dialogue leaders have been motivated by social service in the cause of bringing peace and social harmony. On May 8, 1963, eight students in Vietnam were killed when the government crushed a peaceful demonstration by thousands of Buddhists seeking the same legal status as the Catholic Church.[83] The world learned of this religious suppression on June 11, 1963, when an elderly Zen monk, Thich Quang Duc, sat in the lotus posture at a busy intersection in Saigon, doused himself with gasoline, and set fire to himself. After two years of more demonstrations and self-immolations (called 'Buddhist barbecues' by the Diem ruling family), the School of Youth for Social Service was founded in 1965 by Thich Nhat Hanh to train Buddhists in nonviolent social action based on Gandhian principles to help the poor develop self-reliance in education, agriculture, sanitation, and health care. In spite of their pledge to non-violence, many members of SYSS were killed, badly injured, or imprisoned by the government.[84]

Living in exile in Paris in the mid-1970s, Nhat Hanh told of the death on May 16, 1967 of the Buddhist laywoman, Nhat Chi Mai, a staff member who had immolated herself for peace in front of a Buddhist statue of Quan Am and a Christian statue of Mary.[85] This account by Nhat Hanh was told to his friend, Daniel Berrigan, a Jesuit anti-war activist also living in exile in Paris, after Father Dan had recalled the immolation of a fourteen year old American boy who couldn't bear the horror of the war and had to do something. The death of Nhat Chi Mai expressed an interreligious dialogue that had taken place within herself because of the war, while the dialogue between Father Dan and Nhat Hanh also arose as a human kinship beyond religious boundaries in the name of those who had suffered so much. Beyond this special kinship, Nhat Hanh explained his appreciation for other religions by writing that 'religious life is life. I do not see any reason to spend one's whole life tasting just one kind of fruit. We human beings can be nourished by the best values of many traditions.'[86]

Two points are important here. First is the priority given by Nhat Hanh to life over religion, which means that like many other Buddhists he sees religion as a temporary and inadequate vehicle to enable people to enter more fully into reality: religion should not take precedence over or be a barrier to life. Second is the commitment that Buddhism should be involved in relieving suffering and the conflict of war, and that in the face of suffering and death, religious differences are important only as different sources of nourishment, not as obstacles to collaboration. As a consequence, dialogue is most meaningful when it takes place in the context of trying to heal a world in conflict. This can be called 'socially engaged dialogue.'[87]

Another major leader of socially engaged Buddhism is Sulak Sivaraksa, a prominent Thai Buddhist who is a lay disciple of Buddhadāsa and was the honorary editor of the official journal of the Buddhist Association of Thailand, *Visakha Pūjā*, for thirteen years. After Christian schooling in Bangkok and Wales,[88] Sulak was radicalized by reading the outcry of young writers and poets upon his return to Thailand in 1962 at the age of 29. In response, he founded the journal *Social Science Review* (*Sangkhomsat Parithat*) which became the leading voice for social, economic, and political change in the 1960s and helped generate a climate that led to the mass demonstrations in 1973 that established a democratic regime. Although thrown out of office, anti-democratic forces increasingly kidnapped and assassinated labor and farm leaders, leaving many families and villages destitute. To help relieve their suffering and to form an interreligious coalition to appeal for a nonviolent means to resolve disputes, Sulak collaborated with Christians to form the Coordinating Group for Religion and Society (CGRS)[89] on March 17, 1976; their joint Declaration was printed in the *Visakha Pūjā* B.E. 2519 (1976).[90] After the military coup in October 1976 the CGRS continued to visit political prisoners, look after their families, work with the poor by relieving malnutrition, and to report on abuses of power.

For the past two decades Sulak has worked with Christians and Muslims to help modernize Thailand and promote democracy and social justice while maintaining traditional Buddhist values of collaboration based on mindfulness and compassion. In 1979 he formed the Thai Inter-Religious Commission for Development, and in 1985 it began a regular journal called *Seeds of Peace,* which included reports of the CGRS.[91] In addition, Sulak has been active in numerous dialogue groups,[92] but always to remind them that conceptual categories and religious practices are valuable only to the degree that they are helpful in relieving human suffering, greed, hatred, and ignorance.[93]

The World Conference on Religion and Peace (WCRP) also strives to be socially responsible by developing a worldwide climate to nurture inner and outer peace. The practical focus of the WCRP was expressed in the welcoming remarks by Kosho Ohtani of Nishi Hongwanji in 1970, who recalled that 'Japan is the only country that has been victimized by an atom bomb.' Pointing out that science cannot answer the question about how to realize peace and happiness, he proposed that: 'Understanding towards others and the generosity to forgive are surely the spiritual bases leading to a peaceful world.' As for differences among religions, he asserted that 'There may be differences of opinions, but let us not just be abstract and subjective. It is much more important to be concrete in finding a solution to peace. May we transcend individual feelings and faiths and advance our deliberations by centering our thoughts on the one subject of world peace.'[94] To demonstrate its commitment to action, shortly after the 1970 meeting, a WCRP delegation went to Vietnam and later evolved a series of relief actions that led to help for boat people and resettlement placement in Japan.

Religion has a special responsibility as a peace-maker since it shapes the inner attitudes that are necessary for restraining hostility and building cooperation. However, no one religion has a monopoly in the area of ethics and social relationships. Based on these values, the Dalai Lama flatly states that 'I am not interested in converting other people to Buddhism but in how we Buddhists can contribute to human society, according to our own ideas.' Furthermore, 'the motivation of all religious practice is similar – love, sincerity, honesty – each type of system seeking in its own unique ways to improve human beings. If we put too much emphasis on our own philosophy, religion, or theory, are too attached to it, and try to impose it on other people, it makes trouble.[95]

In contrast to trying to impose one's own religion on others, the Dalai Lama emphasized the need to understand each other, both to avoid trouble and to enhance our life. 'Most important is that we respect each other and learn from each other those things that will enrich our own practice. Even if all the systems are separate, since they each have the same goal, the study of each is helpful.'[96] In emphasizing a common goal of religions, in respecting and valuing the differences among religions, and in seeking to learn from other religions in order to avoid trouble, build cooperation, and to be enriched by them, the Dalai Lama fully embraces all the characteristics of modern interreligious dialogue. It was appropriate, therefore, that he was the featured speaker of the centennial meeting of the World Parliament of Religions held in Chicago in 1993, and was also the featured speaker at the fifth international conference sponsored by the Society for Buddhist-Christian Studies in 1996 and titled: 'Socially Engaged Buddhism and Christianity.'

Conclusion

Interreligious dialogue has been an initiative largely of Christianity. The emergence of dialogue among Buddhists in recent times not only has benefited from Christian impetus, however, but also has been shaped by regional experiences. Particular social factors that have made Buddhist interreligious relations different from the Christian West have been government suppression, colonialism, and war. Appropriately, modern interreligious dialogue has been most strongly motivated among Buddhists as a moral commitment to build a global community of peace through interreligious collaboration, even if that meant temporarily suspending or subordinating the distinctive features of their own religious traditions. While this global mission first appeared during the first World's Parliament of Religions, it has developed as a more dominant theme in Buddhist dialogue than in Christian for two reasons. First, Christianity has had the unusual luxury of freedom of movement at home and expansion globally because of its strength in relation to Western governments (either through sponsorship or separation). This has enabled Western Christianity to become well organized, educated, and strong, as well as to travel with European expansionism into distant lands where contact with other religions could lead eventually to intellectual curiosity and dialogue.

In contrast to modern Christian experience, Buddhism has usually been under government control in Asia that prevented a well-organized religious challenge to secular power. In modern times, this has also meant that in some cultures, especially in Korea and China, it was illegal to evangelize, the Buddhist clergy was not seen as a socially desirable profession, and it was cut off from the world. As a consequence, in spite of the active interreligious dialogue by Chinese and Koreans in the past (as we have seen in the cases of Ta-hui and Hyujŏng), there has been less contemporary interest in dialogue by Buddhists in China and Korea than anywhere else.

Even though Buddhism in Japan was also state controlled, the modern rise of Japan to a world power and to expansionism has enabled Japanese Buddhists to engage the wider world with intellectual interest and rational dialogue. Only in Japan are there great Buddhist universities with the highest quality of secular and religious education. Only in Japan have there been the economic resources for Buddhists to travel as suits their interest. Nevertheless, even there the major reason for dialogue is moral. Nara Yasuaki[97] observed that all members of the Zen-Christian Colloquium 'share a common understanding of the nature and limits of language with the result that the colloquium is a real dialogue instead of a doctrinal debate.' 'Gradually, I have come to realize and have been convinced that it is dialogue when we can move each other to the depths. The necessity of exchanging knowledge and of objective discussion is not to be denied; each has it own interest and significance ... But, at the same time, thanks to my fellow members, I was able to come in touch with the "world of the spirit", which is sharply distinguishable from knowledge.'[98]

While affirming the friendship and cordiality of the meetings, Nara also admitted the danger that dialogues sometimes were less than productive since they emphasized being pleasant. Part of the reason was that the Buddhist members were a selective group 'known in Zen circles as internationalists' who have either lived abroad or who are broadminded, being 'very much concerned about talking to people of other religions in order to establish a spiritual tie by which all religions can cope with the various problems of the world.' Accordingly, in order to develop understanding and solidarity, 'controversial issues, which should have been discussed thoroughly, were consciously avoided lest an unpleasant feeling should be left behind among us.'[99]

Quite different has been the experience of Buddhists in Sri Lanka, Southeast Asia, and Tibet. Certainly the privileged position of Buddhism in these cultures has ensured an inner sense of confidence and talented Buddhist leaders. In Thailand, a country that has been colonized economically but not militarily, two social reformers, Buddhadāsa and Sulak Sivaraksa, became major interreligious dialogue leaders. Similarly, in Vietnam and Tibet, which have entered the modern world as victims rather than conquerors, the two outstanding Buddhist leaders, Thich Nhat Hanh and the Dalai Lama, are both active in interreligious meetings. Living in exile has made them more available to dialogue, while the pain that their communities have experienced may have changed their priorities: certainly neither leader is interested in the inter-institutional rivalries, the ritual boundaries, and the intellectual pride of a privileged elite. Instead, the struggle of their people has caused them to emphasize the strongest resources of their tradition – the clarity of calm mindfulness, the openness of emptiness, and the kinship of compassion – which has enabled them to relate to a common humanity and to collaborate interreligiously with a concern for the welfare of all. Although in Sri Lanka, the leading Buddhist social activist, A.T. Ariyaratne, is not active in dialogue, he at least assumes that the common purpose of all religions is to develop egolessness, and he promotes interreligious cooperation.[100]

Most interreligious dialogue as practiced in this century is a new phenomenon not only for Buddhists, but also in the history of world religions, because it has arisen based on a new sense of responsibility for building a global community. This role of dialogue as an effort to affirm a shared humanity and spiritual values in order to rescue the world from war and conflict is different from the more intellectual view of dialogue that has evolved within the privileged elite of Western Christians that is centered on the theological task of discussing the 'perception and understanding of reality' among themselves. In this latter sense, interreligious dialogue is not new for

Buddhists, but has been a recurring, if infrequent, phenomenon in Buddhist history. Today, however, most Buddhist dialogue efforts imply that the present needs are not primarily intellectual, but moral: how to act as partners to overcome social injustice and economic exploitation in both East and West by cultivating spiritual and communal values that will restore a global kinship and responsibility for each other and our Mother Earth. Contemporary Buddhists who advocate interreligious dialogue see this as a task not just for their minds and mouths, but also for their hearts and hands.

Notes

1 Thich Nhat Hanh, *Living Buddha, Living Christ* (Berkeley: Riverhead Books, 1995), 1–2.

2 For a record of their conversation, see Thich Nhat Hahn and Daniel Berrigan, *The Raft is Not the Shore* (Boston: Beacon Press, 1975).

3 See Eric Sharpe, 'The Goals of Inter-Religious Dialogue,' in John Hick, *Truth and Dialogue in World Religions: Conflicting Truth Claims* (Philadelphia: The Westminster Press, 1975), 77–95 and 'Dialogue of Religions' in Mircea Eliade, ed., *The Encyclopedia of Religion*, vol. 4 (New York: Macmillan, 1987), 344–348.

4 Leonard Swindler, 'The Dialogue Decalogue,' reprinted from *Journal of Ecumenical Studies* 20:1 (Winter 1983; September 1984 revision) that outlines ten points:

　1 The primary purpose of dialogue is to learn, that is, to change and grow in the *perception and understanding of reality*, and then to act accordingly.

　2 Interreligious, interideological dialogue must be a two-sided project – within each religious or ideological community and between religious or ideological communities.

　3 Each participant must come to the dialogue with complete honesty and sincerity. Conversely, each participant must assume a similar complete honest and sincerity in the other partners.

　4 Interreligious, interideological dialogue must not compare our ideals with our partner's practice.

　5 Each participant must *define himself*. Conversely, the one interpreted must be able to recognize herself in the interpretation.

　6 Each participant must come to the dialogue with no hard-and-fast assumptions as to where the points of disagreement are.

　7 Dialogue can take place only between equals.

　8 Dialogue can take place only on the basis of mutual trust.

　9 Persons entering into interreligious dialogue must be at least minimally self-critical of both themselves and their own religious or ideological traditions.

　10 Each participant eventually must attempt to experience the partner's religion or ideology 'from within.'

5 Winston King, 'Buddhist-Christian Dialogue Reconsidered,' *Buddhist-Christian Studies* 2 (1982): 5.
6 See my 'Six Buddhist Attitudes Toward Other Religions' in Charles Wei-hsun Fu and Sandra A. Wawryko. eds., *Buddhist Ethics and Modern Society* (New York: Greenwood Press, 1991), 347–370.
7 *Vinaya, Mahāvagga* I: 10, from Hajime Nakamura, *Gotama Buddha* (Los Angeles: Buddhist Books International, 1977), 83.
8 Marasinghe, M. M. J., *Gods in Early Buddhism* (Vidyalankara: University of Sri Lanka, 1974).
9 See the *Sigālaka Sutta* in the Pali *Dīgha-nikāya* #31 (Cf. the Chinese version, T 1.70–72; 638–642; 252–255) tr. by Maurice Walshe, *Thus Have I Heard: The long Discourses of the Buddha* (London: Wisdom, 1987), 461–469.
10 *Dhammapada*, chapter 26, verses 383–423. The Prakrit version of the *Dhammapada* begins with verses 393, 394, and 392 of the Pali version, thus indicating that the main purpose of the Prakrit text was to offer a more correct interpretation of the qualities of a true brahmin.
11 For example, see Timothy Barrett, *Li Ao: Buddhist, Taoist, or Neo-Confucian* (Oxford: Oxford University Press, 1992); Judith Berling, *The Syncretic Religion of Lin Chao-en* (New York: Columbia University Press, 1980); Robert Gimello, 'Mārga and Culture: Learning, Letters, and Liberation in Northern Sung Ch'an,' in Robert E. Buswell, Jr. And Robert M. Gimello, eds., *Paths of Liberation: The Mārga and Its Transformation in Buddhist Thought* (Honolulu: University of Hawaii Press, 1992), 371–437; Robert F. Rhodes, 'Shin Buddhist Attitudes Towards the Kami,' *The Eastern Buddhist* 27:2 (Autumn 1994): 53–80.
12 For example, see the recent interaction between spirit worship and Buddhism in Sri Lanka in Richard Gombrich and Gananath Obeyesekere, *Buddhism Transformed: Religious Change in Sri Lanka* (Princeton: Princeton University Press, 1988).
13 See Thomas Cleary, trans., *The Flower Ornament Scripture*, vol. 3 (Boston: Shambhala, 1987); Jan Fontein, *The Pilgrimage of Sudhana* (Paris: Mouton, 1967).
14 *Bodhisambhāra* (Taishō 32: 517–541), v. 142, translated by Chr. Lindtner, *Nagarjuniana* (Delhi: Motilal Banarsidass, 1987), 245.
15 These prohibitions are found in early Mahayana initiation vows for female lay disciples (T 13.901b.14–15) and are still used today in Taiwan's Fo Kuang Shan community.
16 *Fan-wang jing*, T 24.1005c.5–7 and 1006c.19–23.
17 See Peter Gregory, *Inquiry into the Origins of Humanity* (Honolulu: University of Hawaii Press, 1995).
18 The questions asked in the Fo Kuang Shan initiation ceremony used in 1991 in Honolulu were translated into English as follows: 'Can you respect the Buddha as your teacher in life after life and not take refuge in other religions, devas or demons?' 'Can you respect the Sangha as your teacher life after life without taking refuge in other religious followers?' The social consequences of these vows still need further study by investigating the fate of non-Buddhist religious minorities in Buddhist

cultures, such as the history of the Bon religion in Tibet, or of Muslim or Hindu minorities in Sri Lanka and Thailand.

19 *Upālisutta, Majjhimanikāya,* i.371–387.
20 See Martin G. Wiltshire, *Ascetic Figures Before and in Early Buddhism: The Emergence of Gautama as the Buddha* (New York: Mouton de Gruyter, 1990) and Padmanabh S. Jaini, 'Śramaṇas: Their Conflict with Brāhmaṇical Society,' in Joseph W. Elder, ed., *Chapters in Indian Civilization* (Dubuque, IA.: Kendall Hunt, 1970), vol. 1, 41–81.
21 *Suttanipāta* 1082, tr. H. Saddhatissa, *The Sutta-nipata* (London: Curzon, 1985), 124.
22 See my 'Social Integration for Buddhists: The Mixed Message of Kalyāṇamitras,' in Kamata, Shigeo, ed., *1991 Anthology of Buddhist Studies* (Kaosiung, Taiwan: Fo Kuang Publishers, 1992), 187–192 which discusses such passages as *Saṃyutta-nikāya* #66 and *Dīgha-nikāya* #24 and #25.
23 See Choi, Joon Sik, *The Development of the 'Three-Religions-Are-One' Principle from China to Korea: A Study in Kang Chughsan's Religious Teachings as Exemplifying the Principle* (Ann Arbor, MI: University Microfilms International, 1989).
24 *Zokuzōkyō* I.31.5, p. 473a–b, Translated by Miriam Levering, *Buddhism in Sung Culture: The Ch'an Master Ta-hui Tsung-kao,* unpublished 1989 ms., 175.
25 This distinction between essence and function was first used by Wang-pi (226–249). See Wang Pi, *Commentary on the 'Lao Tzu,'* tr. By Ariane Rump with Wing-tsit Chan (Honolulu: University of Hawaii Press, 1979), 112. This distinction became very popular in Chinese Buddhism, and was used in the earliest interpretation of the *Lotus Sutra.* See Young-ho King, *A Study and Translation: Tao-sheng's Commentary on the Lotus Sutra* (Albany, NY: SUNY Press, 1990) and the *Platform Sutra of the Sixth Patriarch,* tr. by Philip Yampolsky (New York: Columbia University Press, 1967), section 14.
26 *Zokuzōkyō* I.31.5, p. 461a. See Miriam Levering, *Buddhism in Sung Culture,* 176 and 182.
27 Robert Gimello, 'Mārga and Culture,' 383.
28 A model of this approach was the great literati Su Shih (1037–1101), a predecessor of Ta-hui. See the fine recent study by Beata Grant, *Mount Lu Revisited: Buddhism in the Life and Writings of Su Shih* (Honolulu: University of Hawaii Press, 1995).
29 See Young-ho (Jinwol) Lee, '*Samga Kwigam* of Hyujŏng and the Three Religions,' *Buddhist-Christian Studies* 12 (1992): 43–64 and the translation of the *Samga Kwigam* by Young-ho Lee in *Buddhist-Christian Studies* 15 (1995): 139–187.
30 The five delegates were Yatsubuchi Banryū (Pure Land), Shaku Sōen (Rinzai Zen), Toki Hōryū (Shingon), Ashitsu Jitsunen (Tendai), and the lay Buddhist Hirai Kinzō. See James Ketelaar, 'Strategic Occidentialism: Meiji Buddhists at the World's Parliament of Religions,' *Buddhist-Christian Studies* 11 (1991): 47–48.
31 Hirai Ryuge Kinzo, 'The Real Position of Japan Toward Christianity,' in Richard H. Seager, ed., *The Dawn of Religious Pluralism: Voices from the*

World's Parliament of Religions, 1893 (LaSalle, IL: Open Court, 1993), 398.

32 Ibid., 50–51.

33 See Shaku Soyen, 'Arbitration Instead of War' and 'The Law of Cause and Effect, as Taught by the Buddha' in Richard H. Seager, ed., *The Dawn of Religious Pluralism*, 352–353, 406–409. A decade after the Parliament of World's Religions, Suzuki interpreted Shaku Sōen's talks during his tour of America in 1905, which were later published as *Sermons of a Zen Abbot* (LaSalle, IL: Open Court, 1906).

34 Because Merton found the wisdom of the Christian desert fathers 'bore a remarkable resemblance to some of the stories of the Japanese Zen masters,' he contacted Suzuki, who 'received with pleasure the suggestion to engage in dialogue.' See Thomas Merton, *Zen and the Birds of Appetite* (New York: New Directions, 1961, reprinted 1968), 99. The dialogues are found on pp. 99–138. Cf. Thomas Merton, *Mystics and Zen Masters* (1967). Another early response to Suzuki was by the Benedictine monk, Dom Aelred Graham, who wrote *Zen Catholicism: A Suggestion* (New York: Harcourt, Brace, and World, 1963).

35 *Birds of Appetite*, 104–115.

36 Masuo Nezu, 'Interreligious Cooperation and Rissho Kosei-kai,' *Dharma World* 22 (July/August, 1995): 20. Nikkyo Niwano remembers how critics argued that such a group could never survive since the founders of new religions would think of themselves as 'the sole representatives' of the 'true faith.' But instead, 'just the opposite turned out to be true. Our meetings were very harmonious and cheerful.' Nikkyo Niwano, *A Buddhist Approach to Peace* (Tokyo: Kosei Publishing Company, 1977), 70. Nevertheless, contrary to Niwano's optimism, it was not possible for different groups to 'open up their doctrines and learn from one another.' However, the first chair of Shinshūren, Miki Tokuchika (head of the Perfect Liberty Church) wisely avoided doctrinal discussion.

37 Masuo Nezu, 'Interreligious Cooperation and Rissho Kosei-kai,' 21.

38 Nikkyo Niwano, 'The Will of God and the Spirit of Buddha,' in Homer Jack, ed., *Religion and Peace: Proceedings of the Kyoto Conference on Religion and Peace* (New Delhi: Andhi Peace Foundation, 1973), 31.

39 'However, I have come to realize that it is an idea which can only be realized a couple of centuries from now … and have decided to use the term "religious cooperation" or "interfaith cooperation" as a temporary stage toward reaching the goal, and have made every effort for its advocacy and implementation today.' Niwano, *A Buddhist Approach to Peace*, 71–73.

40 We are indebted to Jan Van Bragt and James W. Heisig of the Nanzan Institute for Religion and Culture, Nagoya, Japan, for making translations and studies of the works of Nishida, Tanabe, Nishitani, and Takeuchi available in English for Western audiences. This has not always been uncritical as can be seen in a recent book about the controversy surrounding the roles of the leading thinkers of the Kyoto School in relation to the military regime during the Second World War. See James W. Heisig and John C. Maraldo, eds., *Rude Awakenings: Zen, The Kyoto*

School, and the Question of Nationalism (Honolulu: University of Hawaii Press, 1994).

41 From *Gakkyū seikatsu no omoide* (Memories of My Student Life) in *Tōyō-teki Mu* (Oriental Nothingness), vol. 1 of his *Collected Works* (1969), 415–434, tr. by Masao Abe, 'Notes,' *The Eastern Buddhist*, XIV.1 (Spring, 1981): 143.

42 In 1944, to aid students to realize the insights he was advocating that went beyond rational categories, Hisamatsu formed a group to do Zen practice called Gakudō-dōjō (Place to Practice the Way to Awakening).

43 Tillich confessed that his central religious problem at that time was finding calm in the midst of his busy life, so that he asserted: 'I should like to take a lesson in Zen.' Because Hisamatsu was an authority on Zen art, Tillich also wanted to know how Hisamatsu could 'bring together the Formless Self and the artistic form?' See 'Dialogues East and West: Conversations between Dr. Paul Tillich and Dr. Hisamatsu Shin'ichi,' Part One, *The Eastern Buddhist*, n. s. IV.2 (October 1971): 91–92 and 107; and Part Two, *The Eastern Buddhist*, n.s. V.2 (October 1972): 107.

44 'Dialogues, East and West,' Part One, 107 and Part Two, 111.

45 This group held its first annual meeting July 26–28, 1982. Although it was organized after the Buddhist-Christian conference held in Honolulu in 1980, and was conceived as a branch of its organizer, the East-West Religions Project of the University of Hawaii, and although its first leader was a Christian, Doi Masatoshi, and its secretariat was first located at the National Council of Churches offices in Kyoto, the Tōzai Shūkyō Kōryū Gakkai came to embody many of the people and issues of the Kyoto School. Fujiyoshi Jikai, a Pure Land disciple of Hisamatsu, participated from the beginning, and was soon joined by Tokiwa Gishin, another student of Hisamatsu. A Buddhist reformer and a Rinzai Zen master, Akizuki Ryomin, has published the proceedings of each annual meeting in the journal he edits, *Daijōron*. In recent years, the Buddhist intellectual leader has been Ueda Shizuteru, also of the Kyoto School, who is a specialist on Nishida, Zen philosophy, and German mysticism. The annual meetings are held for three days and involve the presentation of written papers with responses. English summaries of the first three meetings were published in *Buddhist-Christian Studies* 3 (1983): 119–156; 9 (1989): 100–122; and 6 (1986): 97–120.

46 'If, however, space and time were to belong to the awakening itself, then it would not be a true awakening,' claimed Hisamatsu, since it would be conditioned by the finite. While it may be 'my awakening,' this must refer to the ultimate level of the 'formless my' and involves all humanity. See 'Dialogues, East and West,' Part Two, 124–127.

47 The basic argument against reversibility is that the past and the future do not disappear into each other, that God and humans could not totally include each other, that space-time distinctions make a difference, that historical events matter and are not reversible, and that ethical distinctions between good and evil remain at the ultimate level. See the interchange of Masao Abe with the Christian and Jewish dialogue partners in John B. Cobb, Jr. and Christopher Ives, ed., *The Emptying God: A Buddhist-Jewish-Christian Conversation* (Maryknoll, NY: Orbis

Books, 1990); and Christopher Ives, ed., *Divine Emptiness and Historical Fullness: A Buddhist-Jewish-Christian Conversation with Masao Abe* (Valley Forge, PA: Trinity Press International, 1995). For my summary evaluation of the issues, see the latter book, pp. 14–21.

48 Because of his leadership in Buddhist social and spiritual reform, the Thailand Theological Seminary in Chiang Mai invited Buddhadāsa to deliver three Sinclaire Thompson Lectures in February 1967 where he presented his ideas most fully. Unlike Japanese and Sri Lankan Buddhist scholars, Buddhadāsa was not trained in Western critical analysis, nor has he ever traveled outside of Asia. See Bhikku Buddhadāsa, *Buddhism and Christianity*, Fifth Sinclaire Thomson Memorial Lecture Series, 1967 (Bangkok: Sublime Life Mission, 5/1 Atsadang Road, n.d.)

49 'The ordinary, ignorant worlding is under the impression that there are many religions and that they are all different to the extent of being hostile and opposed. Thus one considers Christianity, Islam, and Buddhism as incompatible and even bitter enemies.... If, however, a person has penetrated to the fundamental nature (dhamma) of religion, he will regard all religions as essentially similar. Although he may say there is Buddhism, Christianity, Islam, and so on, he will also say that essentially they are all the same. If he should go to a deeper understanding of dhamma until finally he realizes the absolute truth, he would discover that there is no such thing called religion – that there is no Buddhism, Christianity, or Islam.' Donald Swearer, ed., *Me and Mine: Selected Essays of Bhikku Buddhadāsa* (Albany, NY: SUNY Press, 1989), 146.

50 For example, in April 1966 the noted Sri Lankan Buddhist philosopher, K. N. Jayatilleke (1920–1970), proposed a shared content for religion when he argued that Buddhism is 'comprehensive enough to contain, recognize and respect the basic truths of all higher religions. All these religions believe in a Transcendent, characterized as Nirvāna which is beyond time, space and causation in Buddhism, as an Impersonal Monistic principle such as Brahman or Tao in some religions and as a personal God in others. They all assert survival, moral recompense and responsibility. They all preach a 'good life,' which has much in common and whose culmination is communion with or the attainment of this Transcendent. The early Buddhist conception of the nature and destiny of man in the universe is, therefore, not in basic conflict with the beliefs and values of the founders of the great religions so long as they assert some sort of survival, moral values, freedom and responsibility and the non-inevitability of salvation.' See K.N. Jayatilleke, *The Buddhist Attitude Towards Other Religions* (Chiangmai, Thailand: Buddhist Publication Foundation, 1987; reprint of the Wheel Publications #216, Kandy, 1975), 25.

51 Gyatso, Tenzin [His Holiness the XIV Dalai Lama], *Kindness, Clarity, and Insight*, trans. and ed. by Jeffery Hopkins, co-edited by Elizabeth Napper (Ithaca, NY: Snow Lion, 1984), 46.

52 See Masao Abe, 'Kenotic God and Dynamic Sunyata,' in Cobb and Ives, *The Emptying God: A Buddhist-Jewish-Christian Conversation*, 1–65 and 'Beyond Buddhism and Christianity: "Dazzling Darkness",' in Ives, *Divine Emptiness and Historical Fullness: A Buddhist-Jewish-Christian Conversation with Masao Abe*, 224–243.

53 See Abe's essay, 'A Dynamic unity in Religious Pluralism: A Proposal from the Buddhist Point of View,' in John Hick and Hasan Askari, eds., *The Experience of Diversity* (Brookfield, VT: Gower Publishing, 1985), 163–190.

54 Nishitani Keiji's core ideas first appeared in 1954–55 and were reprinted in his 1960 book *Shūkyō to wa nani ka* (What is Religion?). This has been carefully translated by Jan van Bragt as *Religion and Nothingness* (Berkeley: University of California Press, 1982).

55 Ibid., 17.

56 'Buddhism and Christianity as a Problem of Today,' Parts I and II, *Japanese Religions* 3.2 (1963): 11–22 and 3.3 (1963): 8–31.

57 The group is focused on discursive dialogue, and most of its meetings since 1984 have been reported in *Buddhist-Christian Studies*. The Theological Encounter with Buddhism Group was hosted by the University of Hawaii (1984), Vancouver School of Theology (1985), Purdue University (1986), Pacific School of Religion (1987), Hsi-lai Temple (1989), Boston University (1992), and Risshō Kōseikai in Japan (1994). Zen and the Kyoto School were present through Masao Abe and Tokiwa Gishin, as well as Frank Cook. Although Shin Buddhist representatives included Taitetsu Unno and Takeda Ryūsei, Tibetan representatives were even more numerous: Rita Gross, Jeffery Hopkins, and two representatives from the Naropa Institute, Judith Simmer-Brown and Reginald Ray (organizers of the Naropa contemplative interfaith dialogues).

58 Jewish dialogue partners have included Eugene Borowitz (see Cobb and Ives, eds., *The Emptying God*, 79–90; *Buddhist-Christian Studies* 13 [1993]: 223–231), Richard Rubenstein and Sandra Lubarsky (see Ives, *Divine Emptiness and Historical Fullness*, 93–126).

59 See my article, 'A Tribute to "Mr. Dialogue",' in Donald W. Mitchell, ed., *Masao Abe: A Zen Life of Dialogue* (Boston: Charles E. Tuttle, 1998), 89–100.

60 The New Testament scholar, Ariga Tetsutarō, who was professor at Kyoto University and editor of the journal *Japanese Religions* for the Natural Council of Churches in Japan, recalls that dialogue with Abe began in 1948 when Abe was an assistant in the department of philosophy. Ariga informs us that based on his experience with Abe, 'It is not his purpose to discuss philosophy in an abstract way. He aims to do so out of his existential concern.' See *Japanese Religions* 4.1 (1964): 3–4.

61 See John Cobb, *Beyond Dialogue: Toward a Mutual Transformation of Christianity and Buddhism* (Philadelphia: Fortress Press, 1982).

62 See Abe Masao, 'The Impact of Dialogue on My Understanding as a Buddhist,' *Buddhist-Christian Studies* 9 (1989): 63–70.

63 *Inter-View* No. 1 (December 1981): 30–31, Newsletter of the East-West Religions Project, University of Hawaii.

64 *Birds of Appetite,* 133. Merton agreed on the 'strongly personalistic tone' of Christianity which 'generally seems to prohibit a full equation with Zen experience' of emptiness, except perhaps in rare Christian mystics such as Meister Eckhart and his student John Ruysbroeck. See the recent study by Paul Mommaers and Jan van Bragt, *Mysticism Buddhist and*

Christian: Encounters With Jan van Ruusbroec (New York: Crossroads, 1995).

65 Nikkyo Niwano, *Lifetime Beginner: An Autobiography*, tr. by Richard L. Gage (Tokyo: Kosei Publishing, 1978), 75–76.

66 Ibid., 76.

67 Ibid., 79. Nevertheless, to show his continuing respect for Shinto, Niwano makes an annual pilgrimage to the national Ise Shrine as an expression of his appreciation of all spiritual traditions.

68 Ariga Tetsutarō recalls being with Douglas Steere as Protestant observers to Vatican II in 1965 when they crystallized the idea of holding an interreligious dialogue in Japan. The Quakers sponsored the first meeting, but included two Rinzai Buddhists, Hisamatsu Shin'ichi and Yamada Mumon, on the original organizing committee. See Ariga Tetsutarō, 'What Zen-Christian Colloquia Mean – Reflection on My Experiences of Nine Years,' in Irie Yukio, et.al., eds., *Zen-Christian Pilgrimage: The Fruits of Ten Annual Colloquia in Japan 1967–1976* (Tokyo: Zen-Christian Colloquium, 1981), 24–31.

69 Irie Yukio, 'Preface,' *Zen-Christian Pilgrimage*, 4–7.

70 See the various works mentioned above by Thomas Merton and Dom Graham, as well as works by William Johnston, such as *Christian Zen* (New York: Harper, 1971), Elaine MacInnes, *Teaching Zen to Christians* (Manila: Buencamino Press, 1986), and Robert E. Kennedy, *Zen Spirit, Christian Spirit* (New York: Continuum, 1995).

71 Hugo M. Enomiya-Lassalle, 'Foreword,' in Ruben Habito, *Total Liberation: Zen Spirituality and the Social Dimension* (Manila: Buencamino Press, 1986), 6.

72 See *'In Memoriam*: A Tribute to Yamada Kōun Roshi, *Buddhist-Christian Studies* 10 (1990): 231–237.

73 It is important to distinguish between someone who has finished their koan training and been confirmed to *teach* Zen, from higher ranks such as someone who has been recognized as *hasansai* and capable of validating the *kenshō* experience, someone ordained as a Buddhist (by accepting the precepts, called *jūkai*), and finally someone promoted to the *junshike* rank, and finally promotion to the *shōshike* rank as a Dharma successor who can *transmit* the Zen lineage. See Robert Sharf, 'Sanbōkyōdan: Zen and the Way of the New Religions,' *Japanese Journal of Religious Studies* 22/3–4 (Fall 1995): 448–450.

74 For example, Yamada's student, Robert Aitken Roshi of the Diamond Sangha, has confirmed Fr. Patrick Hawk as a Zen teacher.

75 Bernard Tetsugen Glassman, 'Forward,' in Robert E. Kennedy, *Zen Spirit, Christian Spirit: The Place of Zen in Christian Life*, 9–10.

76 See Susan Benoit Billot, *Voyage dans les Monastères Zen* (Paris: Desclee de Brouwer, 1987).

77 For reports from the Third East-West Spiritual Exchange, see *Buddhist-Christian Studies* 10 (1990): 189–208.

78 For reports from the Fourth East-West Spiritual Exchange, see *Buddhist-Christian Studies* 12 (1992): 203–225.

79 *Kindness, Clarity, and Insight*, 45. See also Donald Mitchell and James Wiseman, eds., *The Gethsemani Encounter* (New York: Continuum, 1998).

80   The most accessible reports on these activities can be found in back issues of the *Bulletin of Monastic Interreligious Dialogue*, Abbey of Gethsemani, 3642 Monks Road, Trappist, KY 40051-6102: FAX: 502-549-4124. The interest in these intermonastic dialogues is expressed by the many subscribers of the *Bulletin on Monastic Interreligious Dialogue*, which now numbers 2300.

81   The Naropa conference series grew out of conversations in Calcutta between Ven. Chogyam Trungpa and Thomas Merton on his visit to Asia in 1968. As Trungpa recalled: 'I had the feeling I was meeting an old friend, a genuine friend.... He was the first genuine person I met from the West. After meeting Thomas Merton, I visited several monasteries in Great Britain, and at some of them I was asked to give talks on meditation, which I did.... I was very impressed and moved by the contemplative aspect of Christianity, and by the monasteries themselves. Their lifestyle and the way they conducted themselves convinced me that the only way to join the Christian tradition and the Buddhist tradition together is by means of bringing together Christian contemplative practice with Buddhist meditative practice.' From an address given to the Naropa Institute Conference on Christian and Buddhist Meditation, August 9, 1983, reported in Susan Walker, ed., *Speaking of Silence: Christians and Buddhists on the Contemplative Way* (New York: Paulist Press, 1987), v.

82   For current activities, contact the Barre Center for Buddhist Studies, 149 Lockwood Road, Barre, MA 01005 (phone: 508-355-2347).

83   In 1963, nine years after the partitioning of Vietnam in Geneva, the five-colored Buddhist flag (representing faith, diligence, mindfulness, concentration, and wisdom) was banned by the South Vietnamese government.

84   In 1967 after a four-month period in which six members of SYSS were killed, thirty badly injured, and one self-immolated, the staff and students read this pledge at a funeral: 'Now, once again, we solemnly promise never to hate those who kill us, above all never to use violence to answer violence, even if the antagonists see us as enemies and kill until they annihilate us. We recall our pledge that people, no matter what their origins, never are our enemies.... Help us to keep steadily this non-violent mind in our social work by love that asks nothing in return.' James H. Forest, *The Unified Buddhist Church of Vietnam: Fifteen Years for Reconciliation* (Hof van Sonoy, The Netherlands, International Fellowship of Reconciliation, 1987), 7.

85   Thich Nhat Hahn reports on her death as follows: 'Nhat Chi Mai, for instance, prepared everything for her immolation herself – absolutely by herself. Her most intimate friends didn't know a thing about it. She spent a whole month with her parents in order to be a source of joy and pleasure. She was, as we say, honey and sweet rice for her parents. And after that, she came to visit our community. She wore a beautiful dress. We had never seen her in that dress before, and many thought that she was going to marry and that was why she deserted the community for one month. She brought a banana cake that she had made at home. She divided it up and gave it to every one of us. And how she laughed! Many

suspected that she was going to get married. She was so joyful. And then two days later they heard the news. One remarkable thing is that when she knelt to die, she put in front of her a statue of the Virgin Mary and a statue of woman Bodhisattva Quan Am, the Buddhist saint of compassion. And she put a poem there: "Joining my hands, I kneel before Mother Mary and Bodhisattva Quan Am. Please help me realize fully my vow." In the situation of Vietnam, that meant very much, because unless the people of the two major religions of Vietnam – Buddhists and Catholics – cooperate, it will be very hard to alter the course of the war. She saw that.' Daniel Berrigan and Thich Nhat Hahn, *The Raft is Not the Shore* (Boston: Beacon Press, 1975), 63. Nhat Chi Mai left letters behind calling for withdrawal of US troops and for UN-supervised free elections. 'I want to use my body as a torch to dissipate the darkness, to awaken Love among men, to bring Peace to Vietnam.' Her funeral became a peace procession attended by 50,000 people. For a record of her death, and the motivations of many other self-immolations by Buddhists in Vietnam, see James Forest, *The Unified Buddhist Church of Vietnam: Fifteen Years of Reconciliation* (Alkmaar, The Netherlands: Hof van Sonoy, 1978).

86 Thich Nhat Hahn, *Living Buddha, Living Christ* (Berkeley: Riverhead Books, 1995), 1–2.
87 Thich Nhat Hahn is the alleged inventor of the phrase, 'socially engaged Buddhism' and is recognized as the embodiment of its meaning. A helpful introduction to his social activism can be found in Sallie B. King, 'Thich Nhat Hahn and the Unified Buddhist Church of Vietnam: Nondualism in Action,' in Christopher S. Queen and Sallie B. King, eds., *Engaged Buddhism: Buddhist Liberation Movements in Asia* (Albany, NY: SUNY Press, 1996), 321–363.
88 Sulak also received considerable Christian schooling, however, first at Assumption College in Bangkok and later at an Anglican college, St. David's University College in Lampeter, Wales. Sulak's keen sense of social justice was sharpened also by training as a barrister in London. See his autobiography, *Loyalty Demands Dissent* (Berkeley: Parallax Press, 1998).
89 The CGRS publishes reports on human rights violations in Thailand in their quarterly *Human Rights in Thailand Report*.
90 See the discussion of the Declaration in Sulak Sivaraksa, *A Buddhist Vision for Renewing Society* (Bangkok: Tienwan Publishing House, 1986), 80–82, 95–97, 188–190.
91 *Seeds of Peace* had begun briefly as a supplement to *Visakha Pūjā* in 1976, but only had two issues. It continues today as the journal of the International Network of Engaged Buddhists that was formed by Sulak in 1989: P.O. Box 1, Ongkharak, Nakhorn Nayok 26120, Thailand (FAX: 66-37-391-494). The objectives of the TICD are explicitly interreligious, namely to: (1) Coordinate work among individuals, groups of individuals and various agencies dealing with religions and development in thecourse of working together; (2) Share experience in and knowledge of religions and development as well as exploring ways and means of working together; and (3) Offer training and secure resources in terms of man-power and materials to support and enhance the agencies that need help.

92 Sulak has been a member of the Cobb-Abe Theological Encounter with Buddhism Group since 1984.

93 Sulak has been arrested several times for challenging government injustice, and in 1995 was given the Right Livelihood Award. For a recent overview of his life, see Donald K. Swearer, 'Sulak Sivaraksa's Buddhist Vision for Renewing Society,' in Christopher S. Queen and Sallie B. King, *Engaged Buddhism: Buddhist Liberation Movements in Asia*, 195–235.

94 Kosho Ohtani, 'How Shall Man Realize Peace and Happiness? In Homer Jack, ed., *Religion and Peace: Proceedings of the Kyoto Conference on Religion and Peace*, 26–28.

95 *Kindness, Clarity, and Insight*, 49.

96 Ibid.

97 Nara Yasuaki, a Sōtō Zen priest, a scholar of Indian Buddhism, and the President of the leading intellectual center of the Sōtō Zen sect, Komazawa University (1994–1998), has been a regular member of the Zen-Christian Colloquium and the Tōzai Shūkyō Kōryū Gakkai.

98 Nara Yasuaki, 'Zen-Colloquium and Me,' *Zen-Christian Pilgrimage*, 88.

99 Ibid.

100 See scattered remarks in the writings of A.T. Ariyaratne, such as *Peace Making in Sri Lanka* (Moratuwa, Sri Lanka: Vishua Lekha Press, 1987), 13–14; *Religious Path to Peace and Building a Just* World (Moratuwa, Sri Lanka: Sarvodaya Press, 1987), 7; and an interview with Ariyaratne entitled 'For a World Spiritual Awakening,' *Dharma World*, 19 (November–December 1992), 18. I am indebted to Robert Bobilin for these references.

CHAPTER TWO

Response to David Chappell

Winston L. King

It is quite apparent that David Chappell and I have taken somewhat different tacks in our development of the theme of Buddhist-Christian oriented interreligious dialogue. Professor Chappell has written a well-documented and wide-ranging survey and analysis of Buddhist attitudes toward, and historical instances of other religion dialogue, both within Buddhism itself and with non-Buddhist faiths. Perhaps, for symmetry's sake I should have matched this pattern for Christianity.

However, for better or worse, I have taken a different route. My overriding concern here has been to try to define the nature of genuine full-scale interreligious dialogue. The statement that I take to be definitive of true interreligious dialogue is that of Francis Cook quoted in my essay, namely that dialogue partners must admit 'that they are somehow incomplete and that they may be made more complete through the insights of the other party' to the dialogue. And to also requote Franz Brendle, 'True dialogue ... requires readiness for change.' Judged by this standard most of the interreligious 'dialogue' in Christian history has not been dialogue but competition and dispute. Christianity, with its well-defined doctrinal base and rigid organization, has usually viewed proposed concessions as destructive of the True Faith.

What is to be said of Buddhism in this respect? As Chappell portrays it, it too has had its orthodoxies; in his words there *are* instances, 'rare though they may be,' of Buddhist affirmation of the equal validity of other religious traditions. But I would perhaps phrase the matter somewhat differently. Because Buddhism in general has been and is more flexible than Christianity in both doctrinal statement and in practice it has more easily adapted itself to other-religious situations. First, Buddhism has usually been more experience-oriented than rigidly doctrinal Christianity. Through the centuries and in diverse cultures this led to a plethora of 'scriptural' expressions in the Mahayana development – all of them Buddha's words – and to the down-grading of *all* scripture in Zen, in favor of experience only. And this flexibility enabled Buddhism, as it moved out of its native India, to outflank its competitors in Tibet, China, and Japan, by its adaptability and by its co-option of other sacred essences.

Thus in China, rather than declare itself an outright competitor to Taoism and dominant Confucianism, Buddhism entered under some-what of a Taoist 'disguise,' and indeed absorbed, in its Ch'an form, something of the Taoist essence. In Japan, rather than attacking the proto-Shinto *kami*, Buddhism co-opted them. They were made into precursors of the Buddha, his forerunners and worldly assistants, still of legitimate use in *this* world, while the Buddha held the key to the *eternal* world of full salvation. And Hachiman, a Shinto war-god, was promoted to the role of a bodhisattva. Thus Buddhism could eat its religious cake and have it too-a feat almost impossible for more tightly doctrinaire Christianity, even though it too has made its culture-oriented adaptions.

This same semi-amorphousness and flexibility of Buddhism has allowed a kind of Eastern cultural imperialism to enter into its religious interchanges with the West, largely unconsciously. Thus, for example, Hisamatsu Shin'ichi's *Oriental Nothingness* noted by Chappell, is among other things, an embodiment of Japanese-Eastern cultural themes and values presumed to be incomprehensible to the religious and philosophical West and quite different from its blankly nihilistic nothingness. (Of the same genre is the famous remark of D.T. Suzuki to Hisamatsu at Harvard, that he had not found a single Westerner capable of understanding Zen enlight-enment.)

It must be said in all fairness to Hisamatsu that he had no desire or intention of being culturally imperialistic, but always sought to extend his thinking to include all earnest seekers equally, Eastern or Western. (In my two visits to his home in Kyoto I found him to be a friendly, charming host seeking to make his viewpoint crystal clear to any interested person. I highly value his calligraphic *ten* (change, revolve, tumble) which hangs in my living room. And I recall that it was he who urged Masao Abe to study with Christian theologians before he began to try to relate Buddhism and Christianity. As Chappell notes, Hisamatsu 'tried to push beyond both traditions to seek what is common to [all] human existence.' Ironically perhaps this very effort put him at odds with the specifically Christian loyalists in the West and was more accommodative to post-Christian scientific-secular 'God is dead' currents of thought.

What then has been the area of meaningful Buddhist contact with the Christian West, if any? Chappell observes quite accurately, I think, that 'Christian theology has failed to spark any serious interest, challenge, or growth in the Buddhist community.' This situation has *always* been more or less true in my opinion. The earliest Christian attitude toward Buddhism was characterized by an aggressive colonialist-missionary effort to convert Asian polytheists and godless Buddhists. But with the passage of time the passive East became politically independent and religiously self-confident. The West discovered the rich Hindu-Buddhist spiritual traditions and their immense literature, as well as their spiritual methodologies, notably meditation. As a result, Buddhism now speaks confidently out of its great variety and experiential depths to the West, both religious and irreligious, with an assured sense of its own spiritual-psychological superiority, and sends its missionaries Westward. Hence the general Buddhist disinterest in Christian doctrine. This is unlikely to change. What then is the prevailing pattern of Buddhist-Christian interchange as Chappell sees it? To quote:

> Where there is serious interreligious dialogue by modern Buddhists it is often based not on intellectual curiosity but on moral values in an effort to deepen the spiritual life of society, to remove discrimination and exploitation, and to nurture a sense of global community in a divided world.

And he further notes that these cooperative efforts have been undertaken 'even if that meant temporarily suspending or subordinating the distinctive features of their own religious tradition.' If this is destined to be the character of future Buddhist-Christian interaction, even though it falls short of the fully mutual interreligious dialogue as I have conceived it, I can only say that it is to be cordially welcomed over rancorous competition.

In passing, one notable exception to this non-theological pattern of interaction must be noted: that of the vigorous dialogical efforts of Masao Abe. Professor Abe has made a vigorous and continuing effort to dialogue with Christians in fully *theological* terms, especially seeking to relate Buddhist emptiness (*śūnyatā*) and God's self-emptying into Christ. Though he remains a convinced Zen Buddhist, Professor Abe has asserted that his study of Christianity had made a significant difference in his Buddhism – a genuine dialogical result! One can but wonder if Abe is to be the only Buddhist of his kind for the forseeable future.

Returning to the more usual socially and humanistically interactive type of Buddhist-Christian relationship, it is to be noted that there may be at least one type of problem that will plague even this limited interaction, namely the religious value of justice. Justice is a major concept and basic value in Christian and Western civilization. And even though secular and humanistic Westerners may have rejected most Christian beliefs, especially that of a just Providence, *justice* remains a major value. But justice as a social goal is seldom if ever espoused, or even mentioned by Buddhists. The first, and probably the major reason for this in many Buddhist traditions, is the pervasive and persistent Buddhist belief in *karma*. Karma is Justice Incarnate in traditional Buddhism; every deed, good or evil, will in time receive its true reward. Ignorant, clumsy individual efforts at helping karma perform its tasks are best omitted. And though karma is not often mentioned in Western and Zen Buddhist circles, its ghostly influence there is undoubtedly present. The other defect in human efforts to achieve justice, as seen by Buddhists, has been stated by Professor Abe thus: '[J]udgement based on justice naturally calls forth a counter-judgment. Accordingly we fall into an endless struggle between judges and judged.'[1]

He has proposed in consonance with this that the whole world, every one of us, because of 'collective karma,' shares responsibility for the horrors of the Holocaust – thus diluting historical moral responsibility on the part of its deliberate perpetrators to a near zero point.[2] Should this be a pervasive attitude among modern Buddhists it will greatly limit even the type of societal collaboration that now, in Professor Chappell's view, characterizes contemporary Buddhist-Christian interrelationships. Can Eastern Buddhist compassion and Western Christian-humanist justice fruitfully meld? In his last paragraph Chappell offers the hopeful prospect of such an occurrence: 'Today .... most *Buddhist* dialogue efforts imply that the present needs are moral, how to act as partners to overcome social injustice and economic exploitation.' (Emphasis added.)

Notes

1 *Buddhist-Christian Studies* 9 (1989): 67.
2 Christopher Ives, ed., *Divine Emptiness and Historical Fullness* (Valley Forge, PA: Trinity Press International, 1995), 77–8.

CHAPTER THREE

Interreligious Dialogue

Winston L. King

In the ages-long history of interreligious contacts, 'dialogue' – as a friendly interchange of views on some topic or other – has been almost unknown. Confrontation, of various sorts and intensities, has been the more usual mode of interreligious relationship. Examples of this are multitudinous. We have many recorded instances of both intra- and interreligious debate. There have been learned religieux appearing before rulers to represent differing views of the 'same' religious faith or of different faiths, to persuade the ruler to adopt one or the other as the official faith of the realm. In a thousand adversarial encounters, representatives of religion A have sought to confute and convert those of religion B, and vice-versa, to the one true faith.

What is striking in even the mildest forms of religious divergence, even within the same 'great tradition,' is the intensity of the emotions aroused among discussants of religion. The vocabulary of religious disagreement is rich in pejorative terms and invective to describe other-believing religionists: unbeliever, unenlightened, ungodly, heretic, unclean, heathen, pagan, infidel, apostate are a few of them. Fierce anathemas and excommuniations have been launched against schismatics.

Unfortunately, the intensity of religious divergence has not been limited to mere words. Invective has all too often been translated into violent action and used to justify persecution, imprisonment, torture, and holy wars throughout the world. Along with ethnic nationalism religion has been one of the most divisive and explosive forces in human history.

Why should such intensity of emotion characterize everything touched by religion? Though this intensity takes many forms its *raison d'être* is quite obvious: what we term 'religious' is characterized by the ultimacy of the interests involved, what Paul Tillich termed 'ultimate concerns.' In religion one deals with the value and the meaning of human life; in it are found the deepest, highest, and most personal hopes, fears, and aspirations embodied in its beliefs, actions, and institutions. In its various forms religion assures human beings of their intrinsic worth, that their existence has significance beyond its seemingly fragile and insignificant forms. It claims to provide the essential means for the enhancement and final establishment of human worth, happiness, and often the continuance of personal existence beyond death. In a single word, religions promise their adherents some sort of 'salvation.'

The overall effect of this sense of ultimate salvational significance is to give religious life and its structures an absolute value. This absoluteness of value is extended from the salvational goal to the means of achieving it – to the rites, beliefs, and practices of the embodying religious structures. Hence doctrines, institutions, spiritual techniques, and special experiences are all seen as indispensable to one's ultimate salvation – to be maintained at all costs. To distort, misuse, neglect, or deny the efficacy of any of these vital 'means of grace' is religiously, i.e., ultimately, fatal to the believer's welfare in the most fundamental sense. Given this absolutist conviction of the salvational efficacy and indispensability of a religious tradition – perhaps strongest in monotheistic religions – it is not surprising that religious divisions and schisms are among the most intense known to humanity and that the large majority of attempts at interreligious dialogue are no more than nominally modified debates.

Motivation to Dialogue

The most obvious motivation for interreligious dialogue is of course the hope of substituting it for the confrontational modes of interreligious contact, which at their best may be acrimonious and at their worst ugly, even violent. Today, in the wake of the increasingly frequent and substantial intermingling of world populations and cultures, many are asking themselves and each other: 'Is there a better sort of interreligious relationship than wary or hostile religious exchange? Does not the universality of religious hopes call for a joining of human understanding and cultural resources in this area?'

42

A second motivation is the widespread sense of the importance of the spiritual in human life, and the great perils that today threaten its existence and embodiment. 'Spiritual' is a somewhat vague term to be sure, one which has been used in many different ways. Yet it does represent a value, a discernible element in all human cultures. Perhaps it can be termed the 'moreness' of life, the inward dimension that goes beyond the sheerly physical animalistic life of humankind, the seeking of the 'meaning' of human existence, and the pursuit of immaterial 'values.' The persistent search for the 'good', the 'beautiful,' and the 'true' is another statement of the 'spiritual.' Some years ago in a writing I no longer possess, Masao Abe called upon Buddhists and Christians to unite in their struggle against materialistic scientism and communism as destructive of spiritual values.

A third consideration pointing toward dialogue rather than confrontation is that of religious humility. In Buddhist language it is refusing to mistake the pointing finger of religious doctrine for the moon of truth. It is a sense that the Eternal Mystery is so profound that no one statement of its meaning can claim to exclusively comprehend its totality. John Cobb has expressed it thus with regard to Buddhism and Christianity: 'My thesis is that both Christianity and Buddhism need to be transformed through their encounter and that both are capable of the needed transformation.'[1] This goes beyond what orthodoxies-in-confrontation are willing to say. And it goes beyond the religious formulations presented at the Parliaments of Religion, which are usually showcase-type advertisements of the religious wares on hand. Such presentations are not to be disdained, but it is to be doubted that they advance the cause of interreligious dialogue very much. That is better done perhaps in small groupings of individuals who know and trust each other's sincerity.

Dialogue of Concern

One important type of religious interchange which can scarcely be termed interreligious dialogue, but nonetheless embodies an increasingly necessary and important kind of interaction, is what I will term dialogical action, or perhaps simply humanistic cooperation. Those who may not agree in religious faith statements of allegiance can (and do) nevertheless join together in shared concern and action. Whatever the religious explanation of human suffering – sin, predestination, past evil karma, social class structure, innate greed, hatred, and delusion – the call to alleviate it can be responded to by all alike. A very recent and interesting expression of this situation is to be found in an April 1995 leaflet of the Harvard Divinity School. The Alumni/ae Council president writes:

> I was struck at our meetings this year by how much Council members have in common, despite the fact that we are a diverse group in religious affiliation, occupation, gender, race, and geography. What binds us together I think are a commitment to assist social change and social justice, a mix of spiritual 'interiority' and action in the public sphere, and, more concretely, involvement in interracial and interreligious activities of various kinds.

Two further examples of this kind of interfaith 'dialogical' activity may be noted. One is the Quaker example. The religious basis for Quaker activities of this sort has been stated thus:

> The AFSC's [American Friends Service Committee's] task is the same today as 78 years ago: to build peace with justice. The reason is still that we believe in the dignity and worth of each individual and the spark of the Divine in each human spirit.[2]

With this historic sense of 'that of God in every [hu]man' Quakers have been notable in their concern for peace, for disarmament, and for reaching out with 'no strings attached,' i.e., non-proselytizing social services of various sorts, to many disparate groups of varying nationality and religious faith.

The other example comes from Buddhism, that of the activities of Sulak Sivaraksa, a Thai Buddhist. He sharply diverges in attitude and action from the stereotypical Buddhist image of social passivity in dependence upon inexorable karmic forces to bring about punishment of evil, both individual and societal – and a hoped-for achievement of universal peace and justice by means of individual transformation. At considerable personal risk he undertook to promote various humanitarian and social reform programs in his native Thailand in across-the-board cooperation with Muslim and Christian individuals and agencies. He remains a committed advocate of social change along lines suggested by his Buddhist faith but in continuingly friendly interaction with those of other faith persuasions.

It may be noted in passing that there is now the growing possibility of such dialogical interaction between Christianity and Buddhism on the ecological front. Many Christians have at last begun to recognize and acknowledge the evils that have arisen in part from the Judeo-

Christian view of human kind as sub-lords of the universe, entitled by divine decree to exploit the natural world for their pleasure and profit. This assumed lordship has developed into the modern ruthless pillaging of natural resources by industrialized and militarized societies for the benefit of the relatively few and the endangerment of life on this earth. There is a growing appreciation of the validity and importance of the Buddhist sense of the intimate interconnected-ness of the total universe and its implications for a new corporate and individual living style.

Sharable Spiritual Techniques

A second area of joint interreligious action is found in the use of shared spiritual techniques. It seems to be easier, and less religiously dangerous, to share in meditation or prayer than in 'theological' discussion. A Japanese Buddhist monk friend told me of a sharing-meeting with German Catholic monks in which he had taken part. At the conclusion of the joint meditation sessions the participants had embraced each other with tears in their eyes and a strong sense of their shared spiritual quest. But when they turned to discussion, and the German monks used the word 'God,' the sense of intimate fellowship faded and the Buddhists felt antagonism and divisiveness welling up within them. This is of course typical of most doctrinal interchanges; the desire for religious transcendence is common to all, but perceptions of the nature of that transcendence and the means to it are the very stuff of religious disagreement. Hence comes the religious lure of the relatively recent Zen-Christian meditational movement.

The late D.T. Suzuki was a kind of literary/intellectual forerunner of this use of other-religion techniques. Suzuki thought that a Zen-Christian spiritual affinity could be found in Western Christian mysticism. He was especially impressed by the Zen quality of Eckhart's God beyond God, his mystical still-point beyond a conceptualized deity. Toward the end of his life he vigorously repudiated this connection; Zen was simply the essence of veridical human self/other awareness, totally unmystical.

Yet the feeling of Zen-mystical affinity lingered. In a conversation with me on May 15, 1966, about two months before his death, he said:

> I don't think we can say that Zen has a specially Japanese character ... It is everywhere. I would say that Eckhart, for

instance, was one of the most prominent Zen men in the West. When I read his sermons everything he says is Zen.[3]

He went on to include Suso, St. John of the Cross, St. Benedict, and St. Teresa in this Zennish category.

Today the Zen-Christian connection is flourishing. One thinks of Thomas Merton, William Johnston, Enomiya-Lassalle, Ruben Habito on the Christian side and of Harada Roshi and Yamada Roshi on the Zen side.

Ruben Habito gives us his definition of interreligious dialogue in these words:

> Interreligious dialogue is a mode of practice that cuts through two distinct religious traditions in a way that focuses on their mutually resonating elements, and in a way that not only reinforces as well as deepens, but also challenges the traditions involved.[4]

With respect to Zen he notes: '[T]he full engagement of its practice does not require or demand adherence to any propositional statement of religious faith.'[5] And in his volume *Total Liberation* he constantly translates Zen nuances into 'orthodox' Christian experiential overtones. He also gives us Enomiya-Lassalle's and Yamada Roshi's version of the Zen-Christian meditative process. When asked whether he undertook Zen meditation – which he carried on for many years with Yamada Roshi – because he felt some lack in his own Catholic faith Enomiya-Lassalle replied:

> For me it was not a question of something lacking in Christianity, but that I wanted to learn more about the Japanese mentality ... It was actually my contact with Zen that enabled me to appreciate better ... the mystical tradition of Europe.[6]

He further says that he had first read of Zen in Suzuki's books.

Yamada Roshi said that many Christians who first considered doing Zen meditation with him were fearful of 'losing or forsaking their Christianity. And I tell them that Zen is not a religion ... in the sense of beliefs and concepts and practices that demand exclusive allegiance.'[7] In other words, Zen-style *koan* meditation is not religion; specific and divisive doctrinal categories can remain untouched – a viewpoint that Habito espouses enthusiastically, and a practice that is being widely followed in Philippine Catholic Christianity.

Fruitful as such a mingling of spiritual practices seems to be, for our purposes here a basic question remains: is sharing of a meditative technique a genuine interreligious *dialogue*? The answer must be negative. The 'sticking points' of basic viewpoint and doctrine between the two religious faiths remain unaffected; the pristine purity of each remains unsullied. Without denigrating the value of this mode of interreligious interaction, it is only marginally dialogical.

The Interreligious Dialogical Ideal

Some of the most frank and forthright statements of the ideal goals and possible results of true interreligious dialogue came out of an American Academy of Religion session in which I was an organizing agent some dozen years ago. The first two are from the Christian perspective and the third from a Buddhist viewpoint. George Rupp's version was as follows:

> I construe the purpose of dialogue to be the attainment of more adequate religious positions and I therefore place a positive value on the possibility of modifications in each participant's self-understanding.[8]

And John B. Cobb added: 'I was looking for ways in which along different paths both Christianity and Buddhism might move toward appropriation of the truth of the other.'[9] And finally, from the Buddhist perspective, Robert Thurman said:

> Such should be the ideal of dialogue, for all parties to convert. To 'convert' suggests that each party in dialogue 'convert' to the best and highest religious values of the *other* and yet be perfectly free to retain [one's own] cultural identity as 'Christian' or 'Buddhist.' Such would be the ideal of dialogue, for all parties to 'convert' to the full experiential and ethical fruition of their own and the other's tradition. In practice then, in dialogue between Buddhists and Christians, each should [also] feel free to expose in the other any conceptual points of reservation, any anchors of exclusivism in doctrines or understandings.[10]

If we accept such statements as these as the proper ideals for interreligious dialogue, there are several important implications which should be clearly understood by all prospective dialoguers. For one thing, to somewhat repeat, dialogue implies much more than a 'friendly' and tolerant exchange of religious views by the adherents of two or more religious faiths who haven't the slightest intention of changing their pre-dialogue faith stance a hairsbreadth. There must be at least some readiness to accept change, perhaps that of a fundamental sort.

True interreligious dialogue begins within the individual, either prior to or following some dialogical encounter. Sallie King has written as follows about interior dialogue:

> I conceive interior dialogue as follows ... Briefly stated one pays attention to what is happening ... What am I receiving? What is my immediate response? Does it conflict with some other principles or beliefs that I cherish? ... If so, how do I respond?[11]

She goes on to say that whatever one's answer to such internal questions, there needs to be further outside input, for 'internal dialogue cannot proceed alone.' She also suggests that external dialogue will not be more than a superficial exchange of views unless some such internal dialogue has taken place and continues to occur.

In what we may see as an extension of this idea, Robert J. Schreiter speaks of 'multiple belonging,' the same person feeling called upon to assert allegiance to more than one religious tradition at a time. He distinguishes three varieties of this religious multiplicity: 'Sequential belonging,' or moving from tradition A to tradition B, but retaining 'some traces of the earlier belief'; 'dialogical belonging,' exemplified by 'native peoples of the America's'; and 'simultaneous belonging,' which consists in 'finding a way for them to coexist beyond dialogical belonging,' i.e., discussional encounter. Schreiter thinks this third type is very rare, suggesting that Raimundo Pannikar, who calls himself a Christian/Hindu/Buddhist equally and at the same time, might be an example.[12]

The actuality and seriousness of the possible results of such an attitude in genuine interreligious dialogue must be emphasized and fully recognized when one decides to engage in such dialogue. In this connection Franz Brendle, a German Catholic priest, warns would-be dialoguers:

> True dialogue always consists of taking and giving, and that requires readiness for change.... [I]t will always be moving within the area of conflict between one's own religious identity and openness toward others.[13]

But as Masaaki Honda, a Japanese Christian, observes: 'We cannot find the real field of dialogue without our own convictions, however criticized that may be from the academic side.'[14] That is to say, merely intellectual discussion of religious beliefs is not interreligious *dialogue* but merely interreligious discussion. Writes Francis Cook, in a kind of ultimate challenge to all would-be dialoguers:

> [Dialogue] demands of both partners in dialogue that they be prepared to admit as a precondition to dialogue that they are somehow incomplete and that they may be made more complete through the insights of the other party. Given human insecurity and jealously, it will be difficult for either side to stand before the other and say, in effect, 'Teach me what I don't understand about God (or Emptiness).' And yet, is it possible to talk on any other basis?[15]

One possible result of interreligious dialogue that I have never heard discussed is the following: recognizing the validity and/or attractiveness of both traditions A and B – one's own 'native' faith and another one encountered later – the dialoguer ends at a neutral position, the values and claims of A and B canceling each other out for the dialoguer.

The Dialoguers

The twentieth century has witnessed what might be called a dialogue of cultures. In a reversal of the Western colonial and Christian missionary invasion of the Orient, the Eastern cultures have come West. The first trickles of the Eastern wave were the translation of some of the hitherto unknown Theravada Buddhists texts into Western languages in the later nineteenth century. Then the trickle became a solid and continuing stream of Eastern cultural-religious translations finding their voice in the West.

Today there is an abundance of books dealing with and presenting the religious and psycho-somatic spiritual disciplines of the East to any who are disposed to listen. All of this has led to a tide of professional and personal interest in Eastern spiritual traditions and practices. On the professional level it has produced many books on and courses in 'comparative religion.' In such courses students are treated to a purportedly dispassionate comparison of the world's religions, East and West, North and South, with each other, with neither favor nor disfavor shown to any. Sometimes, representatives of the 'other,' i.e., non-Christian faiths, are brought in to present their own traditions.

Can such encounters be termed interreligious dialogue? Scarcely, if we follow the guidelines already set forth, that of a situation in which the discussants put their own professed faith on the line of 'live' discussion and with a willingness to accommodate changes therein. Indeed, in the professional world that has presided over most of the 'comparative' religious discussion in academe, there are many who perceive themselves only as neutral referees whose religion is religious neutrality.

It is obvious that most of the staunchly orthodox believers, the ranks of the run-of-the-mill believers, West *and* East, will have no interest in such interreligious dialogue. The typical reaction is fear of and hostility to anything that might call upon them to change their faith stance. The thought of modifying or 'surrendering' any portion of, say, literally true and inerrant scripture, essential ritual, unchallenged ecclesiastical authority, or established doctrinal stance is totally unacceptable because theirs is the one and only True Faith, and because the surrender of any sacred territory might breach the ramparts of the True Faith and in the end lead to its total destruction.

Given this situation, genuine dialoguers will almost certainly come from the ranks of professionals: writers, scholars and professional religieux (ministers, priests, monks, swamis, gurus). The profession of such persons calls for extensive knowledge of their own religious faith, practice in presenting it to others, and often a literary knowledge of other religious traditions and personal contact with their representatives. Such individuals being trained in and accustomed to discussions of religious pros and cons will not find the idea and practice of interreligious dialogue either strange or totally abhorrent.

But, as already implied, even such 'qualifications' for dialogue do not guarantee that true dialogue will occur when the intellectuals and professionals of differing religious persuasion meet for discussion. For some, their very professionalism will be an obstacle; the 'true person' of faith or no faith may not be willing to show him/herself. Interreligious discussions may have inoculated them against the alteration of their own personal faith-stance. The camel of religious commitment may not be able to go through the needle's eye of creative interreligious dialogue.

Are There Non-negotiables Between Religious Faiths?

Even though there is the sincere desire among dialoguers to gain new religious insight from dialogical encounters and the genuine willingness to 'convert' to the other's insight while remaining within one's own tradition, to use Robert Thurman's terminology, a final question must be asked. Are there elements – values, stances, basic convictions, doctrines so basic and so divergent between the major religious traditions that they cannot be altered or modified but only respectfully and tolerantly recognized? If so, it will be of no real benefit to anyone to pretend to agreement. And the facile harmonist suggestion that all paths of sincere spiritual effort lead to the same mountain top of final attainment is really beside the point of attempted interreligious dialogue altogether.

To make the discussion here more concrete it will be useful to choose two specific religions for our examples and not deal with vague generalities. I shall, for various reasons, choose Buddhism and Christianity for discussion here. Since the total range of differences cannot be considered, I shall focus on three themes. The first of these is God versus Emptiness (*śūnyatā*). Some thirty years ago I proposed in *Buddhism and Christianity* that the Buddhist equivalent of the Christian God was Dharma (ordered cosmic reality), Karma (morally just world order), Buddha (revealer, example), and Nirvana (final salvation). Apparently I was the only adherent of that suggestion. And in recent years, due to the fact that most Buddhist dialoguers have been Mahayanist Buddhists, the discussion about ultimate religious reality has been in terms of Zen Buddhist notions of Emptiness and Christian notions of God. Superficially the contrast seems absolute: God, the fullness of creative, sustaining, and redeeming power over against non-substantiality, non-conceivability, a conceptual nothingness. Can these two come even within speaking distance of each other?

Masao Abe, from the Zen Buddhist side, has made a valiant effort to bring these two 'entities' into meaningful relation to each other. On the basis of Philippians 2:58 he has written as follows: 'In the case of Christ, Kenosis [emptying] is realized in the fact that one who was in the form of God emptied himself [of his divine substance] and assumed the form of a servant.' For Abe, this means that 'God is something – or more precisely that God is each and everything – by his total self-emptying. Only through this total *kenosis* is God truly God.'[16] That is to say, God is not God by virtue of a monarchical sovereignty over the world – a common Christian stereotype – but by virtue of the universe being his emptied-out, self-diffusing being.

It is perhaps in some such terms that some Buddhists can 'believe' in the Christian 'God' and some Christians come to think of 'God' in

Buddhist-friendly terms. Process theologians such as John Cobb have shown some Christian friendliness to this approach. Whether this interreligious meeting of ideas and values will ever be of major religious significance remains to be seen. Most Christians, Catholic and Protestant, will continue to think of Jesus as the God-man, the truest and fullest revelation of God to humanity, the hope of human salvation. And on the Buddhist side Gautama Buddha, Amida Buddha, and the great bodhisattvas will continue to be mediators of true salvation.

In passing it may be remarked that it seems strange that D. T. Suzuki, writing from a Zen viewpoint, should have found the Christian symbol of the cross so repulsive. He wrote:

> When I see a crucified figure of Christ, I cannot help thinking of the gap that lies deep between Christianity and Buddhism. The gap is symbolic of the psychological division separating the East from the West. . . . Could not the idea of oneness [with Christ] be realized in some other way, that is, more peacefully, . . . less militantly, and less violently?[17]

Suzuki once said in conversation with me that the Western cross symbolized the need for the vertical Western ego to be flattened; the East, having no such sense of self (no-self, *śūnyatā* of Buddhism) needed no cross.

And there is another kind of strangeness with Abe's presentation of the idea of the self-emptying God. Why did he not relate this to the figure of the bodhisattva who vows to reenter human life endlessly till all are saved, who in Śāntideva's words says:

> My own being and my pleasure, all my righteousness in the past, present, and future, I surrender indifferently that all creatures may win to their end. . . . I yield myself to all living things to deal with me as they wish.[18]

Perhaps this kind of self-emptying does not have the *cosmic* significance of the self-emptying Christian God, and maybe Zen *śūnyatā* has no room for such pietistic themes.

Tangential to this, but of the practical and atmospheric rather than the strictly doctrinal, is the matter of worship versus meditation. Worship appears to be essentially theistic in nature, in which the devotee offers petitions and adoration to God. Meditation is a withdrawal from the outer world of sights and sounds, a retirement into one's inwardness for concentration of attention on some theme of intensive self awareness, which is the Buddhist spiritual method par excellence. Of course, the two are not necessarily mutually exclusive. Christian mystics are both intensive meditators and worshippers. But for lay and evangelical Christians, prayer, hymns, and worship are the most usual spiritual techniques, contrasting sharply with the Buddhist pattern of contemplative religiousness.

However, in Buddhist actuality the line is sometimes crossed. A Singhalese monk (date unknown) expressed himself thus about the Buddha:

> Him do I worship, the guide to deathlessness, the Noblest Sage and Peerless One.... He ... whose glories fill the entire universe.... Him do I worship.... Him, with the lotus-bud formed by my hands reverently clasped and raised above my head, do I worship.[19]

This is of course atypical and strictly unofficial, even 'heretical.' But even today, something of the nature of petitionary prayer is sometimes used in orthodox Buddhist circles. I quote from an experience in Burma:

> After [we had] discussed the power of the Buddha in his lifetime to 'scan' the universe for those souls in need of help, I asked a well-educated, middle-aged layman whether there was anything comparable today in Buddhist thinking. If someone in spiritual need should send out an SOS, would there be a dependable and helpful response? While the precise nature of this power was not made clear, the unhesitating answer was 'Yes.'[20]

At least in Southeast Asia the tone of the voice in which 'Buddha' is said, and the body language before Buddha images in pagodas seems to be 'worshipful.' So too the quality of Pure Land Buddhist reverence for Amida Buddha and the salvation-confirmatory faith-experience would seem to be worshipful in quality. Thus the most professional dialoguers of Buddhist persuasion would be unlikely to plead guilty to 'worship,' but their rank and file fellow Buddhists may not follow them here, at least in practice and attitude.

A second area of important Buddhist-Christian divergence is that of the respective views of human existence. The historic Christian view is that each human birth is an absolutely *de novo* beginning of existence which will last one lifetime in human form and then at death be saved in heaven or damned to hell. (The Catholic belief in limbo and purgatory somewhat soften the absolutism of this version of final destiny.) Contrastingly, for Theravada Buddhism there is a pattern of beginningless and endless non-substantial composite being in many forms; purgatorial, animal, spirit, human, and godling. These forms are determined by karmic justice and represent the maturing of the good or evil deeds done when in a human state. Nirvana is the name given to final release from all embodied existence, achieved by good moral living and meditational discipline.

Mahayana Buddhism complexified and subtitilized this schema with its samsara/nirvana equivalence language, climaxing in its (Zen) existentialist devotion to each present moment of existence in its concrete, circumstantial fullness. The Theravada schema might seem to have disappeared from Mahayana Buddhist consciousness, especially in Zen. Yet at least its ghostly presence persists. Two quotations from Zen sources will illustrate the point. The late Yasutani Roshi spoke thus from a Zen perspective: 'Now in our subconscious are to be found the residual impressions of our life experiences including those of previous existences going back to time immemorial.'[21] And Masao Abe speaks of acting 'in wisdom and compassion ... operating to emancipate innumerable beings from transmigration.'[22] When this viewpoint is tied to a conviction of the reversibility of temporal progression (Eastern Cyclism?) and the declaration that the future can determine the past,[23] how can it be reconciled with, or even come into conversational range with, the Christian-Western sense of the irreversible temporal currents of events and beinghood?

One final area of considerable difference between Buddhists and the modern Christian viewpoints must be noted, that of religiously inspired social action. It is quite true that early Christianity was not so minded, but waiting in readiness for the Divine Apocalypse that would end earthly history. And it is also true that some modern Christians view individual conversion to the Christian faith as the basic solution to social problems. But the culturally dominant Christian tone is humanisticlly inclined, socially activist in nature. The Christian should vigorously seek to right social wrongs.

The traditional Buddhist view is one version of the Indian-Asian view of the world as an organic unity, as one writer phrases it: 'When the various parts, the different groups and individuals are in harmony with each other, justice [a sacrosanct Christian-Western value] automatically results.'[24] Thus as the same author goes on to say, Buddhism in general does not conceive that the radical evils in the world must be vigorously, even forcibly, opposed. The Buddhist view is that 'suffering' is effected by our own mental creation; it is we ourselves who [individually] weave the fabric of our own sufferings in many forms,' – and that suffering in any case is endemic to space-time existence.

There is some evidence that this traditional Buddhist view may be changing as Buddhism 'comes West.' Some Western-educated Buddhists are social activists and even suggest that the ancient individualistic karma teaching might be abandoned, replaced by a sense of societal karma.[25] And to this writer it seems that perhaps Buddhism might employ its bodhisattvic motif more effectively and imaginatively, developing it in a social-action mode.

In conclusion, does dialogue have a viable future? Will more dialogic efforts lead to further progress? Should it be continued? Yes to all of these. Will a considerable body of believers in each religious camp remain in their traditional positions? Will some items of belief-practice remain non-negotiable? Will continuing dialogue lead to blunting the sharp edges of religious animosities, and some degree of better mutual understanding? Yes again to all of these.

Notes

1 *Buddhist-Christian Studies* 3 (1983): 42.
2 *Quaker Service Bulletin* (Spring 1995): 1.
3 *The Eastern Buddhist*, n.s. 21 (1988): 98.
4 *Dialogue, New Series*, 19–20, 105.
5 Idem.
6 Ruben L. F. Habito, *Total Liberation: Zen Spirituality and the Social Dimension* (Maryknoll, NY: Orbis Books, 1989), 87–88.
7 Ibid., 85.
8 Ibid, note 1, 47.
9 Ibid., 41.
10 Ibid., 34.
11 *Buddhist-Christian Studies* 10 (1990): 123.
12 Robert J. Schreiter, *Studies in Interreligious Dialogue* (Kampen: Kok-Pharos Publishing House, 1994), 72–73 and *Christian Identity and Interreligious Dialogue*, 72–73.
13 Franz Brendle, *Dharma World* 21 (1994): 11.
14 Masaaki Honda, *A Zen-Christian Pilgrimage: The Fruits of Ten Annual Colloquia in Japan, 1967–1976*, the Zen-Christian Colloquium, 1981.
15 *Buddhist-Christian Studies* 3 (1982): 142.
16 James W. Heisig, 'Sunyata and Kenosis,' *Academia Humanitatis*, Social Science Volume, Section 43, Extract, January 1986, 17.
17 Ibid., 7.
18 James B. Pratt, *Pilgrimage of Buddhism* (New York: Macmillan, 1928), 219.

19 Winston L. King, *A Thousand Lives Away* (Cambridge: Harvard University Press, 1964), 176.
20 Ibid., 178.
21 Philip Kapleau, *Three Pillars of Zen: Teaching, Practice, Enlightenment* (Tokyo: John Weatherhill, 1965), 10.
22 Quoted in Frederick J. Streng, 'Nāgārjuna,' *Encyclopedia of Religion* (New York: Macmillan and the Free Press, 1987), 43.
23 *Buddhist-Christian Studies* 7 (1987): 43.
24 George Evers, *Studies in Interreligious Dialogue* 4 (1994): 215.
25 See Ken Jones, *The Social Face of Buddhism* (London: Wisdom Publications, 1989).

CHAPTER FOUR

Response to Winston King

David Chappell

It is a pleasure to be lifted into the wide horizons of Winston King's views of dialogue based on more than a half-century of experience in Burma, Japan, and the West. I agree with him that the reason traditional interreligious encounter was largely contentious, and even violent, is because strong emotions aroused by religious differences challenged the ultimate identity and worth of other people. But I suspect that the more violent forms of interreligious encounter were often caused by the addition of tribalism and greed for political power. Also, I agree that there are at least three values that reach beyond the individual's personal religious hopes, shared spiritual values by all religions over against more egoistic, materialistic values, and a humble quest to improve one's religious life by learning from others.

Where Winston and I differ, however, is in our interpretation of what Winston calls the 'dialogue of concern' or 'dialogical action.' While acknowledging the 'increasingly necessary and important' role of dialogue for social action, he claims that it 'can scarcely be termed interreligious dialogue,' and then gives a variety of examples. Similarly, Winston finds that there are religious practices that can be shared, such as silent meditation, but he rejects these joint practices as not 'genuine' interreligious dialogue since the 'sticking points' of 'basic viewpoints and doctrine' remain unaddressed: for example, in the claim by Ruben Habito that 'dialogue is a mode of practice that cuts through two distinct religious traditions in a way that focuses on their mutually resonating elements.' Apparently genuine dialogue also needs to include those differences that produce discord and sour notes.

Somewhat in contradiction to this argument, however, Winston then proposes the 'dialogical ideal' as based not on intellectual 'sticking points' but on the individual's willingness to change one's 'self-understanding' (Rupp) by 'appropriation of the truth of the other' (Cobb) in order to convert to 'the full experiential and ethical fruition of their own and the other's tradition' (Thurman) that must involve an 'internal dialogue' (Sallie King) 'either prior to or following some dialogical encounter' (Winston King). It seems to me that none of these points about dialogue by these various authors are restricted to doctrinal sticking points, but could involve a much broader and multi-dimensional range of experience, including social responsibility and joint meditation. Instead of rejecting interreligious social action and joint silent meditation as not genuine dialogue, perhaps it is more precise to say that these two practices function more fully as dialogue when the practitioners admit 'that they are somehow incomplete and that they may be made more complete through the insights of the other party' (Cook), and are open to receive the truth of their dialogue partners at every level possible in the course of time.

Very few people have as much dialogue experience as Hans Ucko, who is responsible for facilitating and overseeing Jewish-Christian-Muslim dialogue for the World Council of Churches in Geneva. Yet the Buddhist-Christian Symposium held in July 1994 in Switzerland[1] came as a big surprise to him. He commented to me that in most dialogue meetings between Christians and Jews, or between Christians and Muslims, the partners came with clearly articulated theological positions and attempted to persuade the others of the validity of their viewpoints. In contrast, the technique used by the directors of the 1994 Symposium, Pia Gyger and Niklaus Brantschen, was to break the Symposium into small groups which began with personal sharing by each person of their inner thoughts on that day. Instead of being challenged by the others, the response invariably was an empathetic sharing of similar or complementary inner experiences by others in our group that expanded and clarified the inner experience by placing it in an interfaith context. Hans Ucko found this group of interfaith seekers and sharers to be in profound dialogue, but unusual because of its mutual sympathy and support. But these dialogues would not fit Winston's concern to face the differences of doctrine and worldview!

In spite of the harmony of the 1994 Symposium, I must admit that several academics who attended were very frustrated because the emphasis was on personal experience (specifically on Zen-Catholic joint practice) rather than on conceptual viewpoints. It is important to acknowledge, therefore, that any dialogue usually can emphasize only certain dimensions at any one time, and may not be meaningful to everyone. This became clear during the final review panel that acknowledged that the Symposium had been a dialogue of the heart (focused on spirituality), but that dialogue of the head and hands (implying intellectual discussion and sharing social responsibility) were other dialogue dimensions that deserved attention.

Even though religious traditions differ, I would argue that individuals within each tradition are predisposed to different ways of being religious, both for social and biological reasons, and that several broad categories that appear universally are social, meditative, intellectual, devotional, and ritual forms of religious experience.[2] A person who emphasizes one of these ways of being religious will probably get along better with similarly inclined people from other traditions than they do with people from their own tradition who emphasize other ways of being religious. For example, meditators or social activists usually find greater affinity with meditators or social activists from other traditions than they do with intellectual or ritual purists from their own traditions. On the other hand, those multi-dimensioned people who are able to integrate equally the different ways of being religious in their own tradition, as well as in another tradition (as Raimundo Pannikar and Ruben Habito are able to do), are the exception rather than the rule. As a consequence, I would argue that dialogue is communication between people, and for those religious people who communicate best through non-verbal forms, such as social action, ritual, music, meditation, and devotion, then dialogue can be genuine if they are sharing with an openness to learn and grow, even if they fail to deal with doctrines and worldviews.

In spite of Winston's concern about doctrinal differences, the 'dialogical ideal' that he constructed does not emphasize any one form of religious experience, inasmuch as all the people he quotes urge that dialogue involves openness to all dimensions and should be as inclusive as possible. Rather than focusing on intellectual sticking points (which highlights only one way of being religious, the intellectual), the main emphasis of the thinkers quoted by Winston seems to be concern to improve one's religious life by learning from the religious experience of others as broadly as possible. Even though the dominant Western form of dialogue is discussion about world-views and the major sticking points are theological, I would argue that for many other Western and Eastern people, there is equally valid dialogue focused on religious values, practices, and self-understanding that are better communicated in other ways. Interreligious dialogue is primarily communication between people, and if one partner is an adherent of Shinto who emphasizes ritual practice and aesthetics more than doctrine, then the form of dialogue will involve participation and practices as a major component.[3]

There are other reasons why I would be less quick than Winston to reject interreligious cooperation as not dialogue. Personal changes are usually piecemeal and gradual, and we often show only part of ourselves even to ourselves. In this connection, I totally agree with Winston that 'the intellectuals and professionals of differing religious persuasion' are especially prone not to show other dimensions of themselves that lie outside their roles. For this reason, I question Winston's assertion that 'genuine dialoguers will almost certainly come from the ranks of professionals.' In my own experience, many of the most moving and profound dialogues have involved not professionals, but laity. This was especially true in 1980 when we prepared for the first international Buddhist-Christian conference in Hawaii by holding over thirty local dialogues between lay leaders of various neighboring churches and temples. Sitting in a circle, the discussions began with the clergy being limited to a five minute opening statement that had to be focused on personal experience. Since most of the laity in Hawaii have interfaith experience in their families and jobs, they had all developed forms of self-understanding, world views, values, and ethics that somehow integrated this religious diversity. Nevertheless, the reason they attended the dialogue meetings was not only to share, but to learn and clarify. The discussion was very multi-dimensioned, but clearly dealt with the major 'sticking points' of interfaith practice and thought in the experience of the participants. While in 1980 the laity in Hawaii may have been atypical, pluralism is growing everywhere and is increasingly a part of everyone's living situation.

Winston raised three concrete 'sticking points' in dialogue: views of God, human existence, and social action. It seems that all three areas are undergoing change in both traditions for a variety of reasons, especially since the center of authority for an increasing number of people has shifted from traditional hierarchies within their own culture to a new sense of the global community and environment. Certainly in the area of social action, I would argue that differences between Buddhism and Christianity quickly disappear whenever Buddhism is freed from political suppression. Also, I applaud

Winston's proposal that the Buddhist complex of Dharma, karma, Buddha, and Nirvana as a group are functional equivalents for God. However, bodhisattvas and local spirits should also be added since these often serve as the objects of petitionary prayers for practical benefits (healing, prosperity, children, protection). However, aren't these insightful parallels that Winston proposes the very kind of 'mutually resonating elements' that Ruben Habito was affirming and Winston was rejecting earlier in his essay? It is just because of the positive role that can be played even by differences that I would argue that dialogue need not always involve intellectual conflict based on differing worldviews, but can involve expanding our understanding based on seeing parallels or contrasts in other traditions. Instead of changing a religious position, dialogue can also involve mutual support and enhancement. This would then uphold the dual emphasis of John Cobb that dialogue involves both *enrichment* as well as *purification* (namely, changing or abandoning trivial and distorted ideas and practices).

Are there non-negotiables between religions? President Ikeda of Soka Gakkai International has rejected the religious unity of the ecumenical movement as false since any religion 'to remain a religion, must be convinced that its own doctrines are uniquely correct and that other doctrines are mistaken.' While reverence for Nichiren as the eternal Buddha and practice involving the *daimoku* and *gohonzon* are non-negotiables for SGI, it is clear that there is much room for dialogue resonance since, as Ikeda has insisted, 'cooperation among religious bodies, though impossible on the plane of doctrine and teaching, is not only possible, but also essential, on the quite different planes of politics, economy, industry, and culture.' Furthermore, perhaps because he also believes that 'Christianity, Islam, and Buddhism have taught love and compassion transcending differences of race and ideology as the ways to promote mutual understanding and to bring about a kind of ecumenical union of mankind,'[4] SGI has already begun dialoguing with Roman Catholics at Nanzan University (Jan VanBragt, Jim Heisig, and others).[5] Because of the diversity of any world religion, and of the different interpretations and priorities that arise based on individual needs and abilities, there will always exist shared ground for dialogue even if for the moment there are areas that are held in suspension as non-negotiable.

In sum, I agree with Winston everywhere except in his effort to narrow dialogue to discussion over doctrinal sticking points. Because

I assert a multidimensioned view of religion, as well as the dual function of dialogue as enrichment and purification, and use a longer time line that may require preliminary periods of building trust and sharing values, I am more liberal in including many forms of interreligious cooperation and discussion under the general term 'interreligious dialogue.' But even though we may disagree on how to use the term 'dialogue,' we probably both want to support interreligious dialogue and cooperation in as may ways possible, no matter what name it is called. Given the sorry history of past religious conflict, any and all cooperation is a welcome change. And as Hans Küng keeps emphasizing: No world peace until there is peace among the religions; and no peace among the religions until there is dialogue among the religions.

Notes

1 See my report in *Buddhist-Christian Studies* 15 (1995): 239–240.
2 Cf. Dale Cannon, *Six Ways of Being Religious: A Framework for Comparative Studies of Religion* (Boston: Wadsworth, 1996).
3 For example, as a social activist, Sulak Sivaraksa often tries to develop new understanding in other people through new experiences, not just by intellectual argument. At an annual meeting of the International Network of Engaged Buddhists, Sulak includes visits to areas of social change in Thailand, not just reading newspapers and having discussion. Also, when Sulak received the Right Livelihood Award before the Swedish Parliament on December 7, 1995, he asked that Buddhist monks be invited to chant scriptures to grace the occasion. *See Torch of Wisdom* (Taipei), No. 219 (February 10, 1996): 7.
4 Aurelio Peccei and Daisaku Ikeda, *Before It is Too Late* (Tokyo: Kodansha International, 1984), 98.
5 These dialogues are scheduled to appear in a book, and in spite of Ikeda's earlier claim, the dialogues did include discussion about doctrine, as well as dialogue about clergy, practice, and the future.

PART TWO

Ultimate Reality

CHAPTER FIVE

'In the Beginning ... God': A Christian's View of Ultimate Reality

Bonnie Thurston

At the outset of *Emptiness: A Study in Religious Meaning,* Frederick J. Streng noted that in the West religious discourse begins with God and God's self-revelation, and in the East it begins with the human condition.[1] Streng's insight is fundamental to this chapter, for their observation is where biblical theology, the perspective from which this chapter is written, also begins.

The term 'ultimate reality' is taken from the writings of Paul Tillich. He summarizes his discussion of the term in *Christianity and the Encounter of the World Religions.*

> Religion is the state of being grasped by an ultimate concern, a concern which qualifies all other concerns as preliminary and which itself contains the answer to the question of the meaning of our life. Therefore this concern is unconditionally serious and shows a willingness to sacrifice any finite concern which is in conflict with it. The predominant religious name for the content of such concern is God.[2]

Biblical religion, while conforming to Tillich's definition, quickly moves away from abstractions like 'ultimate reality,' and, as Streng notes, speaks instead about God. The existence of God is presupposed by the writers of the Bible. Indeed, the Psalmist notes that only 'fools say in their hearts, "There is no God."' (Psalm 14:1)[3] Popular Christianity assumes the existence of God, even if a great many non-foolish Christians through the centuries have offered proofs of God's existence. I will not deal with the vast literature presenting philosophical proofs for the existence of God or the systematic descriptions of God's essence or nature. Philosophical approaches to the Judeo-Christian-Islamic God finally fall short for the simple reason that our God cannot be comprehended by the finite minds of human beings. Most serious writers on the subject begin with that admission. For example, the great Christian philosopher and theologian, St. Augustine, practically admitted as much.

> What then, brethren, shall we say of God? For if you have been able to comprehend what you would say, then it is not of God. . . . If you have been able to comprehend Him as you think, by so thinking you have deceived yourself. This then is not God, if you have comprehended it. But if it be God, then you have not comprehended it.[4]

Ancient Christian liturgies, as well, note the incomprehensibility of God. In the Orthodox Liturgy of St. John Chrysostom as the service moves toward Holy Communion the priest prays, 'For you are the ineffable God, inconceivable, invisible, incomprehensible, existing forever and yet ever the same...' God may be understood to be 'inconceivable, invisible, and incomprehensible,' but God is assumed to *be*. In fact God has been understood as Being itself. Etienne Gilson noted, 'in a Christian metaphysics of being . . . the supreme principle is a God whose true name is "He who is." A pure Act of existing...'.[5]

But the Christian's ancient Israelite ancestors in faith were not philosophers or especially philosophically minded. For the Hebrews, God was person. Nor, according to Gilson, were the early Hellenists, the other intellectual 'parents' of Christianity, abstract in their 'god talk.' A Greek god, he notes, 'is never an inanimate thing; he is a living being, just as men themselves are.'[6] For the ancients, God was not disembodied Being, but was personal. The following observation conjoins the notions of God as Being and God as person:

> There is no other way to talk about who and what God is other than to say that God is existence itself. Am-ness. God is the holy ground of being. At the bottom of the universe is not some mindless grinding machinery or evolutionary process. What moves everything, from stars to human hearts, is personal existence.[7]

For Biblical religion, 'personal existence' rather than pure Being (or Emptiness) is at the root of reality. Tillich articulated it this way: 'The center of the antiontological bias of biblical religion is its personalism. According to every word of the Bible, God reveals himself as personal.

The encounter with him and the concepts describing this encounter are thoroughly personal.'[8] Christianity functions with an understanding of God as personal. And that is because Christianity inherited its basic notion of God from Israelite monotheism.

From the outset, the God of Israel was described simply and concretely, not metaphysically or abstractly. God was called 'Yahweh' 'a distinctly personal name, going back to pre-historic times.'[9] The God of the Patriarchs was understood to be 'one, personal, almighty, transcendent, eternal, and deeply interested in Israel.'[10] This personal God was described in human terms. One of the earliest statements about God in Hebrew Scripture is that humankind, both male and female, is God's image. 'Then God said, "Let us make humankind in our image, according to our likeness,"' (Genesis 1:26) and 'God created humankind in his image, in the image of God he created them; male and female he created them.' (Genesis 1:27) The attempt of the Hebrew writer, as Jack Miles' popular book, *God: A Biography*, points out, is to make some sense of God in human terms.[11] Throughout scripture God is described in human terms with, for example, a face (Ex. 33:20), back (Ex. 33:23), arms (Deut. 32:40), and legs (Na. 1:3, Zec. 14:4). God is also characterized in terms of human activity, for example as a warrior (Ex. 15:3, Ps. 24:8), and as exhibiting human emotions like jealousy (Ex. 20:5, Deut. 4:24), slowness to anger (Ex. 34:6), and forgiveness (Jon. 4:1).[12]

Many other examples can be given of God described as carrying out human activity as exalted as that of king (Ps. 95:3) and judge (Ps. 96:12) or as common as that of shepherd (Ps. 23:1) or woman giving birth and nurturing children (Is. 66:9, Numb. 11:12).[13] The point is not to anthropormorphize God, and certainly not to suggest that Christian faith is anthropocentric, but to underscore that God was understood as person. Yahweh was 'at once the most transcendent God of the ancient Near East and the most human.'[14] Two biblical depictions of God's personhood are especially illuminating in this context: God's giving of the Divine Name to Moses in Exodus 3, and God's incarnation, the foundational understanding of Christianity which is variously described in the New Testament. Both depictions underscore how basic is the Christian understanding of God's personhood.

The book of Exodus chronicles the 'root experience' of Israel: God's deliverance of the Hebrews from slavery in Egypt, their covenant with God, and God's providential care for them in the wilderness of Sinai. God chooses Moses, a fugitive from Egypt living in Midian, to lead the exodus from Egypt. Chapters 3 and 4 of Exodus describe Moses' call, focusing on his reluctance and God's patience. The fact that, in these chapters and elsewhere in Exodus, God's relations with Moses are described in terms of conversation underscores the personal dimension of the understanding of God.[15] God promises Moses, 'I will be with you,' (Ex. 3:11, about which more will be said shortly), but Moses demands further assurances, the most startling of which is the demand to know God's name. (cf. Ex. 3:13)

In the context from which Hebrew scripture comes, names were more than labels for identification; they were expressions of the essential nature of the bearer. The soul found expression in the name of the person. To speak in someone's name was to speak with that one's authority. And it was believed that knowing someone's name gave the knower power over that person, potentially the ability to manipulate him or her.[16] Thus it is shocking, first, that Moses asks God's name and, second, that God answers.

'God said to Moses, "I AM WHO I AM."' (Ex. 3:14) The answer is an etymology of the cultic name, Yahweh (designated by the tetragrammaton, YHWH). It does not describe God's being so much as God's *personal* presence in the affairs of people. Because tense is not inflected in the verb structure of Semitic languages, YHWH is variously translated from the root verb 'to be' as 'I am,' 'I cause to be,' and/or 'I will be.'[17] The present tense translation, 'I am,' emphasizes God's eternal being and divine will. According to the Masorites (rabbinical scholars ca. 700 CE) YHWH was based on the causative form of 'to be,' thus emphasizing God as creator and lord. Finally, the name can be translated by the simple future tense, 'I will be,' which gives promise of God's presence; God's being is understood to be turned toward God's people.

In the context of the Christian view of ultimate reality two points are noteworthy. First, Exodus 3 unites the concepts of God as Being and God as personal being. Indeed, it includes the personal as an essential aspect of God's being. Second, the name God gives Moses reveals nothing but God's Is-ness, the existence of God as one who is. Again, to belabor the point, God's existence is understood personally. And that 'person' promises, 'I will be with you.' (Ex. 3:12)[18]

This brings us to the second, and for Christians the defining, depiction of God as personal. We call it the incarnation. Christians believe that God took human form or appearance[19] in Jesus of Nazareth. In the words of St. John, God 'became flesh and lived among us.' (John 1:14) For Christians, this is both a great mystery and an extension of the personal nature of God. Hebrew scripture records that God spoke to the prophets (of whom Moses is understood to be the greatest. cf. Deut. 34:10). 'But when the fullness of time had come, God sent his Son, born of a woman.' (Gal. 4:4) The earliest Christians believed the incarnation was an extension of what God had been doing in history, in the words of the Pauline school, 'a plan for the fullness of time.' (Eph. 1:10) After telling the story of Jesus' birth, Matthew, a Jewish Christian writing about 85 CE, noted, 'All this took place to fulfill what had been spoken by the Lord through the prophet: "Look, the virgin shall conceive and bear a son, and they shall name him Emmanuel," which means, "God is with us."' (Matthew 1:22–23)

Christians believe that God created human beings and, in sympathy (literally 'feeling with'), God communicated with them. God's communication first occurred directly (for example in Genesis 1 and 2 God is said to have walked in the garden of Eden with Adam and Eve, or in Exodus, spoken directly with Moses) and then by means of the Torah (law) and the prophets. Finally to perfect that communication and sympathy, God took on human flesh. In the words of the writer of the New Testament book of Hebrews,

> Long ago God spoke to our ancestors in many and various ways by the prophets, but in these last days he has spoken to us by a Son ... He is the reflection of God's glory and *the exact imprint of God's very being*, and he sustains all things by his powerful word. (Hebrews 1:1–3. Italics mine.)

Christians believe that God made the Divine Self most fully available to human knowing in Jesus. In St. John's gospel Jesus says, 'If you know me, you will know my Father also. From now on you do know him and have seen him.' (John 14:7) If one has 'seen' Jesus, she or he has 'seen' God. The most important thing about Jesus in this discussion, then, is not Jesus-the-individual, but Jesus-as-God-incarnate. In other words, for our purposes we can set aside questions connected with the 'historical Jesus,' and think solely in terms of Jesus as a self-manifestation of God. As Tillich noted, the central event of Christianity 'is a personal life, the image of which ... shows no break in his [Jesus'] relation to God and no claim for himself in his particularity.'[20]

The analogical language that speaks of God as a Father who sends a Son will lead us to the second major point of this chapter, that Christians believe God's personal existence is relational. But first a word on the metaphor of 'fatherhood.' The language of the Father-God does not mean either that God is male or that God engages in sexually generative activity.[21] To say nothing of the unacceptability of material, bodily aspects in God, such an implication would not only be sexist, but would 'undermine the human equality of women made in the divine image and likeness.'[22] (See the quotation of Genesis 1:26, 27 above.) Christians refer to God as Father after the example of Jesus who called God, *Abba*, the Aramaic word for 'father.' Hebrew scripture and the Jewish tradition in which Jesus grew up certainly knew God as 'father,'[23] a concept that presupposed a quality of relationship with God.[24] As Joachim Jeremias has noted in his extensive study of the term *Abba*, Near Eastern religions are familiar with the mythological idea that the deity is the father of humankind or of certain human beings. 'When the word "Father" is used for a deity in this connection it implies fatherhood in the sense of unconditional and irrevocable authority.'[25] But the word 'Father' as applied to God also 'encompasses, from earliest times, something of what the word "Mother" signifies among us.'[26] That is, absolute authority *and* absolute tenderness and nurture are both implied by *Abba*.

When Christians speak of the Fatherhood of God, then, we mean to imply something about both the personal being of God and the relational nature of that person-hood. It implies the will of God to bestow and to nurture life (about which more will be said presently). To speak of God as Father is to speak of God as 'the homeland of all people.'[27] 'To call God "Father" means that life and death are not handed over to a vitalistic randomness...'.[28] As Soelle asserts, to regard the world as God's creation means to regard it as planned and good.

The incarnation, then, raises the tricky issue of one God in multiple persons, what Christianity calls 'Trinitarian theology.' Christianity asserts that God is made known in Jesus Christ and sends the Holy Spirit,[29] the third 'person' of the Trinity, to abide with believers. St. John's gospel refers to the Holy Spirit as the *parakletos*, the paraclete, comforter or advocate. In that gospel Jesus says, 'I will ask the Father, and he will give you another Advocate, to be with you forever.' (John 14:16) '... the Advocate, the Holy Spirit, whom the Father will send in my name, will teach you everything, and remind you of all that I have said to you.' (John 14:26) The Holy Spirit, the third 'person' of the Trinity, insures God's continued presence 'with us.'

Again, there is a vast and historic literature on the Trinity. But what I want to stress in this discussion is that speaking of God as manifested in a Son and a Holy Spirit is a way of asserting that God's fundamental nature is relational. God's very self can be understood as a relationship. Tertullian, writing at the end of the second century, asserted that the three persons of the Trinity are one in substance, condition and power, but three in *relation*, mode of existence, and special characteristics. (Italics mine.) In the fourth century the Cappadocian Fathers of the Eastern church pursued this idea of God's internal relationality.

> ... the radical move of the Cappadocians was to assert that divinity or Godhood originates with personhood (someone onward another), not with substance (something in and of itself).... Thus personhood, being-in-relation-to-another, was secured as the ultimate originating principle of all reality.[30]

What this means is that the relatedness of the three 'persons' of God is the model for all of reality. The essence or heart of God is 'to be in relationship ....'[31] Or as Elizabeth Johnson says in her powerful book, *She Who Is*, 'the one God is God in the threefold mode of his own self-relatedness.'[32] At heart, God is community; in the ontology of the triune God, priority can appropriately be given to relation.[33] As Johnson points out, this fact has profound implications for both Christology (the doctrines about Jesus Christ) and ecclesiology (the doctrines about the church).[34] Johnson's observation leads us to our next consideration, the nature of God's relationality.

To summarize the point about God's relational nature in the words of Nels Ferré, 'The very nature of the ultimate, the absolute, God as love, a self-existing and self-directing being, is to have relations.'[35] We might say the inner life of God is a life of relationship, a community of love. Writing about Buddhist *śūnyatā* and the Christian Trinity, Michael von Brück has put the matter as follows: Love, 'as symbolized in the innertrinitarian relationship, is the ultimate nature of Reality.'[36] Ferré also asserts that God's relational nature is characterized by love. That, of course, is why God had to be manifested as, and in, a person, Jesus of Nazareth; '... for love is not basically a philosophical term. Love is a personal term.'[37]

The witness of Christian scripture is that God's relational nature is characterized by love. Love 'is the nature of ultimate being.'[38] The writer of I John states simply, 'love is from God' and 'God is love.' (I John 4:7–8 and 16b) Henri Bergson writing of God notes that God is love; the description of God is interminable because what is described is ineffable, but 'divine love is not a thing of God: it is God himself.'[39]

71

And, for Christians, God's love is seen most clearly in Jesus. Again, I John:

> God's love was revealed among us in this way: God sent his only Son into the world so that we might live through him. In this is love, not that we loved God but that he loved us and sent his Son to be the atoning sacrifice for our sins. (I John 4:9–10)

To paraphrase Paul's letter to the Philippians, although Jesus was in the form of God, he took human likeness and humbled himself to the point of death on a cross. (Phil. 2:6-11) The cross, that great stumbling block to belief in God the Father of Jesus, is seen by Christians not in its torturous cruelty (which, of course, it was), but as the ultimate expression of God's love.[40] The great paradox is that God loved human beings enough not only to become one among them, but to die for them, and to bring life from that death. The doctrine of God in the modern period dwells on this immanent God, and its incarnational theology focuses on God who humbles the Divine Self and suffers in order to redeem. God who is essentially love shows the Divine Self most clearly in self-sacrifice.[41]

Obviously, then, the nature of the love here discussed is not the emotional, or even hormonal, reaction of American afternoon television! It is not 'luv,' not a matter of 'feeling' at all. Christian love as demonstrated by God is a consciously chosen act of will, a choice to act for the benefit of the other in spite of the consequences to one's self. My own sense is that Winston King is correct when he describes Buddhist loving kindness 'as systematic and calculated, indirect and impersonal, and atomistically individualistic' and describes Christian love as 'spontaneously and intensely personal in spirit, practical and direct in its expression, historically and socially minded in viewpoint.'[42]

Christian love is the 'form of being which acts out of complete concern not only for all, in all dimensions of life, and the conditions which sustain, promote and enhance life, but also for ever new life and new conditions of life.'[43] Or, as LaCugna notes, 'God by nature is outgoing love and self donation.'[44] In short, the love which is God and is *of* God is characterized by generativity and generosity. The two characteristics are closely related and one does not take precedence over the other.

God's generativity is the note on which the biblical account opens. 'In the beginning ... God created the heavens and the earth.' (Gen. 1:1)[45] The writers of Genesis stress from the outset that God made from nothing everything that exists. Being complete in the Divine Self, 'perfect' to use a philosophical term, God did not have to create anything else. But God chose to do so. Reflecting on the creation of human beings, but with general applicability to this point of God's generativity, Gilson notes,

> The only possible explanation for the presence of ... finite and contingent beings is that they have been freely given existence by 'Him who is,' and not as parcels of his own existence, which, because it is absolute and total, is also unique, but as finite and partial imitations of what He himself eternally is in his own right.[46]

The love exhibited by the Christian God is always generative, always creative, always productive, always bringing into existence. So that which is *of* the love of God is always life giving, generative, having the potential power of bringing into being.

If that which is of God is always generative, so it is also always generous, giving, and especially self-giving. Christians believe that the creation itself is witness to the abundance, the magnificent open-handedness of God. 'This ontological surplus of Being in the face of Nothingness is what the Christian religion ... tries to articulate.'[47] God's generosity and liberality is seen not only in the bewildering variety of the created universe, but most astonishingly in God's willingness to give the only Son (God's *monogenous*, cf. Jn. 1:14) to redeem that creation. Or, put another way, God's generosity is seen most clearly when God 'empties himself' (*ekenosen*, cf. Phil. 2:7) to take human form. Masao Abe is exactly correct that emptying is 'the fundamental *nature* of God himself,' and that 'we should understand the doctrine of Christ's *kenosis* to mean that Christ as the Son of God is *essentially* and *fundamentally* self-emptying.'[48] (Italics his.)

Because the love which characterizes the Christian God is generative and generous it is always becoming. 'God as reality both is and becomes by nature, for He is love, but this relation cannot be considered merely as such, ... but must also be considered in terms of a progressive process with unrepeatable points.'[49] To suggest that God is always becoming is not to say that God is incomplete or imperfect. It is to say that if the nature of the Christian God is love, then it is characteristic of that love perpetually to be *being* given.

Perhaps a more concrete way to make this point is to say that God was once incarnate in Jesus Christ (an 'unrepeatable point'), and is always 'incarnating' (a 'progressive process') in those who love as

God loves. Christianity believes that God continues to 'be with us' in love which, in the human sphere, is never perfected, always becoming perfect. John writes in his first epistle, '... if we love one another, God lives in us, and his love is perfected in us.' (I John 4:12)

The three elements that Arnold Toynbee suggested are the essentials of Christianity are helpful at this point. First, according to Toynbee, Christianity has a vision of God as loving his creatures so greatly that He sacrificed himself for their salvation. Second, humans should follow the example God set for them in His incarnation and crucifixion. And, finally, human beings should act on this in so far as they are able.[50] Thus, to return to the point about God's becoming, when Christians see generous and generative love in action, we are seeing God's nature 'becoming' among us. And for us Christians, to be devout means first to give ourselves to God (as God gave the Divine Self to us), and then 'to take part in the movement of love in the world and to become love [ourselves].'[51] The beauty and splendor of God is visible and is becoming in those who, to use the language of the prophet Isaiah, 'prepare God's way' by being lovers.[52]

Thomas Merton, one of the great pioneers of Buddhist-Christian dialogue, articulated this point very clearly. God, Merton asserted 'seeks Himself in us.' Indeed, 'we exist solely for this, to be the place He has chosen for His presence, His manifestation in the world, His epiphany.'[53] And how does this astonishing thing occur? Through love.

It is the love of my lover, my brother or my child that sees

> God in me, makes God credible to myself in me. And it is my love for my lover, my child, my brother, that enables me to show God to him or her in himself or herself. Love is the epiphany of God in our poverty.[54]

Merton asserts, and it is the quintessential Christian assertion, that 'whether you understand or not, God loves you, is present to you, lives in you, dwells in you, calls you, saves you...'.[55] Here is a fundamental difference in the Christian world-view from that of Buddhism. We Christians do not believe that, in the final analysis, we can be 'lamps unto ourselves.' It is just too dark. We need 'the life' that is 'the light of all people,' Jesus Christ, both to enlighten and to save us. (cf. John 1:1–5)

For Christians, 'Ultimate Reality' is personal, but much more than a personal being 'out there' somewhere, a God Who is well disposed toward us humans, but far away. God has chosen to come among us (as Jesus Christ) and to remain with us (through the Holy Spirit). We Christians have not only the gift of physical life that God has given us, but we have the awesome privilege, and also the responsibility, of sharing in the very essence of God which is love. Our 'charge' as Christians is to love as God loved, to be generative and generous in our loving, indeed, to 'be perfect ... as [our] heavenly Father is perfect.' (Matt. 5:48)

Notes

1 Frederick J. Streng, *Emptiness: A Study in Religious Meaning* (Nashville: Abingdon Press, 1967), 21.

2 Paul Tillich, *Christianity and the Encounter of the World Religions* (New York: Columbia University Press, 1963), 4–5. (Hereafter *Encounter.)*

3 Unless otherwise noted, all biblical quotations are from the New Revised Standard translation of the Bible (New York: Oxford University Press, 1991).

4 *Sermons on Selected Lessons of the New Testament* 52:16.
When it occurs in the original quotation I have retained the use of the male pronoun for God with the understanding that it is traditional usage and does not imply God's 'maleness.' In the body of the essay I have made an attempt to use the inclusive language which reflects more contemporary thought about God.

5 Etienne Gilson, *God and Philosophy* (New Haven: Yale University Press, 1961), 51.

6 Ibid., 9.

7 John F. Kavanaugh, 'Holy Ground of Being,' *America* 172/8 (March 11, 1995), 39.

8 Paul Tillich, *Biblical Religion and The Search for Ultimate Reality* (Chicago: University of Chicago Press, 1955), 22. (Hereafter *Search.)*

9 W.T. Davison, 'God (Biblical and Christian)' in James Hastings (ed.) *Encyclopedia of Religion and Ethics* (New York: Charles Scribner's Sons, 1914) VI: 253–254.

10 R.T.A. Murphy, 'Concept of God in the Bible,' in *The New Catholic Encyclopedia* (New York: McGraw-Hill, 1967) VI: 539.

11 Jack Miles, *God: A Biography* (New York: Alfred A. Knopf, 1995), 14.

12 S. David Sperling, 'God in the Hebrew Scriptures,' in M. Eliade (ed.), *The Encyclopedia of Religion* (New York: Macmillan, 1987) VI: 6–7.

13 For a fuller discussion of Biblical 'god language' see Phyllis Trible, *God and the Rhetoric of Sexuality* (Philadelphia: Fortress Press, 1978).

14 Sperling, 7.

15 I am grateful to Fr. James A. O'Brien, S.J. for pointing this out to me.

16 For further discussion of the concept of the name see Chapter 4 'The Name,' in Bonnie Thurston, *Spiritual Life in the Early Church* (Minneapolis: Fortress Press, 1993).

17 In her book, *Theology for Skeptics: Reflections on God* (Minneapolis: Fortress Press, 1995), Dorothee Soelle notes Mary Daly as having said

that a noun was not an appropriate word for speaking about God. A verb, active and dynamic is needed. (p. 46) The name God gave Moses *was* a verb!

18 A very helpful discussion of this remarkable phrase occurs in Donald E. Gowan, *Theology in Exodus* (Louisville: Westminster John Knox Press, 1994) chapter 3.

19 The Greek word Paul quotes is *schemati,* outward form, which is contrasted with *morphe,* nature. See Phil. 2:6–11.

20 Tillich, *Encounter,* 81.

21 This is a crucial point, the one on which Muslims differ with Christians in their understanding both of the nature of God (*Allah*) and of the origin of Jesus. Surah 112 of the Holy Qur'an, a cornerstone of Muslim piety, notes that God is 'the One.' God 'begetteth not nor was begotten.' And to the degree that God's 'begetting' of Jesus was not sexual generation, Christians could agree.

22 Elizabeth A. Johnson, *She Who Is: The Mystery of God in Feminist Theological Discourse* (New York: Crossroad, 1992), 18.

23 See, for example, Isaiah 63:16 at which point the prophet declares, 'For you [God] are our father.'

24 Reginald Fuller, 'God in the New Testament,' in M. Eliade (ed.), *The Encyclopedia of Religion* (New York: Macmillan, 1987) VI: 8.

25 Joachim Jeremias, 'Abba,' *The Prayers of Jesus* (Philadelphia: Fortress Press, 1978), 11.

26 Ibid.

27 Soelle, 20.

28 Soelle, 31.

29 The Eastern and Western branches of Christianity divide over the question of whether the Holy Spirit 'proceeds from the Father and the Son' or just 'from the Son,' but both members of the 'family' are strongly Trinitarian in their understanding of God.

30 Catherine M. LaCugna, 'God in Communion With Us: The Trinity,' in Catherine M. LaCugna (ed.), Freeing Theology: The Essentials of Theology in Feminist Perspective (San Francisco: Harper, 1993), 86–87.

31 LaCugna, 106.

32 Johnson, 206.

33 Johnson, 216.
   Again, this was the genius of the Cappadocians in their discussion of God, to give priority to relation not substance (as per Aristotle and St. Thomas).

34 See Johnson, chapter 10, 'Triune God: Mystery of Relation.'

35 Nel F.S. Ferre, *The Christian Understanding of God* (New York: Harper and Row, 1951), 19.

36 Michael Von Brück, 'Buddhist Sunyata and the Christian Trinity,' in *Buddhist Emptiness and Christian Trinity,* Roger Corless and Paul F. Knitter eds., (New York: Paulist Press, 1990), 61.

37 Ferre, 29.

38 Ferre, 18.

39 Quoted in Maritain, 93.

40 In the context of Buddhist-Christian dialogue Von Brück rightly notes, 'The importance of the Cross ... is that it points up the necessity and

value of becoming a no-thing. The cross symbolizes the devoiding or transcending turn into the other and finally into the Whole.' Von Brück, 65.

41 Davison, 268–269.
42 Winston L. King, *Buddhism and Christianity: Some Bridges of Understanding* (Philadelphia: Westminster Press, 1962), 91.
43 Ferre, 16.
44 LaCugna, 87. Philosophically this should not be construed to imply that God *had* to create, that creation was a necessity. God was not under duress to create, but freely and generously created all that is.
45 According to St. Thomas Aquinas, that the world had a beginning is an article of faith, not something that can be proved. (*Summa Theologica*, 1, 46, 2) See Maritain, 40.
46 Gilson, 53.
47 Soelle, 112.
48 Masao Abe, 'Kenosis and Emptiness,' in Corless and Knitter, 18 and 13. For a fuller discussion of this point see Abe, 'God, Emptiness, and the True Self,' in Frederick Franck, ed., *The Buddha Eye* (New York: Crossroad, 1982) and chapters 9 and 10 in Hans Waldenfels, *Absolute Nothingness: Foundations for a Buddhist-Christian Dialogue* (New York: Paulist Press, 1980).
49 Ferre, 23.
50 Arnold Toynbee, *Christianity Among the Religions of the World* (New York: Charles Scribner's Sons, 1957), 106.
51 Soelle, 117.
52 Soelle, 126.
53 Thomas Merton, *The Monastic Journey*, ed., Brother Patrick Hart) (Kansas City: Sheed Andrews and McMeel, Inc., 1977), 172.
54 Ibid.
55 Merton, 173.

CHAPTER SIX

Response to Bonnie Thurston's '"In the Beginning ... God": A Christian's View of Ultimate Reality'

Malcolm David Eckel

It is now widely understood that the most lively and serious interreligious dialogue occurs between individuals rather than between abstract systems of thought, and the dialogue that takes place in the public sphere mirrors a dialogue that goes on in the minds and hearts of the participants themselves as they grapple with the force of another person's words. The scholar's role in such encounters is not so much to determine which views are 'true' or 'false' but, in Winston King's words, to build the bridges that help this lively exchange take place.[1] In that respect Bonnie Thurston's '"In the Beginning ... God": A Christian's View of Ultimate Reality' is a delightful success. She has opened up important lines of investigation for anyone interested in the connections between Buddhist and Christian views of ultimate reality. In this response I will follow the direction she has so ably charted and attempt to show how a Mahayana Buddhist in the Indian and Tibetan tradition might respond to her account of the nature of God.

'For the ancients, God was not disembodied Being, but personal.'

After a modest acknowledgment of the abstract, disembodied God of the philosophers, Thurston focuses her attention on the personal God of the Biblical tradition. She then uses the concept of 'person' to draw a contrast with the Mahayana Buddhist view of ultimate reality: 'For Biblical religion, "personal existence" rather than pure Being (or Emptiness) is the root of reality.' To Buddhist eyes this contrast certainly has the appearance of truth. There is a long Buddhist tradition of denying the existence of a personal creator God. Buddhist philosophers in India argued for many centuries with their Hindu counterparts about the existence of a divine creator, until the Buddhists ceased to be an active voice in Indian philosophical debate.[2] The controversy continues in a contemporary form in California, where the Buddhist Churches of America have pressed the Boy Scouts of America to remove references to God in the Boy Scout oath. Not only do Buddhists deny the reality of a creator God, they also deny the reality of a 'person.' If ultimate reality is Emptiness (as it is understood in the Mahayana) and Emptiness is the absence of a self-existent reality in all things (as in the momentary phenomena that make up the flow of experience as well as in persons themselves), there ultimately is no 'person,' divine or otherwise. The Buddhist position seems doubly opposed to the idea that ultimate reality takes the form of 'personal existence.'

Buddhists constantly remind us, however, not to be deceived by appearances. The concept of Emptiness seems abstract, disembodied, and negative, like many of the philosophical formulations of the concept of God as 'Being,' but there is a concrete, embodied, affirmative dimension of Emptiness that is built into the concept itself. On the most fundamental etymological level, the concept of Emptiness is based on the idea that one thing is empty of another. It is true, of course, that Emptiness is omnipresent, since all things are equally empty from the ultimate perspective. But in practice one comes to know Emptiness by perceiving that a certain place is empty in a certain way. The place might be a natural setting, as in the tradition of Japanese contemplative poetry, or it might be a shrine associated with an event in the life of the Buddha or a Buddhist saint. But behind all of these localizations of Emptiness stand the 'persons' in whom Emptiness is known and, in that sense, made present: the Buddhas of the past and future, Buddhist saints, teachers of every variety, and finally the personal mental continuum of the individual practitioner.

This is not to say that abstract, philosophical expressions of the concept of Emptiness are mistaken. The Indian and Tibetan traditions were much enamored of abstract expression. The point is that there is no fundamental barrier between the Emptiness of the philosophers and the 'person' who constitutes the Buddha of popular devotion. The philosophers' own works make this clear. Śāntideva's great poem on the practice of the bodhisattva (*Bodhicaryāvatāra*), contains long, abstract accounts of Emptiness, but the text itself takes the form of a Mahayana liturgy and contains lively invocations of powerful Buddhas and bodhisattvas.[3] Bhāvaviveka, another Indian philosopher, depicts the most accomplished bodhisattvas, in the tenth stage of the bodhisattva path, as turning toward the Buddha and weeping tears of devotion (*bhakti*).[4] In a modern setting, it is not farfetched to perceive an invocation of the power of emptiness in the chant of the *nembutsu* ('Homage to Amida Buddha') in the Buddhist Churches of America, in the chant of the name of the *Lotus Sutra* among the heirs of Nichiren, or in the deeply personal encounter between student and teacher in the practice of Zen.

In her discussion of the personhood of God, Thurston mentions the ideas that God has a name and is capable of incarnation. Bridges can be built between the two traditions using these ideas as well. The chant of a Buddha's name to invoke the power of the Budda's compassion was a common practice in the early Mahayana and has become a central feature in some of the most important varieties of modern Buddhism. Buddhist uses of the sacred name draw significance from a general Indian reverence for the power of sacred words and are not dissimilar to the Hindu tradition of chanting the name of God, a tradition that Americans would know best perhaps from their encounters with the impassioned utterance of the words 'Hare Krishna.' On the question of incarnation much can be said. It is plausible, in the terminology of the Mahayana, to describe Emptiness as a 'body.' Texts often equate Emptiness with the 'Dharma Body' of the Buddhas. The meaning of this doctrinal formula depends very much on what one means by 'Dharma' and what theory one holds about the different 'bodies' of the Buddhas.[5] This is not to say, of course, that Buddhist ideas of the sacred name or incarnation are the 'same' as comparable Christian ideas. It is meant to suggest simply that important bridges can be built, lines can be drawn, or sparks can be struck across the divide that seems to separate even these very disparate aspects of the Buddhist and Christian traditions.

'... Christians believe God's personal existence is relational.'

Thurston moves on from the question of God's personhood to make an important point about the internal relationship of the Godhead, expressed in Christian theology by the doctrine of the Trinity. To respond to such a claim from a Buddhist point of view one could explore the 'internal' relationship of Emptiness and compassion in

Mahayana practice. Each is the mirror of the other, and the two develop side by side as a bodhisattva cultivates the 'mind of enlightenment' (*bodhicitta*). To extend the discussion from two to three, one might follow the lead of Christian hymnody and speak of the Trinity as 'wisdom, love, power.' Mahayana texts have much to say about the power that proceeds from the union of wisdom and compassion.[6] But Thurston's point has to do less with the triune character of the Trinity than it does with love itself. The crux of her essay lies in the Johannine claim that God is love. Borrowing the words of Michael von Brück, she says that Love 'as symbolized in the intertrinitarian relationship, is the ultimate nature of Reality.'

Here Thurston stands on the edge of one of the great issues in the Buddhist-Christian dialogue. To put the matter simply, it seems possible for Christians to admire the Buddhist tradition for many things, but Christians seem committed to the notion that their tradition knows best what it means to love. This seems such an odd position in a dialogue where the purpose is to cultivate mutual tolerance and respect, but it appears so often in Christian accounts of Buddhism that it needs to be taken very seriously. This idea is echoed in Winston King's claim (quoted by Prof. Thurston) that Buddhist loving kindness is 'systematic and calculated, indirect and impersonal, and atomistically individualistic,' while Christian love is 'spontaneously and intensely personal in spirit, practical and direct in its expression, historically and socially minded in viewpoint.'[7] It appears in Toynbee's suggestion (also quoted by Thurston) that there are three essentials of Christianity: the idea that God loved his creatures so greatly that He sacrificed himself for their salvation, the idea that humans should follow God's example, and the idea that human beings should enact this example in practice.[8] Pope John Paul II made a similar point when he said that Christian mysticism 'is not born of a purely negative "enlightenment"' but by 'the Revelation of the Living God,' a revelation that comes through the theological virtues: 'faith, hope, and, above all, love.'[9]

What makes Christian love so distinctive? According to Thurston, it is not a quality of emotion but a conscious choice to act for the benefit of others in spite of the consequences for oneself. In relation to God this conscious act of love represents the unfolding of two ideas. The first is an impulse toward creativity ('In the beginning ... God created the heavens and the earth,' Genesis 1.1). The second is is the overflowing of an 'ontological surplus of Being': God creates because God is, or, rather, because God wishes to become. Both of these ideas have a strange ring to Buddhist ears. It is not that a bodhisattva would be reluctant to love, and even to love self-sacrificially. Buddhist moral discourse abounds with examples of self-sacrifice. The sense of strangeness comes from the idea that a bodhisattva should love out of an impulse toward creativity and 'an ontological surplus of Being.' If one probes the mythic substructure of the Buddhist tradition for the counterpart of the Christian story that God once looked into nothingness and made something come to be, one discovers a narrative that moves in precisely the opposite direction. There once was a Buddha who saw that the world had always been, and he, in his wisdom, found a way to allow some of it to stop. His gift to us – his act of greatest compassion – was to teach us that way. Who is to say that this is finally any less loving than the Christian drive to mimic God's sublime generosity in a never-ending round of action and creativity?

On this point too, of course, I can only raise questions and suggest lines for further exploration. Thurston's admirable comments about the nature of God show how much more work remains to be done on the relationship between Christian love and Buddhist compassion. I am grateful to Thurston for raising this issue so gracefully, and I look forward to seeing it explored more deeply as this rich dialogue continues to unfold.

Notes

1 Winston L. King, *Buddhism and Christianity: Some Bridges of Understanding* (Philadelphia: Westminster Press, 1962).
2 An amusing remnant of this controversy is found in a verse by the Hindu philosospher Udayana, spoken, tradition tells us, when Udayana was denied entrance to a temple: 'Drunk with the wine of your own Godhood, you ignore me; but when Buddhists are here, your existence depends on me.' The Sanskrit verse is quoted by George Chemparathy in *An Indian Rational Theology: Introduction to Udayana's Nyāyakusumāñjali* (Vienna: De Nobili Research Library, 1972), 28.
3 Śāntideva, *The Bodhicaryāvatāra*, trans. Kate Crosby and Andrew Skilton (Oxford: Oxford University Press, 1996).
4 Malcolm David Eckel, *To See the Buddha: A Philosopher's Quest for the Meaning of Emptiness* (1992; reprint ed. Princeton University Press, 1994).
5 Ibid., 97–109.
6 I have addressed some of these issues in 'By the Power of the Buddha,' *Dharma World* 22 (Sept/Oct. 1995): 9–15; (Nov/Dec. 1995): 14–18.
7 As quoted by Thurston.
8 Summarized by Thurston from Arnold Toynbee, *Christianity Among the World Religions* (New York: Charles Schribner's Sons, 1957).

9 His Holiness, John Paul II, *Crossing the Threshold of Hope* (New York: Alfred A. Knopf, 1994), 87–88. Another way to frame the argument is to put the stress less on love than on social and historical *action*. Max Weber invoked the distinction betwen Protestant 'inner-worldly asceticism' and the 'inner- or other-worldly mysticism' of the Buddhist tradition to explain the success of Western industrial societies in controlling and shaping the historical process. John B. Cobb, Jr. has argued that the Buddhist tradition can be challenged and enriched by the Christian idea of justice, especially as it is rooted in the nature of ultimate reality itself. See *Beyond Dialogue: Toward a Mutual Transformation of Christianity and Buddhism* (Philadelphia: Fortress Press, 1982).

CHAPTER SEVEN

The Concept of the Ultimate in Madhyamaka Thought: In Memory of Frederick Streng

Malcolm David Eckel

Since the appearance of Thomas Kuhn's *The Structure of Scientific Revolutions* in the late 1960's the secret hope of scholars, even scholars in the humanities, has been to provoke a paradigm shift, not merely to add incrementally to the knowledge of a particular field but to move the foundations of the field itself. The sad truth is that such fundamental shifts are rare and come when the conventional approaches to a problem seem to have been worried to death and no one seems able to break their iron grip. Looking back over the last fifty years of Buddhist studies, it is clear that Frederick Streng had this kind of liberating effect on the study of his field. His most important book, *Emptiness: A Study in Religious Meaning*, brought about a fundamental shift in the interpretation of Buddhist philosophy. He stepped into a field that had been dominated for decades by a single issue, 'the Problem of the Absolute,' and he did something more important than propose a new 'solution.' Other scholars had argued for years about whether Mahayana philosophers intended the concept of Emptiness to serve as a veiled reference to a real Absolute. Streng showed how the traditional formulation of this question misrepresented the intentions of the Mahayana philosophers themselves. Mahayana philosophy, as he saw it, was not simply an attempt to account for the reality or unreality of the Absolute: it was an intellectual and spiritual discipline aimed, in his words, at a goal of 'ultimate transformation.' This simple formulation was enough to free the study of Mahayana thought from the futility of defining the indefinable and redirect it toward the rich and varied world of religious practice.

Nowhere was the effect of Streng's innovation more keenly felt than in the Buddhist-Christian dialogue. By opening up the discussion of the great issues of Mahayana thought to questions of transformation, Streng gave benign intellectual warrant to the whole range of conversations that now constitute the dialogues between Buddhists and members of other religious traditions – conversations that now include as much discussion of spirituality, ecology, social engagement, and religious practice as they do of philosophy or theology. Frederick Streng may not have been widely known in the popular circles of Buddhism in this country, but he had a deep and lasting influence on the way Buddhists have learned to speak their own convictions in the public arena. While he never ceased to speak as a Christian in the Buddhist-Christian dialogue, his work has helped to shape what it means to articulate a Buddhist point of view in the modern world. This alone has made him an important figure in the historical evolution of the Buddhist tradition.

I can think of no better way to honor the memory of Frederick Streng than to develop his concept of 'ultimate transformation' in a direction that he himself would have recognized as significant. In this respect I have the advantage of receiving a suggestion from the mouth of the master himself. As a young professor, I asked Fred Streng how he would like to see the next generation carry forward his work on emptiness. His answer was that we should explore the historical and conceptual differences that distinguish the different branches of Mahayana thought and show how their approaches to emptiness are related to different modes of 'transformative' practice. He was particularly interested in seeing how his study of Nāgārjuna's Madhyamaka philosophy could be extended and elaborated by probing the complex and conflicting interpretations of Nāgārjuna's commentators in India and Tibet. Like others of us, he had come to see the Madhyamaka tradition as a great treasure chest, full of family heirlooms, and our job was to dig through its contents and discern, in the tarnish of a button or the worn collar of an old jacket, clues about the people who once brought its contents to life. In fact, the Madhyamaka tradition is more like a great storehouse full of chests, each one of which contains variants of the contents of all the others, and the experience of entering the storehouse comes close to the experience of the young pilgrim Sudhana when he entered Maitreya's palace in the *Gaṇḍavyūha Sūtra*: each room was different and yet each room contained a reflection of every other room. Change the storehouse or the halls of Maitreya's palace into a library and you have entered the world of Madhyamaka scholarship. At some point you have to take a book off the shelf, open it, and begin to read. The words of the text then function like artifacts of a world long past, each one worn with use and capable of unfolding a story.

Which book should come down from the shelf? Frederick Streng started with the words of Nāgārjuna and studied the meaning of the tradition from its beginnings. His choice was partly a matter of principle ('begin at the beginning') and partly a matter of necessity. Relatively little was known then about the development of the Madhyamaka commentaries after Nāgārjuna. Now the history of Indian Madhyamaka has been much more deeply studied. There are still corners of the tradition that remain unread and many perplexities yet to be unraveled, but it is now possible to adopt a synoptic view of the tradition in a way that would have been impossible in Streng's day. My proposal is to reverse Streng's procedure and begin not from the beginning of the tradition but from a text that looks backward over the history of the Indian Madhyamaka and develops a synoptic view of its arguments and questions. The text is the *Legs-bshad-snying-po* ('The Essence of Eloquent Statements') by the fourteenth century Tibetan scholar Tsong-kha-pa. Tsong-kha-pa has become one of the most authoritative voices for the interpretation of Madhyamaka in Tibet. In the dGe-lugs-pa tradition, represented by the Dalai Lama, Tsong-kha-pa is *the* authoritative voice. One could justify the choice of Tsong-kha-pa based on his historical significance alone. But it is the inclusiveness and critical intelligence of his work that particularly commend it: to read through its pages is genuinely to sense that one has opened up the treasures of the Madhyamaka.

One of the key elements in Streng's study of the Madhyamaka was the claim that concepts do not merely have a reference, they have a function. The function of the concept of emptiness, as he saw it, was to transform a person's understanding of reality through a dialectical process, in which the false reifications that afflict a person's ordinary understanding of the world are stripped away and a person is enabled to see the world as it is. Behind this dialectical process lay a basic Buddhist vision of the problems and possibilities of the human condition. According to the first of the four noble truths, life is infused with suffering. According to the second noble truth, suffering itself arises from a network of causes that have their root in craving and ignorance. According to the third noble truth, suffering is capable of cessation. And according to the fourth noble truth, the cessation of suffering is accessible through the eight-fold path. Study of the concept of emptiness helped promote the achievement of cessation by removing the ignorance that lay at the root of suffering. The work of the philosophers, in other words, was a form of discipline. It was intended not merely to describe the world but to change one's awareness of it so that one could become less attached, more wise, and more free.

Philosophy as a Journey

How did Tsong-kha-pa visualize the process of philosophical discipline? A useful way to start reading Tsong-kha-pa is to ask, in the most simple and literal way, what Tsong-kha-pa himself thought he was *doing* when he elucidated the concept of emptiness. That he was promoting a change of understanding is clear, but how did he picture this change for himself in the language of his text? A possible answer lies in the title of the text itself: *Drang-nges-legs-bshad-snying-po* ('The Essence of Nondefinitive and Definitive Eloquent Statements'). The text deals with the 'essence' (*snying po*) of 'eloquent statements' (*legs bshad*) that are either 'nondefinitive' (*drang*) or 'definitive' (*nges*) in meaning. The phrase 'eloquent statements' refers to the teachings of the Buddha. The terms 'nondefinitive' and 'definitive' refer to a common Buddhist hermeneutical distinction between statements that are provisional in character and those that can be taken at face value. In Sanskrit, the distinction is between statements that 'have to be led to' the proper meaning (*neyārtha*) and those that 'already have been led to' the proper meaning (*nītārtha*). The text presents itself, in other words, as an act of hermeneutics: it is an attempt to sift through the disputes that separate different Indian Buddhist schools and discern the correct meaning of the Buddha's words.

It is easy to understand why the issue of interpretation loomed large in Tsong-kha-pa's intellectual milieu. In the fourteenth century, when Tsong-kha-pa was active in Tibet, the great monasteries of India had ceased to exist as living centers of Buddhist practice. It was no longer possible for the Tibetan tradition to rely on Indian authority to resolve doctrinal disputes. Scholars from all the branches of Tibetan monasticism faced the challenge of systematizing and harmonizing the different strands in the Indian teaching, and they had to do it without the direct guidance of Indian teachers. The interpretive problem was not new, however. Buddhist tradition had been well aware that different situations called forth different teachings, not just in the larger relationship between Mahayana and the schools of Nikāya Buddhism, but within individual traditions and schools, and there always had been a challenge to move beneath the surface of a text and discern the deeper meaning of the Buddha's teaching.[1] But for Tsong-kha-pa the interpretive problem was sharpened by the presence of two radically different traditions of Mahayana thought: the Yogācāra and the Madhyamaka. The formal structure of Tsong-kha-pa's text is governed by this division. He sets out first to analyze the Yogācāra and show its shortcomings, then he investigates the way the Madhyamaka 'leads to' the definitive interpretation of the Buddha's teaching.

What does it mean in this context to use the word 'lead'? The 'nondefinitive' (*neya*) and 'definitive' (*nīta*) meanings are related etymologically to a Sanskrit word *naya* that often is translated 'method.'[2] In the hands of some of the Indian Madhyamaka authors this word was used in a way that was quite close to its literal meaning. They took it as a 'way of leading' or, more appropriately in English, an 'approach.' We find, for example, that Bhāvaviveka presents his controversy with the Yogācāra as a dispute about the proper 'approach' to the perfection of wisdom. Why would he dispute the correct 'approach'? Because only the correct approach makes it possible for a person to make 'progress' (*pratipatti*) toward the goal. Here, in the combination of these two words, we come face to face with the Indian metaphor of knowledge as motion, a metaphor that had significant consequences for Nāgārjuna's own understanding of emptiness. Nāgārjuna said: 'Dependent origination is what we call emptiness. This [emptiness] is a dependent designation, and it alone is the middle path'.[3] The commentators explained that emptiness is 'middle' in the sense that it avoids the extremes of existence and non-existence. But the most important point to glean from this passage is simply that emptiness is a way of following a path, or, better yet, emptiness is just the path itself. Much is said in the literature of the Madhyamaka about the emptiness of emptiness, with the intention of avoiding the mistake of reifying the means by which one avoids reification, but there is no better way to visualize this aspect of emptiness than to think of emptiness as a *way* rather than a reality. It is a way that cannot, at any point, be allowed to settle down (or wander away) into the extreme positions of considering conventional reality to be ultimately real or denying conventional reality altogether.

What kind of way did the philosophers follow? In his account of the Yogācāra, Bhāvaviveka speaks of the importance of following a 'rational' (*yuktiman*) 'approach' (*naya*). Tsong-kha-pa makes the same point at the beginning of the *Legs-bshad-snying-po*.

> Having seen that it is difficult to understand the reality of
> *dharma*s and that, without such understanding, there is no
> liberation from samsara, the compassionate Teacher introduced
> that understanding with many skillful methods and rational
> procedures.
> Therefore, those who are capable of analysis should apply
> themselves to the method of understanding reality. This [effort]
> depends on a distinction between the teachings of the Buddha
> that are definitive in meaning and those that are not. This
> distinction cannot be made just by using scriptural statements
> that say: 'This is definitive in meaning, and that is not definitive
> in meaning.' Otherwise there would have been no reason for our
> great predecessors to undertake to untie the knot of the
> distinction between definitive and nondefinitive [teachings].
> The scriptures contain many different claims about definitive
> and nondefinitive [teachings]. A scriptural statement that makes
> a particular claim is not necessarily [applicable] in the same way
> elsewhere, and, if it is not generally applicable, a scriptural
> statement about particular definitive and nondefinitive [teach-
> ings] cannot prove anything.
> This is why our great predecessors, who were predicted to be
> the ones who would distinguish definitive and nondefinitive
> teachings, have untied the knot of definitive and nondefinitive
> [teachings]. We have to untie the knot by following their correct
> determinations, using rational procedures in which one refutes
> [the possibility] of interpreting definitive teachings any other
> way (lit. of 'leading them elsewhere') and prove that, when
> [teachings] cannot be interpreted any other way, they are
> definitive in meaning. If we accept doctrines that contradict
> reason, the one who taught [those doctrines] cannot be the
> embodiment of the means of knowledge. And the reality of
> things requires means of proof that consist of logically
> established reason.[4]

Tsong-kha-pa clearly emphasizes *rational* procedure (*rigs pa = yukti*). But what is the status of 'reason' in Madhyamaka tradition, and how is it related to emptiness? Tsong-kha-pa signals one of the important features of rationality in this tradition when he speaks of the Buddha as the 'embodiment of the means of knowledge' (*pramāṇa-bhūta*).

Ultimate Reality

The phrase comes from the opening verse of Dignāga's *Pramāṇasa-muccaya* ('The Compendium of the Means of Knowledge'). Dignāga's text was the source of the tradition of Buddhist logic that dominated many aspects of Buddhist philosophy in India from about the mid-sixth century until the demise of Indian Buddhism in the twelfth century. Why would it have been so influential? If suffering came from ignorance, then the cessation of suffering had to come from knowledge, and systematic reflection on the means of knowledge was a crucial device to distinguish true and false interpretations of reality. This was not to say that rational investigation could get a person to reality directly. Mahayana Buddhists always insisted that reality could not be turned into an object of rational thought. But Indian Mādhyamikas treated rational analysis as essential for removing illusions about the nature of things, as Bhāvaviveka says in one of his most important arguments against the Yogācāra.

> [Yogācāra objection:] It says in scripture that the ultimate (*paramārtha*) cannot be investigated and is not accessible to logical reasoning (*tarka-gocara*), so the ultimate cannot be expressed by inference (*anumāna*).
> [Madhyamaka reply:] This is wrong. Inference that follows scripture negates all concepts and brings about non-conceptual insight. The ultimate, therefore, is not an object of inference, but it has priority, because there is no other way of investigating what is true and false.[5]

The Madhyamaka emphasis on rational analysis gave rise eventually to a distinctive treatment of the concept of 'ultimate reality' itself. Mādhyamikas of all sorts, especially in the tradition of Bhāvaviveka, make arguments that start: 'Ultimately such and such a thing is not the case.' What can the word 'ultimately' (*paramārthena*) refer to? Ultimately there is nothing to serve as the referent of the word, since nothing ultimately has any identity. But it is possible to use the word conventionally to designate a mode of reasoning that allows a person to investigate the reference of words, including the reference of the word 'ultimate' itself. To distill these points into a single sentence, one would say that, while ultimately there is no ultimate, conventionally the ultimate is a rational cognition. Bhāvaviveka drew the distinction between these two types of ultimate quite clearly in his *Flame of Reason* (*Tarkajvālā*): 'There are two kinds of ultimate: the first is effortless, transcendent, free from impurity, and free from discursive ideas; the second is accessible to effort, consistent with the prerequisites of merit and knowledge, pure, and inaccessible to discursive ideas.'[6] Other Mādhyamikas distinguished simply between the expressible (*paryāya*) ultimate and the inexpressible (*aparyāya*) ultimate.

To carry the point a step further, the Madhyamaka commentators also distinguished between the ultimate as cognition and the ultimate as the object (*artha*) known by this cognition. The distinction is suggested by the meaning of the term 'ultimate' itself. *Paramārtha* literally means 'ultimate' (*parama*) 'object' (*artha*). Bhāvaviveka explained that the Sanskrit grammatical tradition allowed the compound to be analyzed three ways: As a descriptive (*karmadhāraya*) compound, the term could refer to something that is both 'ultimate' and an 'object.' As a dependent (*tatpuruṣa*) compound, it could refer to the 'object' of the 'ultimate.' And as a possessive (*bahuvrīhi*) compound, it could refer to 'that whose object is ultimate,' in other words to an act of cognition. Bhāvaviveka explained that, in his understanding of Nāgārjuna, the compound should be interpreted in the third way, as a reference to a particular kind of cognition. But the word 'object' comes up in other settings as well. *Madhyamakakārikā* 24.7 speaks of 'the object of emptiness' (*śūnyatārtha*), that is, 'emptiness as object.' Other Madhyamaka writings speak of 'the object of reality' (*tattvārtha*) or 'reality-as-object.'[7] The commentators generally take the compounds 'emptiness-as-object' and 'reality-as-object' as references to propositional expressions of emptiness. Bhāvaviveka, for example, explains that 'emptiness-as-object' means 'thusness' (*tathatā*), and his sub-commentator Avalokitavrata explains that 'thusness' refers to the negation of the ultimate arising of things.[8] Candrakīrti takes 'emptiness-as-object' as a reference to 'dependent arising' (*pratītya-samutpāda*), with the understanding, no doubt, that 'dependent arising' is equivalent, in the words of the first of the *Madhyamakakārikās*, to 'no-arising' (*anutpāda*). Jñānagarbha takes the compound 'reality-as-object' as a reference to the ultimate negation of arising.

Putting all of these distinctions together results in four possible explanations of the word 'ultimate' (*paramārtha*). For a thorough and lucid account of this four-fold scheme it is hard to do better than quote the Tibetan philosopher lCang-skya:

> The object (*viṣaya*), which is the nature of things (*dharmatā*), can be referred to as ultimate (*paramārtha*), and the subject (*viṣayin*), which is a rational cognition, can also be referred to as

ultimate. Each of these in turn can occur in two forms. The object, which is emptiness, is the actual ultimate in a pure state of concentrated awareness, free from discursive ideas (*prapañca*) of the duality [of subject and object] and discursive ideas of real existence. In a conceptual, rational cognition, [this object] is free from discursive ideas about real existence but not from dualistic discursive ideas, thus [in a rational cognition] it is only partially free from discursive ideas. In general, then, emptiness-as-object is the actual ultimate. But [the emptiness that is known] in a conceptual, rational cognition is not an ultimate that is free from both kinds of discursive ideas. These are the two ways of talking about the ultimate-as-object. When the non-conceptual aware-ness of a saint in a state of concentration (*samādhi*) is focused on reality (*tattva*), it is capable of eliminating both kinds of discursive ideas. Thus this [non-conceptual awareness] also is the actual ultimate. Through logical marks (*liṇga*), a conceptual, rational cognition of reality is capable of eliminating discursive ideas of the real existence of its objects, but it cannot eliminate dualistic discursive ideas .... These are the two ways of talking about the ultimate-as-subject.[9]

Clearly Tsong-kha-pa was not speaking in a vacuum when he said that 'the ultimate reality of things includes means of proof through logically established reasoning.' Not only did he mean that the ultimate reality of things was known by logical reasoning, but the ultimacy of 'ultimate' reality itself was established by logical reasoning.

When these observations about the rationality of the ultimate are put together with the earlier point about emptiness as a 'way' or 'approach,' they show some important things about the Madhyamaka attitudes toward the philosophical process more generally. The four-fold exegesis of the term 'ultimate' might easily be ignored for most practical purposes in the study of Madhyamaka, but it provides an important explanation of what Frederick Streng meant when he said that emptiness was a 'dialectical' process that leads to an 'ultimate transformation.' The Indian commentarial tradition identified the 'dialectic' as a process of rational analysis that stripped away illusions about the nature of things in order to approach a complete understanding of their emptiness. Emptiness functioned, as it were, as both goal and process, and it constituted both the object of awareness and awareness itself. The Indian exegetical tradition also made it clear why the dialectic is a *process*. We are here in the metaphorical realm of the path, where knowledge unfolds gradually through a series of stages. In Tsong-kha-pa's case these gradual stages took him from a consideration of the Yogācāra into deeper and more discriminating discussion of the differences that separate the interpretive traditions within the Madhyamaka itself.

Philosophy as an Act of Vision

One of the most important sequences in Nāgārjuna's account of ultimate reality occurs in chapter twenty-four of the *Madhyamaka-kārikās*, the chapter on the Four Noble Truths:

> Buddhas teach the Dharma based on two truths: ordinary, relative truth and ultimate truth.
>
> Those who do not know the distinction between these two truths do not know the profound reality in the Buddhas' teaching.
>
> One does not teach the ultimate without resorting to the conventional, and one does not attain nirvana without understanding the ultimate.[10]

For interpreters of the Madhyamaka, these verses make a crucial point about the concept of the ultimate. Ultimacy is not known by itself; it is known through conventional discourse or conventional usage. And it is impossible to understand the nature of the ultimate without understanding the distinction between the ultimate and the conventional. From this passage grows the long tradition of Madhyamaka discussion of two truths.

If the distinction between the conventional and the ultimate is necessary to understand the ultimate, what is meant by 'conventional'? Some help is provided by the words themselves. 'Convention' is, as it were, the conventional English equivalent of the Sanskrit word *vyavahāra*, a word that, in Sanskrit lexicography, has a distinctly practical focus. Among its standard dictionary definitions are 'doing, performing, action, practice, conduct, behavior.'[11] It also can refer to custom or ordinary life, a mercantile transaction, or a lawsuit. In the usage of the Pali Canon, the most common meaning of the word is 'current appellation, usage, designation, or term.'[12] Madhyamaka commentators generally stress the verbal dimension of the word but also make room for its practical function, as in Candrakīrti's explanation that the word *saṃvyavahāra* refers to practical injunctions such as 'Do! Cook! Eat! Stand! Go! Come!'[13] English and French translators have often attempted to capture both dimensions of meaning by translating *vyavahāra* as 'usage.'

Strictly speaking, however, Nāgārjuna distinguishes ultimate truth not from 'conventional usage' but from 'ordinary, relative truth' (*loka-saṃvṛti-satya*). The origin of the word *saṃvṛti* is, perhaps appropriately, obscure. The Pali equivalent, *sammuti*, is derived from *sam-man* ('to think together') and is interpreted as meaning 'consent, choice, general opinion, or convention.'[14] The Sanskrit commentators, however, derive the word from *sam-vṛ* ('to cover'). Candrakīrti explains that *saṃvṛti* means to 'cover' (*varaṇam*) 'completely' (*samantād*), and says that the term refers to 'ignorance' (*ajñāna*) because *saṃvṛti* 'conceals the reality of all things.'[15] To say that there are two truths is to say, then, that there are two perspectives on things. There is an ultimate perspective from which it is possible to see things correctly, and an ignorant perspective from which the truth about things is concealed. The challenge of the philosopher is to remove the 'coverings' that conceal reality and allow a person to see them directly.

I speak deliberately of this process as one of gaining 'perspective' and 'seeing' reality. To say that *saṃvṛti* 'covers' or 'conceals' reality, draws us directly into the realm of another important metaphor in Madhyamaka thought, the metaphor of philosophy as an act of vision. Candrakīrti gives a vivid picture of this act of vision in the well-known comparison of the *taimirika*. (A *taimirika* is someone who suffers from an eye ailment that obscures ordinary vision.)

> *Taimirikas* wrongly see such things as hairs, mosquitoes, and flies, and they cannot understand, as those who are not *taimirikas* do, that the actual nature of the hairs should be understood by the method of no-seeing (*adarśana-nyāyena*). From the teaching of those who are not *taimirikas* they understand only that [the nature of the hairs] is false. But, when the eyes of their intelligence are anointed with the ointment of the correct vision (*darśana*) of emptiness, they obtain the knowledge of reality. Then they understand the reality of these [hairs] for themselves by the method of no-understanding (*anadhigama-yogena*).[16]

It is slightly incongruous, perhaps, to say that the 'vision' (*darśana*) of emptiness functions as an eye-ointment to remove faulty vision. It might make more sense to say that it is an antidote. But the picture becomes clear when one understands that the word 'vision' is the word that is translated as 'philosophy' when one speaks of the 'philosophy' of emptiness. Candrakīrti has in mind a situation in which the philosophical process itself anoints the eyes so that a person can see the world for what it is. Philosophy removes the *saṃvṛti*, the covering that obscures ultimate reality, and allows people to see ultimate reality for themselves.

The implications of this image of vision can be pursued in a number of ways. It is useful, for example, to scan Buddhist sources that are not as self-consciously analytical as Tsong-kha-pa and Candrakīrti to see how deeply the image of the eye is woven into the discourse of Buddhist narrative. The Buddha's first sermon, for example, opens with an account of the middle path and says that 'the middle path, realized by the Tathāgata, gives vision.' For Mādhyamikas (the followers of the middle path), the middle path is emptiness, and it too gives vision. Vision can also be related, as this use of the metaphor suggests, to the journey of the middle path. Bhāvaviveka thinks of the practice of philosophy as the process of ascending a mountain in order to gain clear vision of the surrounding landscape.[17] He even pictures the compassion of a bodhisattva as the tears that a bodhisattva sheds when he or she reaches the top of the mountain and looks back on those who suffer in the valley below. The image can be related to Buddhist pilgrimage, in which Buddhist pilgrims are advised to 'see' and 'be shaken' by sites that are associated with important events in the Buddha's life. It is related to the practice of *darśan* in Hindu worship.[18]

The connection that is most important for our purposes, however, is the connection to the exegetical technique of Tsong-kha-pa himself. When Tsong-kha-pa turns his account of the Madhyamaka 'approach' to emptiness into an examination of the disputes that seem to divide different representative of the Madhyamaka tradition, he moves naturally from the question of definitive and nondefinitive meanings to a consideration of the two truths.

> The Lord Nāgārjuna and his immediate followers did not base the distinction between definitive and nondefinitive [meanings] on a direct quotation from a scriptural source that makes this distinction, but they did so by implication, in the way they explained the meaning of scripture. In [Candrakīrti's] *Prasannapadā*, [Avalokitavrata's] commentary on the *Prajñāpradīpa*, and [Kamalaśīla's] *Madhyamakāloka*, the *Akṣayamatinirdeśa*

[*Sūtra*] is taken as the source for explaining definitive and nondefinitive [meanings]. So this [sūtra] is taken [as the source] here as well. It says in the *Akṣayamatinirdeśa* [*Sūtra*]: Which sūtras are definitive in meaning, and which are nondefinitive in meaning? The sūtras that establish relative (*saṃvṛta*) [truth] are nondefinitive. The sūtras that establish ultimate (*paramārtha*) [truth] are definitive. The sūtras that teach various words and letters are nondefinitive. The sūtras that teach what is profound, hard to see, and hard to understand are definitive. . . . The first of these pairs relates definitive and nondefinitive [sūtras] to the two truths and distinguishes definitive and nondefinitive [sūtras] by subject matter.[19]

Tsong-kha-pa goes on from here to discuss the differences between the two different branches of the Madhyamaka (the Svātantrika and the Prāsaṅgika). The argument is far too complex to summarize in detail, but its structure reproduces the image of philosophy as vision. Tsong-kha-pa explains that the schools differ in their presentation of relative truth and says that the Svātantrika view of conventional reality is like a subtle veil over the eyes. To remove it takes just the right application of the ointment of emptiness so that the eyes can see reality as clearly as one can see the autumn sky, without seeing anything at all.

Emptiness as an Empty Place

To say that the function of philosophy is to strip away the veils that obscure correct vision of reality helps makes sense of the visual metaphor, but problems still remain. Think, for example, not of the illusory hairs, mosquitoes, and flies that appear before damaged eyes of a *taimirika* but of the eyes themselves. Should we assume that the challenge of philosophy is to remove the illusion that the mind sees external objects in order to allow the self-evident clarity of the mind to be revealed? Does consciousness remain, in other words, when the illusion of objects has been stripped away? Or is the existence of consciousness itself one of the illusions that needs to be overcome? Tsong-kha-pa's comments on the *Akṣayamatinirdeśa Sūtra* lead him to precisely this question.

[This account of the two truths] does not take some other eternal phenomenon as its foundation (*gzhi* = Skt. *āśraya*) and call it 'no-arising' and so forth. The ultimate is nothing more than the negation of the real existence of these foundations, and that [negation] should be considered the ultimate teaching.[20]

The opponent who lurks in the background of this passage is the Yogācāra philosopher who thinks that consciousness, stripped of the illusion of external objects, is what we designate when we use words such as 'emptiness' and 'no-arising.' Tsong-kha-pa is arguing that the negation involved in the concept of emptiness is not meant to leave behind a 'foundation' or 'place' that has been emptied of illusions. It is meant to negate even the foundation itself. Emptiness, in other words, is not a veiled reality. It too is empty of identity or self. To understand emptiness correctly is to understand also the emptiness of emptiness.

Much has been said about the disputes between Madhyamaka and Yogācāra about the mind as 'foundation.' Most intriguing, however, is not the doctrinal significance of this point but its metaphorical echo in the tradition of Buddhist practice. Buddhist pilgrimage makes little sense as a religious phenomenon unless one comes to grip with the dialectic of presence and absence. Buddhist sites are made holy by the presence of the Buddha, but the Buddha himself is no longer present at these sites, either in a physical sense or, if the canonical literature is to be trusted, in a spiritual sense. What 'remains' are his relics and a certain 'power' that is imbued in the relics by the Buddha's former presence. In a cultic sense, the Buddhist tradition is built on a tradition of relic worship, and relic worship is built on the recognition that the saint to whom one wishes to pay homage is no longer present to receive one's worship.

In my recent study of Madhyamaka approaches to the Buddha, I discuss a number of the ways this complex relationship of presence and absence work their way out in Buddhist thought. One of the more intriguing is the dynamic that seems often to be at work when a pilgrim or devotee confronts the signs of the Buddha's absence and sees in them an indication that the proper way to understand the Buddha is not to worship him as a literal, physical being but to study and internalize the Buddha's Dharma. The same dynamic is at work in different approaches to the Dharma itself. The Dharma can be worshipped as a physical object, such as a book placed in a shrine, or it can be studied as a teaching. And as a teaching, it can be treated as a series of positive assertions about certain realities or as a teaching about the reality that is, in the words of the *Akṣayamatinirdeśa Sūtra*, 'profound, hard to see, and hard to understand.' This is the reality that is no reality, the reality that can only be seen, as Candrakīrti says, by the method of no-seeing and understood by the method of no-understanding. Perhaps the most intriguing implication of the antifoundational stance of the Madhyamaka is found in the view of nirvana. Nāgārjuna said that there is no difference between nirvana and samsara. For Bhāvaviveka and other followers of the Mahayana, this translated into a concept of 'nonfoundational' (*apratiṣṭhita*) nirvana, a 'nirvana' that is not located firmly in either samsara or nirvana:

> [The bodhisattva] does not leave samsara, but is free from the harm of samsara.
> [The bodhisattva] does not attain nirvana, but it is as if [the bodhisattva] were located in nirvana.[21]

One is reminded of Keiji Nishitani's description of the breakthrough of the 'field of consciousness':

> Only when the self breaks through the field of consciousness, the field of *beings*, and stands on the ground of nihility, is it able to achieve a subjectivity that can in no way be objectivized. This is the elemental realization that reaches deeper than self-consciousness. In standing subjectively on the field of nihility (I use the term 'stand' and refer to nihility as a 'field,' but in fact there is literally no place to stand), the self becomes itself in a more elemental sense.[22]

The bodhisattva practice is not an attempt to become fixed in the state of nirvana, but to break through the tendency toward reification that even the concept of nirvana suggests, to be free, in other words, from the dichotomy of samsara and nirvana itself.

Conclusion

Looking back from Tsong-kha-pa's perspective over the Indian tradition that Frederick Streng used to develop his concept of emptiness as 'ultimate transformation,' a number of points become clear. First, the aspect of the tradition that Streng referred to as 'Nāgārjuna's dialectical structure' takes on a distinctly logical flavor. The Indian Mādhyamikas were very much under the spell of Indian logic and epistemology. They saw the quest for the ultimate as a quest for rational certainty, so much so that the word 'ultimate' itself came to name a rational cognition. This is not to say that the ultimate in its inexpressible mode can be reduced to a syllogism, but the rational interpretation of scripture is the device that rules out false under-standing and brings one to a certain understanding of emptiness. Second, the ultimate is not a concept that can stand on its own. It always has to be understood together with and by means of the concept of the 'conventional.' Ultimacy is known, in fact, by the process of criticism in which the 'conventional' is criticized and stripped of false reifications. Finally, the process of investigation and analysis that leads from the conventional to the ultimate does not lead to a real or stable 'foundation.' The understanding of ultimacy in this tradition is deeply critical of foundational thinking. All three of these points have profound significance for our understanding of the 'transformative' dimension of the ultimate in the Madhyamaka. One is transformed by rational investigation, by a dialectical appreciation of the relationship between the ultimate and the conventional, and by a form of practice that never quite stands still but is always moving forward in a quest for deeper insight and more inclusive expressions of compassion.

But the metaphorical dimension of Madhyamaka thought allows us to say much more than this about the concept of ultimate transformation. The quest for ultimacy involves the pursuit of a path, a sharpening of vision, and a confrontation with an empty place. All three of these images are deeply congruent with the practical dimension of Buddhist discipline. Reading the rational claims of the Indian and Tibetan Madhyamaka can sometimes give the impression that one is dealing only with a group of bookish scholars, who see enlightenment as the pursuit of nothing more than logical coherence. But the world of their imagination was much wider than this. They 'walked,' 'saw,' and 'uncovered' in their texts, just as Buddhist practitioners did in their everyday lives. More needs to be learned, of course, about the kinds of practices they engaged in, but the world of practice echoes strongly in their words. In this respect Frederick Streng was right. Emptiness is a profoundly practical concept, and one can hardly claim to have understood it if one is blind to its transformative value.

Notes

1 See, for example, the articles collected in Donald S. Lopez, Jr., *Buddhist Hermeneutics* (Honolulu: University of Hawaii Press, 1992).
2 As in Edward Conze's *Materials for a Dictionary of the Prajñāpāramitā Literature* (Tokyo: Suzuki Research Foundation, 1973).

3 Nāgārjuna, *Root Verses on the Middle Way (Mūlamadhyamikakārikās)*, ed J.W. de Jong (Madras: Adyar Library and Research Center, 1977), 24.18.

4 Tsong-kha-pa, *Drang-nges-legs-bshad-snying-po* (Sarnath: Gelugpa Students' Welfare Committee, 1973).

5 Translation adapted from Malcolm David Eckel, 'Bhāvaviveka's Critique of Yogācāra Philosophy in Chapter XXV of the Prajñāpradīpa,' in *Miscellanea Buddhica*, ed. Chr. Lindtner, Indiske Studier 5 (Copenhagen, 1985): 73–74.

6 The Tibetan text of this passage is found in Shotaro Iida, *Reason and Emptiness: A Study in Logic and Mysticism* (Tokyo: Hokuseido, 1980), 86. For further discussion of this point and those that follow see Malcolm David Eckel, *Jñānagarbha's Commentary on the Distinction Between the Two Truths* (Albany: State University of New York Press, 1987), 113.

7 *Jñānagarbha's Commentary*, 77.

8 For a discussion of this and the points that follow, see *Jñānagarbha's Commentary*, 126.

9 Translation of lCang-skya quoted from *Jñānagarbha's Commentary*, 112. It is an adaptation of Donald Lopez's translation of *The Presentation of Tenets* in 'The Svātantrika-Mādhyamika School of Mahāyāna Buddhism' (Ph.D. Diss.: University of Virginia, 1982), 506–507.

10 *Madhyamakakārikās* 24.8–10.

11 Sir Monier Monier-Williams, *A Sanskrit-English Dictionary* (1899; reprint ed. Delhi: Motilal Banarsidass, 1963): s. v. *vyavahāra*.

12 T.W. Rhys Davids and William Stede, eds., *The Pali Text Society's Pali-English Dictionary* (1921–25; reprint ed., London: Pali Text Society, 1972): s. v. *vohāra*.

13 Candrakīrti, *Mūlamadhyamakakārikās (Mādhyamikasūtras) de Nāgārjuna avec la Prasannapadā commentaire de Candrakīrti*, ed. Louis de La Vallée Poussin. Bibliotheca Buddhica 4. (St Petersburg: 1903–1913). Reprint edition Osnabrück: Biblio Verlag, 1970.

14 *PTS Dictionary*: s. v. *sammuti*.

15 *Prasannapadā*, 492.

16 *Prasannapadā*, 373. For a useful discussion of this comparison in Madhyamaka literature, see Louis de La Vallée Poussin, 'Madhyamaka,' *Mélanges chinois et bouddhiques* 2 (1932–33): 30–31.

17 The use of the metaphor of vision in Madhyamaka literature is discussed in Malcolm David Eckel, *To See the Buddha: A Philosopher's Quest for the Meaning of Emptiness* (1992; reprint ed., Princeton: Princeton University Press, 1994), Part III.

18 Diana L. Eck, *Seeing the Divine in India* (Chambersburg, Pennsylvania: Anima Books, 1981).

19 *Legs-bshad-snying-po*, 91.

20 Ibid.

21 Eckel, *To See the Buddha*, 173.

22 Keiji Nishitani, *Religion and Nothingness* (Berkeley: University of California Press, 1982), 16–17.

CHAPTER EIGHT

Response to: 'The Concept of The Ultimate in Madhyamaka Thought'

Bonnie Thurston

I must confess at the outset my lack of competence to respond to this chapter. First, it is unseemly for me to critique Professor Eckel because he was my teacher at Harvard and first introduced me to the work of Fred Streng in the Spring of 1983. It is still I who learn from him because, interestingly, having read this chapter I think now, 13 years later, I finally have a sense of what Streng was about in *Emptiness: A Study in Religious Meaning*. Second, I am not trained in the philosophical traditions of Buddhism and therefore am not fully able to evaluate in any scholarly sense Eckel's work.

And, finally, of course Christianity and Buddhism approach the questions of Ultimacy with very different premises. Christianity asserts an Ultimate, though not necessarily substantive, Reality called God. Part of the classic discussion of God's ultimacy has always included God's immutability. In order for God to be 'perfect,' it is argued, God must be unchanging. From the point of view of Biblical theology, this presents some problems, but it has always been part of the tradition of philosophical theology and its discussion of God. Although process theology is now introducing language which suggests that God might be better understood in terms of process rather than essence, the academic and ecclesiastical jury on the viability and accuracy of such a formulation of the concept of God is still out. As a Christian the simple premise from which I begin is, first, that God is 'Ultimate Reality,' and any discussions of the nature and/ or essence of that Reality follow from its existence.

This brings me to eight brief reflections on Professor Eckel's work on the concept of transformation in Madhyamaka thought.

1. First, there is the issue of the apparent dichotomy between essence and transformation, or between absolute reality and ultimate transformation. As Streng has pointed out with regard to Buddhism, in Christianity, too, it is a false dichotomy precisely because the will of God as revealed in Holy Scripture is to re-create humanity, to transform it if you will, to reflect the divine nature which is love. (See my essay.)

2. 'Modes of transformative practice,' might be the way we Christians could describe how this comes about. The question of how we can live to reflect the nature of the Reality which has claimed us and to which we owe fealty is a, if not *the*, basic question of Christian practice.

3. That concepts don't merely have a reference, but a function also has deep resonances in Christian tradition. In Christianity, God's nature is understood to be revealed or 'seen' in Jesus Christ who is described as 'the image of the invisible God' (Col. 1:15) and 'in him all the fullness of God was pleased to dwell.' (Col. 1:19) This concept of God-seen-in-Jesus has as its function modeling or shaping *us* Christians in that image, after that concept.

Christ, too, is the 'embodiment of the means of knowledge.' Scripture is clear that the best worship rendered to Jesus is to do what he says. ('Those who love me will keep my word.' John 14:23) Jesus declares his family are those who follow his teachings, (Mk 3:35), who 'internalize his dharma,' (which, of course, we Christians can do both by word and sacrament). And in Matthew's gospel Jesus says explicitly that his followers are to 'Be perfect, therefore, as your heavenly Father is perfect.' (Mt. 5:48)

We become what we desire. If we desire the perfection of God, to 'know God' and to be changed by that knowing (with all the rich, deep, intimate associations of 'knowing' in Biblical tradition), then we *shall* be transformed, remade in the image of God who is our 'original face.' (See Genesis 1:26–27.)

4. The concept of Emptiness as a means to Cessation or Emptiness as a 'way of following a path' also has deep echoes in the life and teaching of Jesus. When we know Reality, we re-orient ourselves with regard to that Reality and leave behind appearances that are deceptive and that distort the image of God in us and in the world. This is the meaning of teachings like the 'lilies of the field' passage in Jesus' Sermon on the Mount (Mt. 6:25–34) which points to the folly of temporal concerns, the injunction of Jesus' 'do not labor for the food that perishes' (Jn. 6:27), and the admonition to 'seek first the kingdom of God' (Mt. 5:33).

5. For Christians, Reality is and is not 'an object of rational thought.' Philosophical Christianity has objectified God, made of God an object of inquiry. But, as Streng has insisted, religious statements, even philosophical ones about God, 'are a means of apprehending Truth, not the Truth.'[1] How easy it is to mistake the finger for the moon!

More mystical Christianity has understood that Christians, themselves, are part of, participate in the very Reality which transforms them. Paul consistently uses the language of Christ 'in us.' In Christ 'all things hold together' (Col. 1:7); we live our lives 'in Christ.' The phrase 'your life is hidden with Christ in God' (Col. 3:3) suggests that Ultimate Reality may not be 'out there' but 'in here.' Thomas Merton has continually insisted that the deeper Christians delve into their true selves, the closer they come to God. As Streng himself put it, '"the real" is something existing which "is there" – there all the time not "out there" to be discovered.' Existence speaks an intrinsic relationship to the real and urges one to find the real in the self.[2]

6. Here, then, this Christian parts company with the view that 'nothing ultimately has any identity.' The Christian's identity is precisely in *identification* with Christ whom we 'put on' at baptism. (See Ephesians and Colossians.) If Christ is Ultimate Reality then those 'in Christ' share that Reality.

7. On philosophy as an act of vision, again, there are many parallels in Christianity. For Christians, too, God is known through 'conventional discourse,' because conventional discourse is practical. And in that conventional discourse one of the crucial Christian metaphors is that of sight. Stories in which Jesus grants sight to the blind (Mk. 8:22–26, 10:42–52 and parallels and John 9) are stories about faith and spiritual understanding. Jesus' invitation to 'come and see' in the beginning of John's gospel (1:39) introduces a controlling metaphor for the first twelve chapters of that gospel. To be invited to 'see' is to be invited to participate in Reality. In John's gospel to see is to believe in Jesus, and to believe in Jesus is to have life.[3] (John 3:36a) However, it is not emptiness, but Jesus Himself who serves as the 'eye-ointment.'

As in Buddhism, the metaphor of vision or of sight runs throughout Christian tradition. In the context of these remarks, one example is particularly potent. Meister Eckhart, the Dominican Friar and Rhenish mystic (ca. 1260–1327/28), noted 'the eye wherein I see God is the same eye wherein God sees me.' Certainly this is seeing with the 'wisdom eye!' To 'see' is not only to understand the nature of Reality, but the very seeing, itself, is to participate *in* Reality, to share its identity.

8. Finally, however, the desire for or quest for Ultimacy in Christianity can never be a quest for rational certainty. If it is, it is doomed to failure at the outset. Paradoxically in light of our discussion of seeing and of the eye, Christians do live by faith and not sight, knowing that 'faith is the assurance of things hoped for, the conviction of things not seen.' (Heb. 11:1 Compare Romans 8:24–25.) For us there will always be the tension between faith and 'sight.'

And so, interestingly, we too are transformed 'by a form of practice that never quite stands still, but is always moving forward in a quest for deeper insight and more inclusive expressions of compassion.' Like Paul, we Christians have not 'reached the goal,' but we 'strain forward to what lies ahead,' 'we press on toward the goal' which is the 'call of God in Christ Jesus.' (Phil. 3:12–14)

Notes

1 Frederick J. Streng, *Emptiness: A Study in Religious Meaning* (Nashville: Abingdon Press, 1967), 178.
2 Streng, 123.
3 For a fuller discussion of this point see my article 'The Gospel of John and Japanese Buddhism,' *Japanese Religions* 15/2 (1988): 57–68.

PART THREE

Nature and Ecology

CHAPTER NINE

The Buddhist Conception of an Ecological Self

Alan Sponberg

Traditional Buddhist sources have little to say about Nature in the often abstract and romanticized sense in which we use the word today, and still less to say about ecology understood in contemporary scientific terms. Why then is there so much interest in Buddhism among environmental ethicists and activists? And why so much concern for environmentalism among contemporary Buddhists both Asian and Western? In the latter half of the twentieth century the problem of environmental degradation has become increasingly the focus of both philosophers and theologians, many of whom see in this particular manifestation of human delusion a crisis more ethical and spiritual than technological.[1] As we in the West re-examine our own religious and philosophical traditions, seeking both an etiology and a solution to the current predicament, it is hardly surprising that many have sought to mine the traditions of Asia to see what alternative perspectives they might offer.[2] Buddhism has provided this quest with a particularly rich, if sometimes ambivalent vein of reflections and values, expressing a fundamental attitude of compassion and non-injury, yet also a seemingly anthropocentric perspective in its valorization of human consciousness as a necessary requisite for the universal goal of enlightenment.[3] Clearly Buddhism offers a different approach to the environmental problem, and we – Buddhists and non-Buddhists alike – have only begun to fully appreciate what this tradition can add to current efforts to transform our attitudes towards the world in which we live.

Previous expositions of the place of nature and environmental concern within Buddhism have most often sought to compile appropriate passages from the canonical literature and to document environmentally sensitive practices and institutions within the tradition, both historical and contemporary. Some have further sought to extrapolate from these sources a Buddhist environmental ethic.[4] My approach here will be different. Rather than to reiterate the now readily available data on traditional Buddhist attitudes towards nature, what I shall undertake in this chapter is an examination of how a cluster of key assumptions shape Buddhist perceptions of nature and ecology at the most fundamental level. I shall argue, moreover, that both the role and the outcome of these axiomatic assumptions in shaping Buddhist attitudes is particularly easy to overlook precisely because they are assumptions radically contrary to those we take for granted in the West.

While recognizing that the traditional sources do report a number of distinctly Buddhist attitudes that bear on the topics of nature and ecology, I feel these attitudes can only be properly understood when they are considered within the context of Buddhist notions of the self and its relation to the rest of existence. We shall see that these basic notions in Buddhism differ significantly from our own Western presuppositions regarding the self and that this difference has significant implications for the way in which Buddhists will approach the topics of nature and ecology. This difference of assumptions is so basic in fact, that the respective presuppositions on both sides of the cultural divide tend to remain virtually invisible to the other, precisely because they remain largely unconscious. For Westerners seeking to understand traditional Buddhist attitudes towards nature, and also for contemporary Asian Buddhists seeking to articulate a Dharmic perspective in inter-faith discussions of environmental ethics, it is thus crucial to appreciate more fully just how differently the two cultural traditions have constructed their respective notions of the self and its relation to the world.[5]

Buddhist Conception of the Self

Western thought and Western ethical theories in particular have tended to begin with some notion of the person as an autonomous, rational individual. The first thing to note about the Buddhist conception of ethical agency is that it posits a notion of the self that is both dynamic and developmental. Taken together, these key features of Buddhist thought present a radically different notion of the ethical self, one that challenges Western assumptions of both rationality and autonomy. Buddhist ethics and soteriology do indeed require a significant integrity or coherence of personal identity, yet that identity or individuality of the self is seen as a dynamic karmic continuity rather than as an essential ontological substantiality – as an ongoing *process* rather than an underlying *thing*. And this dynamic nature of the self is seen, moreover, as significantly teleological or developmental, in that it includes the potential for (and inevitability of) change directed towards a distinct transformative goal, one with both soteriological and ethical dimensions. The Buddha was much more concerned to characterize the nature of the self in terms of its end or purpose than in terms of its original cause, seeing the latter question as one of those 'unanswerable' (*avyākṛta*) questions that are not conducive to the task at hand, namely the realization of one's potential for enlightenment and the elimination of suffering. Both these features of the Buddhist conception of the self, the dynamic and the developmental, have significant implications for the relationship of that self to the rest of existence including nature and the environment. But before considering these implications, we must first explore more carefully how Buddhists have traditionally framed their understanding of the self.

Perhaps the single most distinctive and radical of the Buddha's teachings was the notion of the non-substantiality of the self, the doctrine referred to in the Pali scriptures as *anattā* (Sanskrit: *anātman*) and usually rendered in English as the view of 'no-self' or 'non-self.'[6] As a corollary of the principle of conditionality (*pratītya-samutpāda*) and as one of the three marks of samsaric existence (along with impermanence and unsatisfactoriness), the doctrine of the non-substantiality of the self lies at the very of heart of the Dharma. With the emergence of modern scientific notions of change and indeterminacy it is easy to loose sight of just how radical this idea would have seemed in the Buddha's day. The notion of an essential, enduring, and immutable 'self' (*ātman* or *jīva*) lying at the core of personal identity was one of the central themes of the diverse Upanishadic speculations characteristic of the Age of the Wanderers into which the Buddha was born.[7] While other thinkers of this period also challenged the notion of an essential or substantial self, the Buddha's rejection of an *ātman* was unique in that, unlike the skeptics and materialists of his day, he simultaneously maintained a notion of ethical or karmic continuity, one that persisted not just throughout the life of the individual, but over multiple lifetimes as well. Indeed the Buddha went so far as to assert that his notion of 'no-self' was actually necessary to sustain any theory of ethical continuity and efficacy over time. But how then was this continuity to be secured? How could actions performed in the past effect consequences at some point in the future?

Those among the Buddha's contemporaries who accepted the continuity of karmic efficacy over time felt that it would be quite impossible without a substantial and immutable essence or *ātman* to which the karmic accretions could accrue. If there was no *ātman*, they reasoned, there was nothing that would hold together the series of lives (or even moments within a life for that matter). There would be literally nothing to be 'reincarnated,' nothing that could carry the karmic impurities from one embodiment to the next. The coherence or integrity of personal identity over time would, they argued, fall apart just as a necklace of pearls would scatter across the floor if one removed the string (i.e., the *ātman*) that linked together all the separate parts. And not only was any theory of ethical justice, of karmic reward and retribution, at stake – without a secure basis for karma, the whole soteric enterprise would be meaningless as well. For the future liberative outcome of one's present spiritual practice would not be secure. Nothing would guarantee that the positive benefits of spiritual practice performed today would accrue to the *same* individual later, within the same or subsequent lifetimes.

Among the various new soteriologies emerging during the Age of the Wanderers, the necessity of some *ātman*-like essence or soul was a virtually ubiquitous assumption. Yet the Buddha asserted that the supposition of such a notion of essential self-hood was as false as it was unnecessary. He did indeed recognize the necessity of securing the integrity of karmic efficacy, but he felt that positing an essential *ātman* was too high a price to ensure the continuity of the self, a price not only unwarranted, but even detrimental, to attaining the soteric goal as he understood it. The liberation he had realized was, in his view, so utterly transformative, that it could only be obstructed by clinging to any view of a 'self,' especially one that posited a core or essence that was not subject to change – and hence not subject to transformation. The integrity of personal identity and of ethical efficacy, required not some substantial permanence, he asserted, but only the continuity of the karmic conditioning itself. Herein lies the crux of the Buddhist conception of the self, and we can understand the Buddhist notion of how the self is related to its environment only if we fully appreciate the implications of this conception of the self.

110

What then constitutes 'personal identity,' if not some essential self or *ātman*? In the Buddhist view, the self is nothing more or less than the dynamic aggregation of a bundle of interrelated causal processes. This aggregation was variously analyzed, most simply into its basic psycho-physiological polarity (*nāma-rūpa*), and that in turn was further analyzed into the five parallel processes of physiological form (*rupa*), karmic formations (*saṃskāra*), cognition (*saṃjña*), feeling (*vedanā*) and discriminative perception (*vijñāna*). Later Buddhists in the Abhidharmic tradition carried the analysis still further, eventually recognizing 75, 85 or even 101 principal components of the process conventionally designated as 'the self.' It is important to stress that the point of this analytic Abhidharmic enterprise was much more soteric or therapeutic than descriptive. It was *systematic* but not scientific, in that its primary objective was to deconstruct all clinging to any false essentialist conception of the self, and not to exhaustively catalog all possible elements of existence. The transformative spiritual value of the analysis was seen to lie, in other words, not in the resulting products of the analysis but rather in the analytic process itself, in its salutary effect on the human tendency to cling to a substantial rather than dynamic notion of personal identity.

Of the various constituent processes making up the self, the karmic 'formations' or predispositions are of the greatest ethical interest. These were identified as the latent or unconscious traces (*bīja* or *vāsanā*) laid down as patterns of habituation through the performance of action (*karman*), actions not just of the body, but of speech and mind as well. Arising thus from previous activity, this karmic conditioning in turn shapes future actions, and these conditioning forces or energy patterns are not only multiple but of varying direction and intensity. We are, in this view, quite literally the (ever changing) sum of our habits. Or we might imagine the self as an extremely complex vector problem, the sort of mathematical exercise where one must identify both the direction and the velocity of different forces operating on an object in order to determine its trajectory from that point forward. In the Buddhist conception of the self, the particular ethical tendency or force of each of the currents of karmic conditioning is playing itself out, influencing and being influenced by each of the others. The self is thus a complicated and ongoing interactive process, the immediate configuration of which determines the overall trajectory of the being, a trajectory that is constantly being altered as each moment brings a new equation of interacting conditionings – some newly created through current activity, others carrying over as the continuing influence of previous actions. But does this conception of the self allow any degree of choice or creativity? Obviously one's response in any given situation must be strongly shaped, indeed determined, by those very patterns of habituation that are the sum of one's identity. Where is there opportunity for any new input, for any new departure seeking to break out the well-worn ruts of previous habituation?

Prior to reaching the goal of enlightenment, the range of possibilities available to a given individual in any given moment *is* significantly restricted or determined – this is precisely point of the Buddhist conception of liberation. Enlightenment is not just *freedom from* suffering; it is *freedom to* act in a creative, compassionate manner, unlimited by the constraints of prior delusion in the form of conditioned reactivity linked to a false and overly self-referential conception of personal identity. But just as the rejection of the *ātman* threatened to undermine karmic efficacy, this non-substantial and dynamic conception of the self seems to allow no opportunity for transformation once the karmic patterns have been established. Once the ruts are set, how is one to break out? Here we encounter another axiomatic assumption of Buddhism, one so fundamental and unquestioned that it is made explicit only in response to later criticism from outside the tradition. The potential for enlightenment is seen as itself part of the karmic conditioning of all beings. Within the *saṃskāras* that constitute one's identity are also certain tendencies conducive to liberation and enlightenment, not just those that tend towards perpetuating the bondage of greed, hatred and delusion. Indeed among these ethically and soterically positive conditionings is the possibility of volitional choice itself (*cetanā*), a karmic formation that emerges in all beings quite naturally once sentience or consciousness is sufficiently developed to sustain that particular degree of self-conscious awareness. These positive conditionings or 'wholesome roots' (*kūsalāni mūlāni*) as they were known in the early tradition are subsequently referred to in the Mahayana as one's Buddha Nature or as the 'embryo' of enlightenment (*tathāgata-garbha*). We can see that the Buddhist understanding of basic human nature is thus profoundly optimistic, even as it stresses just how deeply rooted the inclinations of ignorance and craving tend to be.

While these latent positive tendencies do constitute the *potential* for enlightenment, and while they are considered part of the karmically conditioned endowment of all beings, they must nonetheless be actively cultivated. They must become fully developed before the enlightenment will actually be realized. And this process of cultivation and development is itself part of the on-going process of conditioning and re-conditioning that constitutes the 'individual.' In the last section of this chapter we shall look at some various formulations of the *praxis* the early Buddhists advocated for realizing the goal of enlightenment or liberation. For now it will suffice to point out that this *praxis* is perhaps best understood as a process of cultivating those specific karmic patterns that manifest as a particular set of virtues both cognitive and affective, areteic qualities such as wisdom and compassion associated with the enactment of enlightened awareness.

Buddhist soteriology thus manifests many features of an Aristotelian virtue ethic, but with one significant difference.[8] Since the basic nature of the self is dynamic rather than substantially fixed or given, the *telos* towards which the Buddhist develops, indeed the *logos* that he or she eventually realizes is something that must be cultivated or developed. And this process of development extends beyond one's immediate existence as a human self. Unlike the substantialist notion of personal identity deriving from both the Judeo-Christian and Greek roots of Western thought, the Buddhist self is seeking to realize a set of virtues that are not understood as innately given human qualities. They are qualities potential in our very sentience, yet they are neither *given* nor *human*. They are 'trans-human' potentialities and in actualizing them one must go beyond the very 'humanness' of one's sense of identity. Human beings are thus 'half-baked beings' as it were, beings who have made significant progress in cultivating and refining their basic sentience into progressively higher degrees of awareness, yet beings that have some way to go nonetheless. Through this *praxis* of cultivating the perfections of the enlightened being, the *arhat* or *buddha*, the human Buddhist is moving well beyond what it is simply to be human, just as he or she began that process well short of what it is to be human. There is a clear ontological continuity from human to Buddha, indeed from banana slug to buddha – certainly no discontinuity of the degree that distinguishes the Creator from the created. It is in this sense buddhahood is seen as 'trans-human,' as a manner of being that takes one well beyond the status of 'human being.'[9]

We must now explore yet another closely related assumption, the notion that the potential for enlightenment is characteristic not just of humans, but of all sentient beings, the view that the eighth-century Buddhist poet Shantideva expresses with the poignant assertion that:

Even those who were gnats, mosquitoes, wasps, and worms, have reached the highest Awakening, hard to reach, through the strength of their exertion.[10]

This assertion of a cosmic 'principle of self-transcendence' as the contemporary Buddhist philosopher Sangharakshita has termed it is one that might well be challenged, to be sure, yet it is one that has remained axiomatic throughout the history of Buddhism.[11] Once we see that Buddhahood is the teleological goal, not just of human existence, but of all sentient existence, we begin to see that the 'human self' must be viewed in a much broader perspective. Not only must it be seen as dynamic and developmental; it is by its very nature a being – or rather a *becoming* – that is thus fundamentally trans-human. And it is only when seen in this broader context that the radical difference between Buddhist and Western views of the self begins to fully emerge.

The Cosmological Context

While it was necessary to begin with the Buddhist conception of personal or individual identity, we must now consider the broader cosmological stage upon which the drama of the dynamic and developmental self is played out, for it is this context that brings out the trans-human nature of the self that lies at the heart of this tradition. As part of the emerging Shramanic culture of the Age of the Wanderers, the early Buddhists accepted the notion of a samsaric cycle of repeated death and rebirth, with the particular form of life one experiences in a given lifetime determined by one's actions. Buddhism added two significant modifications to this view: the emphasis on intention in determining the ethical or karmic significance of actions, which we considered above, and the assertion that the ultimate goal of life lay outside the samsaric cycle entirely, which we take up now.

The Buddhists agreed with other contemporary teachings in seeing life as a kind cosmic 'chutes and ladders' game in which one could, through one's actions, move both up and down a hierarchy of interrelated samsaric life-forms. In its Buddhist presentation this taxonomy of possible forms of life is basically sixfold, although a rich variety of sub-species are recognized as well.[12] One may, in this view, exist as a being suffering the torments of a hellish existence, or as a being of unquenchable craving, as an animal, as a human, as a titan or jealous, warring god, or as a blissful god, one of the 'shining ones.'

Whereas the Buddha's contemporaries within the Brahmanic tradition tended to see existence as an immortal god or deva as the pinnacle of existence, the goal of all religious observance, the Buddha differed, seeing this divine existence as still subject to the same limitations as all forms of conditioned samsaric life, even though it was more pleasant and long-lasting. The gods were thus not seen as immortal, as no longer subject to the delusion and suffering of samsaric existence. Only the realization of nirvana or enlightenment would permanently free one from the bondage of ignorance and craving. All of life, then, was seen as an on-going quest to improve one's lot within samsaric existence, to the point at which one had sufficient insight into the nature of existence to break out of the cycle altogether to become not a god, but a liberated one, either an arhat or a buddha.

Quite explicit in the Buddhist conception of the taxonomy of life-forms is the notion of a qualitative hierarchy of 'interpermeable' life-forms. We must be careful not to misunderstand this classification as a taxonomy of essentially different biological species. What the different life-forms specify is better understood as different points along a continuous line charting the complexification of awareness, awareness expressing itself in different 'biological forms' according to its development. Contrary to the taxonomic principles of biological science, the number of different forms is, in this case, an arbitrary, if pragmatic, division of what is seen as an essentially progressive continuum. One might even say that ultimately there are thus as many different 'life-forms' or 'species' as there are individual karmic streams, since each individual 'stream' of karmic conditioning does differ in some way. But each of these karmic streams also shares a significant number of features and tendencies with beings of similar conditioning from the past, and in this sense it was appropriate to specify the six broad divisions recognized by the tradition.

What differentiates the various life-forms in this classification is not their absolute biological difference, but rather their relative capacity for sentience, and that capacity develops as the individual being succeeds in moving up the ladder of existence. Sentience here is understood quite basically as the ability to experience suffering and conversely the potential eventually to manifest enlightened consciousness, these two being seen as simply different degrees of the same capacity. Over the course of multiple lifetimes beings thus could, and inevitably would, make their way repeatedly up and down this continuum of life-forms, gaining their next rebirth at a level corresponding to the specific configuration of the karmic conditionings they had assembled – not just in their most recent existence, but in prior existences as well. It is thus not at all inaccurate to describe this system as a Buddhist theory of evolution, as long as we are careful to not to overlook how it differs significantly from the currently prevailing views of biological evolution in the West.[13] While Buddhism recognizes a hierarchy of biological complexification at the level of species, its evolutionary interests focus ultimately on the individual, that is to say, on the separate karmic life streams that make their way up the ladder of sentience to reach the point where enlightenment and liberation from the cycle become possible. This process is not only teleological (though not theistic) in a way that most evolutionary biologists would reject, it locates the significant development in awareness or consciousness rather than in biological structure, although the latter are seen as evolutionary expressions of the developing consciousness.

The Buddhist Self in Nature

We have considered the philosophical and cosmological aspects of the Buddhist sense of self, seeing that individual identity is perceived as a dynamic and developmental stream of karmic conditioning persisting over multiple lifetimes during which the individual may have existed not only as a human but as other life-forms as well. Before we can appreciate the implications of this view with respect to environmental ethics and practice, we need to consider at least briefly the manner in which it differs from our own cultural assumptions regarding the self and personal identity. Western culture is woven of an extremely complex mixture of different and often conflicting strands, some Middle Eastern in origin, others Hellenic, some traditional and religious, other contemporary and scientific. Viewed with Buddhist eyes, however, one significant and consistent feature of the Western conception of the self stands out. Indeed it is one we should recognize as one of the few features common to both the traditional Judeo-Christian world view and that of modern science. Although both sides of this fundamental cultural divide in the West would frame their respective conceptions of it in quite different and even antagonistic terms, there is indeed one crucial point on which they are in basic agreement, a point so basic to Western culture, in fact, that it is virtually invisible to us until highlighted against the backdrop of a radically different set of assumptions of the sort we have considered above.

In the West, whether seen in religious or scientific terms, what most constitutes the nature of the self is its very specificity, usually understood as a species-specificity. We are what we are – humans, wolves, banana slugs or mosquitoes – and that we shall remain for the whole of our existence, whether that be for all of eternity in the religious view, or simply until we die, according to the scientific perspective. It may seem overly simplistic to point out such a basic fact, yet precisely because this view of the nature of the self is so axiomatic we fail to see how much it shapes the attitudes we have towards each other, towards our fellow beings, and towards our environment. Hence the importance of clearly identifying the striking contrast in the Buddhist conception of the personal identity and continuity – not just so that we understand Buddhism more accurately, but also because we may, in the process, come to a more accurate understanding of our own cultural roots as well.

My thesis regarding Buddhist attitudes towards nature and the environment is based on the premise that our relationships with other beings, especially those of other species, are significantly shaped by the understanding of personal identity that we bring to those relationships. With a conception of personal identity that is fundamentally trans-human, Buddhists have traditionally shaped the problem of inter-species relationships in quite different terms, and as a result we should expect traditional Buddhist environmental ethics to look quite different from its counterpart in the West. While it is beyond the scope of this chapter to explore the Western side of this comparison, one brief example of a central theme in Western environmental ethics with help us see the contrast more clearly. Consider the place of 'rights' in contemporary discussions of environmental ethics. One major strand of contemporary environ-mental philosophy seeks to secure moral consideration for other species and eventually for eco-systems as a whole through the extension of the concept of individual rights. Problems arise for this effort because the notion of rights has been historically linked with notions of human responsibility and duty, capacities which other species are not seen to share. One solution is to assert the notion of a 'right' to moral consideration tied not to the capacity for an anthropocentric concept of responsibility, but rather to a notion of 'intrinsic value,' an attribute shared by all beings regardless of their species. Both these notions of rights and values, along with their concomitant problems, arise from the same distinctly Western notion of a permanently fixed sense of selfhood, one in which autonomous selves are seen to possess rights and values that must be secured and even protected from the self-interests of other autonomous individuals, whether within one's own species or across the species line. And even if the rights of others (individuals or species) are successfully and convincingly negotiated, the question remains of how to change established behavior patterns that are in conflict with the newly defined rights. And this problem of changing existing behavioral conditioning is all the more intractable if that conditioning itself is tied to the axiomatic assumption of a fixed (and species-specific) self seeking to preserve its own rights. Any ecological perspective grounded in this set of assumptions will result in an adversarial compromise at best, one that will have to be enforced at every point that it runs contrary to the perceived self-interests of the dominant individual.

The traditional Buddhist approach to recognizing moral consideration for other individuals will necessarily proceed quite differently, whether that consideration is extended to other humans or to other species.[14] Rather than reifying the prevailing sense of an autonomous self-interested individual with its complement of rights, Buddhism seeks to transform the very way in which the individual conceives of himself. Traditionally, Buddhist 'environmental ethics' has thus been less a matter of identifying and securing rights. Rather it has been much more a matter of undertaking a practice of affirming and eventually realizing the trans-human potential for enlightenment. Based as it is on cultivating an ever deeper insight into the trans-species mutuality of sentience and hence potential for enlightenment, Buddhist practice can only express itself as a compassionate, environmental sustaining altruism. Śāntideva expresses this eloquently:

> Just as the body, with its many parts from division into hands and other limbs, should be protected as a single entity, so too should this entire world which is divided [into parts], yet not divided in its nature to suffer and be happy....
>
> I should dispel the suffering of others because it is suffering like my own suffering. I should help others too because of their nature as beings, which is like my own being.[15]

To do otherwise, he aptly concludes, would like refusing to use one's hand to remove the thorn in one's foot, because the pain of the foot is not the pain of the hand.

Traditional Buddhist Praxis and Environmental Ethics

It has become commonplace to assert that Buddhism locates the individual in profound inter-relationship with the rest of sentient existence, and ultimately with all of the ecosphere. Most frequently this is argued rather vaguely as an extension of the first Buddhist ethical precept of non-injury or, in a philosophically more sophisticated manner, as an implication of the Mahayana doctrine of emptiness understood as a variety of non-dualism that entails compassionate activity towards all other beings (and the environment that sustains them). This understanding of the emptiness doctrine asserts that, if all things are seen as empty of intrinsic existence, then all things must be seen as interrelated, and the only possible course of action becomes one that seeks to compassionately sustain all of existence.[16] What is often not adequately noted is the fact that this Mahayana notion of inter-relatedness is simply the logical development of the basic Buddhist principle of conditionality, the same principle that underlies the non-substantiality of the self and the interrelatedness of the different life-forms as depicted in Buddhist cosmology. While it is quite appropriate to note the extent to which the Mahayana doctrine of emptiness is useful for bringing out the compassionate dimension of both the practice and the goal of Buddhism, it is important to note simultaneously the extent to which this Mahayana position is continuous with the basic Buddhist doctrines illustrated in the 'cosmic chutes and ladders game' of the samsaric cycle of existence.

Failure to acknowledge this continuity results in a lop-sided view of Buddhism, one that obscures the developmental dimension of the tradition. If contemporary Buddhists seek only to affirm inter-relatedness as a traditional expression of the contemporary ecological perspective, then the real contribution that Buddhism might make to cross-cultural and inter-faith discussions of environmental ethics will be lost.[17] Turning to Buddhism simply as a traditional sanction for an already scientifically established ecological perspective on our problems adds little to what we already have. What is needed is not another affirmation of ecology but rather an actual method for developing an ecological sensibility and then expressing that sensibility in practice. This Buddhism offers, but only to the extent that we recognize that the Buddhist affirmation of interrelatedness is deeply embedded in a comprehensive developmental path or virtue tradition, one that seeks nothing less than the radical transformation of the typically human conception of self and self-interest.

What, then, is this praxis by which Buddhists have sought to express their conception of the self-in-relation to the rest of existence? Having noted the fundamentally different concept of a substantial self with which Western traditions have approached the problem of environmental degradation, we should note before continuing that the Buddhists were quite aware of how commonly human action arises from such a substantialist notion of self and personal identity. From the Buddhist perspective, we are dealing not just with a cultural difference, but more deeply with the nature of human delusion itself. Substantialist notions of the self are not simply a cultural option as it were, but a distinctive stage in the development of awareness itself, a stage still well short of the ethical sensibility that Buddhism sees as the goal. While substantialist views of the self are seen thus to be characteristic of all human culture, they represent in the Buddhist view the very problem itself, the obstacle that obstructs a life of liberated, compassionate activity. The Buddha diagnosed the human predicament as suffering arising from such views of the self, self-views born of ignorance and expressed as insatiable craving. That being the diagnosis, the therapy he advocated involved nothing short of a fundamental reconceptualization of the self, one effected by the cultivation of a variety of virtues that cumulatively would overcome the conditioning of the false self-view at the deepest levels of one's being. It is important to note, moreover, that the problem of an overly fixed self-view was seen as both cognitive and affective, as a malfunction of both reason and emotion, a delusion that could be addressed only through a systematic program of transforming or developing both heart and mind. The actual course of this Buddhist practice was variously mapped by the Buddha himself and further elaborated by generations of subsequent Buddhist teachers. The formulation of the course of practice best known in the West is perhaps the eightfold path, but there are other, equally venerable formulations that illustrate even better the objectives of our present inquiry. We shall consider here the threefold training and the seven factors of enlightenment, both central teachings particularly stressed by the Buddha during the final months before his death.

The 'Mahāparinibbaṇa-sutta' of the *Dīgha Nikāya* relates the Buddha's travels during the final months of his life, a time when he appears to have been particularly concerned to summarize all of his various teachings in terms of a concise and systematic practice. As he traveled from town to town visiting communities of his followers for the last time the most frequently recurring theme of his discourses was the threefold course of training consisting in the cultivation of ethical conduct (*sīla*) meditation (*samādhi*) and wisdom (*paññā*). This concise formulation of Buddhist praxis is especially useful for our purposes because it clearly stresses the developmental nature of the path. While not sequential in the sense that the first is left behind once the second is undertaken, with it in turn yielding to the next, these three components of the path are presented as logically augmentative in that each builds on the foundation of the previous. Thus one might well cultivate all three components from the outset of one's practice, the developmental point being that it is only when ethical conduct is firmly established that meditation becomes truly effective, and only through the integrative effect of meditation that the truly transformative power of wisdom becomes possible.

We can see this basic threefold practice elaborated in somewhat more detail in another prominent teaching of the Buddha's last days, the doctrine of the seven factors of enlightenment: mindfulness (*sati*), discrimination of principles (*dhamma-vicaya*), energy in pursuit of the good (*viriya*), rapture (*pīti*), tranquility (*passaddhi*), concentration (*samādhi*), and equanimity (*upekkhā*). Here we are clearly dealing with the successive cultivation of a set of areteic virtues, specific qualities requisite to the mode of existence no longer constrained by an overly self-referential notion of personal identity. A passage in the *Saṃyutta Nikāya* that treats these seven in greater detail makes clear the developmental nature of the sequence: 'When a monk, thus remaining secluded, recollects and reasons about the doctrine, he initiates the mindfulness factor of enlightenment, which he then develops and perfects. Remaining thus mindful, he discriminates, reflects on and investigates with understanding that doctrine, thus initiating the discrimination of principles factor of enlightenment, which he then develops and perfects....'; and so on until each of the seven is perfected.[18] It is worth also drawing attention to the fact that there is significant emphasis in this list on the process of cognitive and affective refinement in that factors four through seven are also specific faculties central to the theory of Buddhist meditation.[19] And this point becomes even more evident if we take up the still further elaborated version of the path found in the *Saṃyutta Nikāya* passage that presents a progressive twelve-fold path to enlightenment as an alternative to the reiterative twelve-fold cycle of samsaric existence.[20]

So far we have considered basic Buddhist doctrines common to all schools of Buddhism, and this has been intentional because I wanted to demonstrate that there is a characteristically Buddhist approach to trans-human ethical consideration that is part of the core tradition. Yet another source used quite prominently in teaching Buddhist morality in all traditional Buddhist cultures is the collection of *Jātaka* tales, popular fables that recount the earlier lives of the Buddha when he was training as a *bodhisattva* or buddha-to-be. A central theme of these widely read stories is the list of key virtues perfected by the Buddha during the course of his training, a theme that subsequently became a central pillar of the Buddhist revitalization movement known as the Mahayana. Overlapping in part with the factors of enlightenment we considered above, the *Jātaka* list of Bodhisattva virtues included generosity, ethical conduct, renunciation, wisdom, energy or enthusiasm (in pursuit of the good), patience or forbearance, truthfulness, resolution, and loving-kindness. And the perfections of the *Jātakas* overlap substantially, in turn, with the six or ten perfections comprising the Bodhisattva ideal in Mahayana Buddhism. It is particularly important to stress this continuity in the tradition here, because accounts of the Buddhist perspective on environmental concerns often stress only the Mahayana notion of the interrelatedness of all things, without indicating the extent to which this view is derived from the earlier aspects of basic Buddhism that we have considered so far.

We must see specifically that the Mahayana teaching of emptiness and hence the inter-relatedness of all things is practically transformative only to the extent that it constitutes the wisdom component of the traditional Buddhist teaching of the threefold training considered above. And we must remember that a crucial point of that teaching was that one could not expect to penetrate very deeply (or transformatively) into the wisdom phase of the path without first making significant headway with the disciplines of ethical conduct and meditation. This should help us see that environmentally sensitive practice in Buddhism is hardly a matter of simply affirming faith and belief in the ultimate interrelatedness of all things and then waiting hopefully for that truth to manifest itself. Without undertaking the discipline of the threefold training, without seeking to cultivate of the perfections or the virtues enumerated above, one is missing the point of Buddhist practice. And to do that is to miss what Buddhism has most to offer us in our present environmental predicament.

Buddhist Practice in a Age of Environmental Degradation

In considering what a contemporary, environmentally sensitive practice of traditional Buddhism might involve, we must first acknowledge that it will offer no simple solutions, that it will in fact ultimately require nothing short of total self-transformation. The only true solution to the problem, in a Buddhist analysis, will be neither technological nor legal. It must be soteriological. It must involve the evolution of a significant number of us human beings to a higher level of awareness, to a higher ethical sensibility. This is not to say that efforts – both technological and legal – to safeguard the environment are pointless, only that they are at best a stop-gap measure, and not the ultimate solution.

On hearing this, one might be led to despair, thinking that this is far to much to ask. Surely there must be some more immediate solution – otherwise the environment and all of us therein are most certainly doomed. But this would not be a Buddhist response. It is a response arising from an overly fixed conception of human nature, a response that fails to recognize just how optimistic Buddhism is about the potential we have to evolve into a higher ethical sensibility. It is true that this will happen only as a result of concerted practice and discipline, but the whole of the Buddhist tradition consists precisely in a sustained effort to devise effective methods for undertaking this transformation. The task is immense, in the Buddhist perspective, but so are our resources, the tradition would point out – if only we muster the resolve, the energy in pursuit of the good, patience, the loving-kindness, the concentration, and the wisdom to bring those substantial resources to bear.

To conclude this chapter let us explore a single example of how each component of the threefold training might be undertaken by a contemporary environmentally sensitive Buddhist – Asian or Western, monastic or lay. Beginning with ethical conduct it is easy to see that the traditional list of five precepts offers many opportunities for cultivating a heightened ethical sensibility of the sort that will eventually express itself in a transformative (as opposed to simply intellectual) experience of inter-relatedness and its correlative of compassion. Consider voluntary simplicity as an expression of the first precept of non-injury for example. And to focus our inquiry even more we can take just one instance of voluntary simplicity: eating lower on the food chain. This Buddhist practice of voluntary simplicity in eating should not be confused with the Hindu practice of vegetarianism which is more a matter of cultivating ritual purity rather than a practice of non-injury. The Buddhist principle of non-injury recognizes that all samsaric life feeds on other life. Existing (for the present) as a human life-form one cannot avoid the necessity of causing some harm in the sustaining of one's own life. What one can do is to minimize the damage by eating as low on the food chain as possible. The Buddha did specifically allow his monks to eat even meat where necessary, either because they were accepting the generosity of others or because they were ill and required extra nutrition. The point thus was clearly to practice causing as little harm as possible, both because that directly benefited other beings, but also because it was part of cultivating a set of virtues which would eventually be radically transformative, which would in turn have an even greater benefit for all beings. Given the variety of nutritive food sources readily available today, especially in the West, restricting one's diet to vegetable sources is an eminently beneficial practice, in terms of both Buddhism and environmentalism.

The second component of the threefold training is the cultivation of greater cognitive and affective concentration or integration, through the practice of meditation. This is the phase of the path in which the Buddha felt humans could begin to develop well beyond the normal human tendencies toward greed, hatred and delusion. The discipline of meditation must necessarily be initially undertaken in a sheltered, isolated environment free from the usual distractions, yet the goal is to cultivate a greater facility of mind and positive emotion that eventually permeates all aspects of one's life. Buddhist meditation is not done for the experience during the meditation session itself, but rather for the transformative effect it has cumulatively. Of the many and various techniques of meditative practice in Buddhism, Western readers are most likely to have encountered some form of mindfulness practice. While this is indeed a foundational practice for virtually all schools of Buddhism, many also follow the oldest scriptural sources in giving equal prominence to the practice of cultivating the four 'immeasurables' – the positive emotions of loving-kindness, sympathetic joy, compassion and equanimity. Taking the first of these as our example for this aspect of the path, our contemporary, ecologically minded Buddhist would undertake a systematic daily practice of generating the emotion of loving-kindness (*mettā*, Skt: *maitrī*), first towards him or herself, then towards someone who is 'near and dear,' next towards a 'neutral person' and then towards an enemy, and finally, after consolidating those varieties of *mettā*, the practitioner would extend this attitude of care and kindness outward in radiating circles to encompass all beings, near and far, seen and unseen. Again the immediate benefits of such a practice to the environment are not difficult to imagine, but we must remember that the ultimate Buddhist goal of this practice is the even more radical transformation of the underlying self-concept that feeds the tendencies towards greed, hatred and delusion.

There are many interesting variations on this basic *mettā* practice. In one, inspired by the same Śāntideva we encountered above, the practitioner reflects imaginatively on the thought that all other beings have been, at some point in the virtually infinite past of Buddhist cosmology, one's own mother. Recognizing the care extended by each of those beings at that time, one undertakes to relate to them in like manner now. This type of practice, sometimes called 'analytic meditation' leads us to the last phase of the threefold training, the cultivation of wisdom itself. Here we find practices that employ the previously cultivated positive mental and emotional facility to discern ever more deeply the actual nature of reality. In the early tradition these practices sought to penetrate the depths of the four noble truths and the three marks of conditioned existence taught by the Buddha, while in the later Mahayana tradition, the focus was even more specifically on gaining transformative insight into the emptiness or the interrelatedness of all things. Returning to our contemporary practitioner, we might feel that this type of discipline would remain too abstract to be of any immediate environmental benefit, but that would be to overlook the fact that the foundation of this discipline lies in practices of the sort we have considered in the two previous examples. Insight into the ultimate nature of reality can arise only from a deeply integrated attitude of caring and concern cultivated towards all beings. And the culmination of all of this threefold training is the wisdom of a buddha, a wisdom that according to the tradition can express itself only as compassionate activity unbounded by any remaining self-referential craving.

Perhaps this is also why Buddhism has seen no need to develop a special and separate position on nature and ecology. And indeed we might be well justified in concluding that in fact Buddhism *has* no particular environmental ethic at all. By the same token, however, we would have to conclude also that Buddhism *is* an environmental ethic, in that it cannot be put into practice without completely transforming one's every response to nature and the environment.

Notes

1 See *The Liberation of Life: From the Cell to the Community*, by Charles Birch and John B. Cobb, Jr. (Denton, Tex.: Environmental Ethics Books, 1990).

2 J. Baird Callicott and Roger T. Ames (eds.), *Nature in Asian Traditions of Thought: Essays in Environmental Philosophy* (Albany: State University of New York Press, 1989).

3 Lambert Schmithausen, who has done the most thorough study of attitudes towards nature in Buddhist sources, is especially good at documenting the apparent ambivalence in certain texts; see his *Buddhism and Nature*, (Tokyo: The International Institute for Buddhist Studies, 1991) and *The Problem of the Sentience of Plants in Earliest Buddhism* (Tokyo: The International Institute for Buddhist Studies, 1991).

4 See for example the various contributions in *Dharma Gaia: a Harvest of Essays in Buddhism and Ecology*, ed. by Allan Hunt Badiner (Berkeley, Calif.: Parallax Press, 1990).

5 The interpretations I express in this article are based, as much as possible, on the 'Basic Buddhism' of the early canonical scriptures generally accepted, at least in theory, throughout the tradition. With regard to the nature of the continuity of the self, however, these sources were developed substantially and often differently by the various later schools of Buddhist thought. Where different interpretations are possible, I have chosen to follow the classical Yogacara teachings of Asaṅga and Vasubandhu as recorded and developed in the later Mahayana and Vajrayana phases of the tradition, the school of thought within Buddhism that most systematically elaborated earlier views on the concept of the self and the nature of personal continuity.

6 See Steven Collins, *Selfless Persons: Imagery and Thought in Theravada Buddhism*, (Cambridge & New York: Cambridge University Press, 1982).

7 On the Age of the Wanderers see *The Buddha* by Michael Carrithers (Oxford & New York: Oxford University Press, 1983).

8 Damien Keown explores the parallels between the ethics of the Buddha and Aristotle in *The Nature of Buddhist Ethics*, (New York: St. Martin's Press, 1992), esp. chapter. 8.

9 The Buddha makes it quite clear that he is not to be considered a human being (or any other samsaric life-form) in his encounter with the Brahmin Doṇa recorded at *A* ii.37f.

10 *Bodhicaryāvatāra* vii:18, trans. by Kate Crosby and Andrew Skilton, (Oxford & New York: Oxford University Press, 1996), 68.

11 See 'The Bodhisattva: Evolution and Self-Transcendence' Sangharakshita (1983), republished in *The Priceless Jewel*, (Glasgow: Windhorse Publications, 1993).

12 Sometimes only five different life-forms are enumerated, with the devas and the titans counted together, which supports my point below that these categories are not essentially exclusive.

13 The link between Buddhist and Western conceptions of evolution is the theme of *The Evolving Mind* (Glasgow: Windhorse, 1996) by the Cambridge-trained Western Buddhist Robin Cooper (Dharmachari Ratnaprabha).

14 One implication of this point is that the efforts, fashionable in some contemporary Buddhist circles, to 'locate' a basis or rationale for 'rights' within Buddhism are not only superfluous but wrong-headed. In the attempt to make Buddhism more acceptable, by making it more Western,

contemporary Buddhists run the risk of obscuring what Buddhism might best contribute to the discussion: a radically different conception of the self-in-relation to the environment and a praxis based on that notion of the self.

15 *Bodhicaryāvatāra* viii:91–99, p. 96; for the sake of clarity I have slightly modified the translation of Crosby and Skilton (see note 9 above).

16 For an especially accessible example of this approach see *The Heart of Understanding: Commentaries on the Prajñaparamita Heart Sutra* by Thich Nhat Hanh, (Berkeley, CA: Parallax Press, 1988).

17 In 'Green Buddhism and the Hierarchy of Compassion,' *Buddhism and Ecology*, (Cambridge, MA: Harvard, 1997) I have explored the tendency among some contemporary Buddhists to reduce Buddhism to an overly one-dimensional teaching of egalitarian inter-relatedness out of a reluctance to acknowledge the developmental and spiritually hierarchical dimension of the tradition.

18 *Saṃyutta Nikāya*: v.67–68.

19 Cf. the 'factors of meditative absorption' (*jhānāṅga*) discussed in Buddhaghosa's meditation manual the *Visuddhimagga*, section IV; (*Path of Purification*, trans. by Nanamoli Thera, Colombo: Semage, 1956).

20 *Saṃyutta Nikāya* ii:29.

CHAPTER TEN

Response to Alan Sponberg's 'The Buddhist Conception of an Ecological Self'

Paula M. Cooey

The central issue Alan Sponberg raises in his very fine essay to which I wish to respond from a Christian perspective is the issue of trans-human identity and its relation to the cultivation of virtues and practices conducive to promoting ecological repair and sustenance. I wish first to explore briefly the implications of the very important differences between Buddhist and Christian thought and life regarding trans-human identity. I shall conclude by addressing briefly some of the significant differences and commonalties regarding the need for and development of an ecological ethic for both Buddhist and Christian traditions. I shall begin by pointing out what I find to be important functional commonalties and substantive differences surrounding the nature of the self, shared by the two traditions as exemplified in both our essays. These commonalties and differences in anthropological assumptions underlie respectively different soteriologies.

While Sponberg correctly stresses that Western religious and secular traditions construe a human self that remains entirely and solely human, I am struck by how both Buddhist and Christian teachings and practices seek to destabilize the ego as the center of this identity. The Western Enlightenment and post-Enlightenment construal of an autonomous self defined by innate rights and responsibilities is relatively recent even in Western history, a perspective which has received mixed reviews from Christian theologians over its own short history. Christian theologians and ethicists have felt, in some cases, deeply ambivalent toward such a construal, and in other cases, have definitively rejected it.

In the context of Reformed Protestant theology rejection has stemmed from a reading of Christian scripture and teaching as requiring a radical transformation from an identity centered by the ego's narrow interests and cravings to an identity centered by God. The process of transformation itself occurs at the divine initiative, rather than by human initiative. The scriptural discourse that defines this transformation stresses the centrality of the grace of God calling humans to repentance and absolving them of sin that they might experience new birth, new life, a new heart, mind or will, in a new realm imagined as the kingdom of God, a new Jerusalem, or a new heaven and earth. In short, the shift in identity is total, and at least for some theologians, irreversible; it furthermore includes both personal and communal trajectories.

Liberation further involves for most Reformed Protestants a communally oriented life that constitutes through its relations this new identity, now focused on the transformation of the world in which Christians finds themselves toward a more just and harmonious order. This community is thus constitutive to Christian identity and, therefore, not reducible simply to a voluntary compact formed among consenting, otherwise autonomous selves. This conception of the self as constituted by its ethically and spiritually problematic relations to its own interests and appetites, as well as its redeemed relations both to God and to others, including non-human others, is not, technically speaking, a substantialist notion the self. This view of transformation as a total shift in identity, while different in important respects from a Buddhist view, depends like its Buddhist counterpart on conceiving the self as the sum of its habits.

Theological discourse on the self is not unequivocal, however. The new life or birth brought by baptism, while discontinuous in relation to the old identity, is bound by the continuity of the human body. Pharisees and the early Jewish followers of Jesus alike valued this continuity so dearly, as to claim a general resurrection of the body upon the return of God's rule on earth – a claim that forms a central tenet of Christian belief to this day. Theological attempts to explain the perdurance of human embodiment, while claiming disjunction in human identity, parallel the conceptual difficulties surrounding claims about the relation and lack of relation between the world as it is characterized by sin and suffering and the realm of God as it is characterized by justice and mercy. Physicality and location lie at the heart of these twin issues. Irrespective of the different possible meanings attributable to 'resurrection of the body' and 'kingdom of

God' throughout Christian history, from a Christian perspective, humans begin as human and remain human, no matter how radical a spiritual transformation they may undergo. Any suggestion of karma and rebirth, at least as they are conventionally understood by an often ill-informed Christian perspective, would be considered antithetical to Christian teaching. Likewise the notions that one could find salvation apart from God's intervention into human life and thus based solely on one's own efforts, or that salvation or liberation involves release from the human condition, would be antithetical to Christian teaching as well.

Both Buddhist and Christian traditions thus clearly see egocentricity as the root of suffering and damage – an egocentricity that can be transformed, though the conditions for transformation rest on very different assumptions. Although in contrast to Buddhist thought, Christian thought focuses on origins as well as ends, the Christian focus on origin arises less out of metaphysical speculation than out of soteriological and ethical concerns. The claim that the God who redeems is the God who creates assures the initial goodness of each creature as the specific material reality it is; there is no sense of progress or regress to a different material condition. The inherent goodness of divine creation further grants all creaturely existence the *same* initial status as *very good* (Genesis 1:31), thus reinforcing the connection of value among human creatures and across species – a connection that otherwise could not be sustained or, in light of human sin, repaired. This shared status of positive worth not only connects all creatures with one another, but also all creation to its creator and redeemer who ideally constitutes the center of redeemed human identity. Thus this connection of worth serves very practical soteriological and ethical functions, rather than ontological or metaphysical ones.

This series of connections based on worth obviously contrasts with the trans-human karmic trajectory that Sponberg describes that produces in a Buddhist context the capacity to imagine the suffering and release from suffering of all sentient beings as relevant to one's own suffering and release. Nevertheless, given this series of connections based on worth from a Christian perspective, it is not clear to me that humans necessarily need a karmic connection to other sentient existence in order to work to promote their well being. As a Christian steeped in the doctrine of the Incarnation, I have theological and ethical difficulties, rather than conceptual ones, with the idea that liberation, my own or the earth's, depends on humans transcending their own humanity. I likewise have problems with the possible implication inherent in trans-human identity as depicted by Sponberg that non-human sentient existence is what it is by virtue of karma. While I understand that these are soteriological claims rather than ontological ones, I cannot help but find troubling the anti-materialism and the hierarchy of value implicit in the connection between karma and rebirth. I nevertheless fully acknowledge that my difficulties may arise in part from my own lack of sufficient understanding.

Recognizing and living out the ecological implications of these connections of worth for Christians requires a kind of practice not often undertaken, however. The technical theological discourse for Christian processes of socio-personal transformation and practice has historically revolved around the concepts *justification* and *sanctification*. Reformed Protestants have for the most part tended, at least to my mind, to emphasize justification (absolution from sin) without sufficient reference to sanctification (the disciplined process of making holy), probably out of an over-weaning fear of contamination by 'works' without sufficient reference to 'faith.' Nevertheless, sanctification, understood as the ongoing transformation of sinners who have been justified by faith through grace, provides an excellent context for raising the issue of Christian ethics in response to ecological degradation.

Understood properly, sanctification defines a process whereby Christians are 'schooled' in Christian virtues and practice. Exemplary virtues include meekness, humility, hunger for justice, and purity of heart, as reflected in the Sermon on the Mount. Concomitant ethical practices, drawn also from the Sermon on the Mount, as well as from the Law among other resources, include loving God, neighbors, strangers, and enemies, doing good to those who harm one, turning the other cheek, and giving up the very clothes off one's back for those who are in need. Thus sanctification functionally parallels the Buddhist three-fold course of training and the seven factors of enlightenment. Both exemplify a life lived simply.

Once again, however, the substantive differences are as important as the functional commonalties. Outside the Christian monastic orders which stress a life of poverty, chastity, and obedience to God, there is unfortunately little encouragement to practice meditation, particularly as a means of attuning oneself to the depths of meaning and value that saturate life. Though prayer may play a central role in spiritual discipline for lay Christians, prayer and meditation are obviously not identical. Likewise for most Christians there are no dietary restrictions, though individual practices may vary, and some denominations prohibit alcohol and caffeine, while some sects practice vegetarianism. This results in part no doubt from a lack of formal admonishment against violence toward all living things, in contrast to the Buddhist practice of *śīla*.

In regard to the issue of violence in particular, Christians have a long and often bloody history of responses that range from pacifism to just war theory to holy war, the biblical injunction prohibiting killing notwithstanding. There is no explicit, built-in mandate that life, more specifically non-human life, be respected. For this reason, Christian theologians and ethicists need to make far more explicit the ecological implications of Christian ethics than their counterparts may feel necessary in a Buddhist context. The resources are there, as I have tried to make clear in my own essay, but they can be retrieved only in conjunction with serious critique of the problems and the highly ambiguous history that besets Christian faith.

Good dialogue does not admit easily to closure, whereas book chapters necessarily must come to an end. I would be remiss if I failed to express how very much I enjoyed 'Self, Nature, and Ecology in Buddhism,' both for what I learned of Buddhism and for clarifying my self-understanding of my own faith. Though these chapters must end, I look forward to continuing dialogue in other arenas. The ongoing effects of ecological devastation will long outlive Alan Sponberg and me; we need to draw critically on available resources appropriate to our traditions, regardless of their origin, as we continue together the long, arduous task of sustenance and repair. Most importantly we need to pass these resources on to future generations in the hope that they may find them useful.

CHAPTER ELEVEN

Creation, Redemption, and the Realization of the Material Order

Paula M. Cooey

Human beings, particularly from the industrial nations, are daily destroying untold numbers of plant and animal species and may ultimately render the human species itself extinct. As Westerners we find ourselves at the end of the twentieth century heirs to and perpetrators of a death consumed and consuming culture. Whether the processes of destruction can be halted or, better still, reversed, remains to be seen.[1] As numerous other scholars have noted, religious traditions, particularly but not exclusively the religious traditions of Western culture, have historically played an ambiguous role in the destruction of planetary life.[2]

Representatives of both Eastern and Western traditions have engaged in dialogue on this issue on numerous occasions. The interreligious dialogue in which I have been most involved has taken place between Buddhists and Christians. Representatives from both traditions have tended to agree that fundamental distraction from concern with and care for this world characterizes many of the teachings of both traditions. Buddhists often seek liberation from suffering by withdrawing from the world. Christian engagement with the world often occurs ironically within a wider context, framed by a misplaced sense of dominion over the world and a devaluation of the world in relation to some conception of afterlife, perceived as the continuation of individual ego in another world or 'heaven.' Though the teachings within these two great traditions differ in content, they hold in common tendencies to make this world, particularly its materiality, unreal and thereby devalued.

At the same time, representatives from both traditions have found promising resources within them for changing human awareness of the significance of this world. Buddhists have placed great value on Zen Buddhist attunement to 'suchness,' as well as on the Tibetan teaching that all sentient existence possesses Buddha nature and participates in the material order as Buddha body.[3] Likewise Christians have rediscovered dominion over the earth as stewardship rather than tyranny, have sought a spirituality that draws upon the life and teachings of St. Francis of Assisi, and have found new meaning for the doctrine of the resurrection of the body that emphasizes care for this earth.[4] Representatives of both traditions share a serious commitment to finding and developing within the traditions resources that will make real, thereby valuable, to their adherents the material order within which they practice their faiths.

Philosophical and theological critique of problematic teachings and the search for resources, coupled with the reconstruction of teachings in relation to the demands of an ecologically threatened age, continue to make positive contributions to the rejuvenation of the traditions, to the lives of adherents, and most importantly to an activism that seeks to benefit planetary life. We are nevertheless only beginning the prodigious task of healing and repairing the devastation we have wreaked, particularly in ways that intend justice for all creatures including the human creature.

Christians in particular have, with few exceptions, failed sufficiently to allow that the very real and tragic prospect that humans may destroy themselves seriously challenges much traditional Christian teaching on creation and redemption.[5] These central doctrines have remained essentially intact in theologians' refusal to incorporate the possibility of such tragedy into the human drama of sin and redemption. Traditional Christian theological construction of good and evil simply does not easily admit the possibility that history may end badly for humans as a species, indeed may end permanently for the human species, without relocating at least some humans elsewhere in some timeless idealized space.[6] Particularly for conventional, white, middle-class, Reformed Protestant Christian faith, as practiced in the United States, there is little room for the natural, moral, and spiritual ambiguity implicit in tragedy and even less room for an unknown future. From this conventional perspective, in the long run everything will turn out all right, as promised according to a highly selective reading of scripture and according to Church teaching. In short, the material order (including human materiality), in its stubborn resistance to human ideation and in all its finitude, is simply not yet real to most Christians. Until Christians realize the full implications of materiality, most of us will continue to ignore, to abet, or to address only superficially the ecological destruction we commit.

Because of theological resistance to acknowledging the possibility of tragedy, serious critique and reconstruction of the doctrines of creation and redemption initially require turning to resources outside Christian traditions, though in light of critique, we shall discover new resources within the traditions. In my own endeavor as a Christian theologian I have found Frederick Streng's work on the Buddhist concept *śūnyatā*[7] and the work of Elaine Scarry on making as creation and destruction[8] to be of enormous help for understanding both the problems and the resources of my own Reformed Protestant tradition. I propose to draw upon their work as I pose a series of questions in an attempt to find ways to make the material order real for Christians. These questions include: Is divine creativity exclusively good, or does it inherently possess a possibility for the tragic? In other words, is divine creativity itself naturally, morally, and spiritually ambiguous? If divine creativity possesses a capacity for the tragic, does redemption presuppose not only sin, but also tragedy? If redemption presupposes tragedy, what does this mean for a human future? I shall raise these questions rather than answer them, though I hope to give some sense of direction beyond them.

The Realization of *Śūnyatā*

Śūnyatā, commonly translated into English as *emptiness* constitutes, qualifies, and interrelates all existence.[9] Buddhists devote considerable, disciplined practice to the realization, that is, the making real, of emptiness in their own lives. As an outsider to these practices, I shall discuss *śūnyatā* analytically and note early on that such analytical discussions, while important, seriously impoverish the meanings of the concept from the perspective of a practitioner. This limitation notwithstanding, analysis remains beneficial for purposes of rethinking the meaning of creation and redemption in the context of Christian faith.

Śūnyatā has no positive existence. Even to take the concept as the negation of space is to reify it and thereby to distort it. On the contrary *śūnyatā* might be better understood as a process or function, an emptying, that qualifies, indeed constitutes, all space-time as characterized by continual change. To realize *śūnyatā* is to realize the interdependence or interconnectedness of whatever is – past, present, and future. The realization of *śūnyatā*, rather than entailing the negation of things, heightens the awareness of what is, particularly the radically open quality of whatever is, as it is in all its interrelations and in its constant flux.

Śūnyatā, existentially realized in the context of Buddhist practice, dramatizes to the adherent that her ego has no independent existence. Realization destabilizes the ego in ways that release the adherent from bondage to the self as the central driving force for existence. Ideally speaking, *śūnyatā*, recognized as a quality of all life including one's own, alters his orientation to self and to others by freeing him from the needs either to defend or to attack, both of which presuppose an independent and oppositional existence of self and other. Realization itself is an ongoing process of seeking enlightenment or wisdom, grounded in meditation and the cultivation of compassion. Realization is thus an act of valuing.

Because of radical differences in the relationship between ontology and epistemology in Buddhist and Christian contexts, the realization of *śūnyatā* does not transplant easily from one context to the other, nor is it necessarily desirable to transplant. The most notable features of the realization of *śūnyatā* for this discussion cluster around function rather than practice. The realization of *śūnyatā* serves ultimately to derail a human craving for absoluteness. As Streng notes, '... the expression of "emptiness" is *not* the manifestation of Absolute Reality, the revelation of the Divine, but the means of dissipating the desire for such an Absolute' (102). Dissipation of the desire for an absolute reality opens the adherent to life without certainty, without closure, and without terror in the face of a radically unknowable future.

The closest functional parallel in monotheistic symbolism is God realized in a believer's life and practice as *totaliter aliter*, Void, or Holy Nothing,[10] though there are important differences. For example, Christians have serious difficulty not reifying the otherness of God by positing *it* as absolute. In addition, the non-personal quality of *śūnyatā* stands in contrast to the personhood of God (otherness notwithstanding), and the immersion of *śūnyatā* within reality as a quality upholding and involved in other aspects of reality likewise contrasts with many traditional conceptions of God's reality as independent of the reality God qualifies. In this latter respect *śūnyatā*, understood as itself empty of all meaning, more closely resembles substance as conceived by Spinoza, though note that he identified substance both with God and with nature.[11]

I suggest that the most serious obstacle to realizing the material order for Christians is the craving for an absolute reality, one that is metaphorically and theologically temporized in terms of beginnings and ends. I shall shortly try to make a theological case for rethinking creativity in ways that parallel the realization of *śūnyatā*, as modified by my understanding of Scarry's work on making. My aim will be to find ways, that are at once theological and practical, to destabilize Christian craving for an absolute reality. Stated more positively, I seek theological concepts and images that make the material order real in Christian discourse for those who practice Christian faith.

The Making of Making

Elaine Scarry argues that the artifacts of human making reveal the processes of making themselves. By analyzing artifacts she traces human making as processes of projecting sensation through imagination onto material reality.[12] Pain plays a central role, for, according to Scarry, an act of creation is largely a process of seeking relief from pain by externalizing the body into artifacts, for example, chairs and beds to relieve aching muscles or coats to shield the body from the pain of cold. In short, the process of making artifacts makes the world itself, its culture, its social institutions including religious institutions, its economic relations, and by implication the so-called natural order itself. We make things and thereby modify and extend material existence, including our bodies, out of our very bodies themselves, projected through imagination.

Scarry makes several points relevant to a theological critique and rethinking of creation and redemption in light of ecological devastation. These points have to do with the relation of destruction to creation and the reciprocity between made things and maker.

Through her analysis of the discourses of torture and war, she argues that the processes of destruction mimic those of creation and repair in that both are ways of making a world that depend upon symbolic expression as substantiated by the human body. The relationship between the maker's body and imagination and its relation to the bodies of others distinguishes the two processes from one another. In the case of destruction the maker seeks to establish a fiction of power by inflicting pain upon the bodies of others, activity that requires suspension of the ability to imagine the pain of another as if it were her own. A tool, for example, a hammer, becomes a weapon to inflict pain rather than a means to relieve it. The subject inflicting pain thus distantiates from his own sentience and extends his imagination through the bodies of others to establish his power.

This process is hardly confined to war and to the torture of human beings. Other noteworthy examples include wife and child battering, the farming, processing, and eating of animal flesh, and the annihilation of species that results from building a dam to generate electricity. In any case, for Scarry human destruction lies in the inability to imagine the pain of another as if it were one's own, in short, in a lack of compassion. Making is thus a morally ambiguous process and moral failure is at bottom a failure of imagination.[13]

Scarry's position depends heavily upon her analysis of the relation between maker and made thing. Like Feuerbach and Marx before her, she inverts the Christian conception of the *imago dei*. We make our deities in our own very human image rather than the reverse; thus, our deities, like our cultures, are human artifacts. Her interpretation of Hebrew and Christian Bible leads her to conclude that the relations between the human figures and their god that characterize biblical narrative depicts the making of making itself. This relation transmutes over the course of history into a relation between capital and the means of production as Scarry turns from biblical interpretation to an analysis of *Das Kapital*. Just as we have made God in our own image and attributed more reality, and thus more value, to God than to ourselves; so, we have created capital as the central symbol generating an allegedly value-neutral system that is in fact more real and more valued than the workers, the bosses, and the shareholders who participate and certainly more real and more valued than the unemployed and the natural order which are its victims.

In short, our artifacts stand in reciprocal relation to us, redounding upon us and indeed remaking us. Just as chairs reinforce certain kinds of posture and the ways we produce food promote or prevent certain kinds of nutrition and disease; so, our human-made theological and economic systems generate certain kinds of values and produce certain kinds of people necessary to sustain and reproduce these cultural systems. Scarry notes that our artifacts reciprocate disproportionately in relation to their initial creation. In other words, what we make makes us in return in ways we could not have initially intended, anticipated, or fully controlled.

Christian Teaching on Creation and Redemption

Reformed Protestants share with other Christians the teaching that God made the world *ex nihilo* – out of nothing – save the love of God itself. Theological speculation has varied regarding God's end in making the universe. In the eighteenth century Reformed Protestant theologian Jonathan Edwards argued that God created the world for God's own glory, a glory that included from the start the redemption of some human beings and the damnation of others as new creation. God, being omniscient, foreknew the human fall into sin and the bondage of the human will to sin – a bondage that extended to the non-human creature, who likewise awaited release through human redemption. God thus provided for the redemption of some human, as well as non-human, creatures through the incarnation, crucifixion, and bodily resurrection of Jesus the Christ, God's own self. For Edwards, a visionary, mystic, and philosophical idealist, the material order, this world, would end after the millennial rule of Christ, at which time God would transpose the saints to a new creation, where they would spend eternity as incarnations of the Holy Spirit glorifying God.[14]

Edwards's theology differed from that of his forefather John Calvin whose epistemology was that of Medieval realism and who was somewhat less given to mysticism and to apocalypticism. Calvin would have hedged on the extent to which the human fall into sin and subsequent redemption implicated the rest of the creation, and he would have eschewed any speculation of an eschatological nature. Nevertheless, Calvin would have agreed in most other essentials. Having created the world from nothing, God provides for the creation in general and redeems the elect in particular, damning the rest to hell. God's purpose, insofar as humans can know it, by the light of the Spirit and the thread of the Word, is that God created the world for God's sovereignty, if not explicitly God's glory.[15]

Reformed Protestantism still lives with this theological legacy of creation and redemption as double predestination. It furthermore lives a divided life. Whereas many Reformed Protestants do not take literally either these teachings or the Bible they seek to interpret, many fundamentalists, far less cautious than Calvin and less elegant than Edwards, argue on the basis of such teachings for the use of nuclear arms, the deregulation of environmental controls on industry and agriculture, and the gutting of the Environmental Protection Agency. The divine drama of creation and redemption having been set in motion and its conclusion already being known mitigate the need for ecological reform for those convinced of their own election to eternal salvation.[16] By contrast, Reformed Protestants who take the threat of ecological doom more seriously live caught between a scientific world view that can predict pending devastation but cannot account for valuing the earth, on the one hand, and, on the other hand, theological teachings that reflect ambivalence toward the material order by continually pointing beyond it, even when they affirm it.

These latter Christians, among whom I count myself, confront at least two major theological problems: how we imagine time and space in relation to each other and how we construe natural, moral, and spiritual ambiguity. A denial of change lies at the bottom of our difficulties imagining time-space as a continuum. Furthermore, we deny change in an effort to escape its inherent ambiguity, especially its more tragic aspects and their irreversibility. We crave instead an absolute reality rather than the partial, relative, ever changing one within which we find ourselves and of which we are made.

The Denial of Change

Simply as an experiment in imagination, think about how we in the West conceive the material order. First of all, we think we can think of it as a whole, all at one time; this is partly what we mean by 'world,' 'nature,' and 'universe.' This image is one of a comprehensive photograph that captures simultaneously everything that is. But what about everything that was? Or will be? Or all the change that is going on right now? Not only is the photograph specious, but we cannot adequately think 'whole' simply because time itself, as one of its constituents, qualifies the very act of trying to imagine 'whole.' Time is in us and we are in the whole we presume to represent as if we were over against it. All such representations leave out time. We have only some isolated fragment of space as a synecdoche for the time-space continuum. Unfortunately we fail to recognize we are using a part (a fragment of space) for the whole; instead we mistake the part for the whole. Thus we reify space.

By abstracting space from time, and therefore from change, we reify 'world,' 'nature,' and 'universe.' We deny change and its effects. The material order in the long run resists such reification, however. Memory, a look in the mirror, an aching joint, or the birth of one's own child assert the irrefutability of change upon us. So we project a future free of change. The same process of abstracting space from time to get a sense of the material order, if idealized according to one's sense of goodness, can as easily produce another world, different from this one, in that it is not subject either to material or moral and spiritual corruption. Thus we imagine heaven as a space not subject to time.

140

When we do introduce time into a theological conception of the drama of creation and redemption, we likely strip time itself of change and reduce the drama to a linear allegory. Thus, eternal life, instead of meaning 'not subject to time' becomes a place that lasts for all time that will never change, a space placed at the end of time insofar as time involves change. God's creativity and knowledge take place in installments of 'before,' 'during,' and 'after' that produce silly doctrines of predestination out of misguided efforts to preserve God's trustworthiness, while accounting for human suffering and evil. In short, Christian ways of thinking about God, God's rule on earth, the earth itself, and the trustworthiness of human-divine relations often reflect human attempts to circumvent the radical nature of change, attempts that result in absolutizing what is relative.

This low tolerance for change is hardly unique to Reformed Protestants or even to Westerners. On the contrary, it seems to have figured heavily in the existential situation which the Buddha himself sought to address when he preached Enlightenment. His insistence on the insubstantiality of self and world and the irrelevance of God to release from suffering represent strategies for overcoming human attempts to assuage a craving for an absolute reality by reifying and idealizing the reality in which they find themselves. As I have already noted, this dissipation of craving an absolute reaches its fullest expression in the realization of *śūnyatā*.

I have also noted that one can find functional equivalents in Christian doctrine and theology. One that I find particularly promising because of its ongoing implication of God in the material order is Edwards's view of divine providence as continual creation *ex nihilo*. In a notebook he kept, titled 'Things to Be Considered and Written fully about,' he wrote:

> Since body is nothing but the infinite resistance in some part of space caused by the exercise of divine power, it follows that as great and wonderful power is every moment exerted to the upholding of the world as to the creating of it – the first creation being only the first exertion of this power to cause such resistance; preservation, only the continuation or the repetition of this power every moment to cause this resistance. So that the universe is created out of nothing every moment and if it were not for our imaginations, which hinder us, we might see that wonderful work performed continually which was seen by the morning stars when they sang together.[17]

In this short passage, Edwards depicts divine creativity as the continual exertion of power to cause resistance and concurrently defines body or material object as the resistance caused. By conflating the initial creation from nothing with preservation or providence, Edwards makes the material order come alive as an unceasing interaction of power and resistance – resistance to 'nothing' in all its senses of nothingness, non-being, and annihilation. The quality of resistance to nothing makes the material order immediately real. To realize the resistance to nothing inherent in all change as it constitutes and pervades all existence is in short to realize the continual creation of something rather than nothing at all.

The realization of continual creation *ex nihilo* as the realization of the material order parallels the realization of *śūnyatā* in certain respects. To realize the resistance to nothing inherent in all change and constitutive of all existence is to realize the interconnectedness of whatever is – past, present, and future. This realization heightens the awareness of what is, particularly the radically open quality of whatever is, as it is in all its interrelations and in its constant flux. For example, it allows the Christian to reread Genesis 2:7 with new eyes: '... then the Lord God formed a human of dust from the ground and breathed into its nostrils the breath of life; and the human became a living being.'[18] We are, with every breath we draw, connected anew to all other forms of life by virtue of having been created from the dirt of the planet with whose creatures we share life, the dust of the stars themselves. The life we share depends upon the divine breath itself. Our resistance to nothing originates not in the exercise of our own individual wills, but in the exercise of a throbbing divine power fully caught up as an inbreathing in the resistances it produces. We are free from the bondage of the self and its cravings as the central driving force of our individual existences and thereby open to relations with other creatures, both human and non-human. To realize continual creation *ex nihilo* is to dissipate the desire for an absolute reality as a means of escaping the circumstances of our materiality. To live in this image of the material order is to sing with the first witnesses to creation, the morning stars themselves. But for our imaginations which hinder us....

The Denial of Ambiguity

Traditional Christian doctrine has taught that the exercise of divine power is by definition always and everywhere good. What may appear from a human perspective to be morally and spiritually ambiguous or even evil, appears so only due to the incommensurability between the divine imagination and human imagination. Any failure in progress toward this goal is attributable to human sin, or for some Christians to the power of Satan. From a more aerial point of view, namely, the divine perspective, good wins out in the end. As theologian Kathleen Sands has pointed out, this construal of goodness tolerates two different accounts of evil, namely, a monistic view that defines evil as the privation of good and a dualistic view that attributes positive existence to evil though it claims the ultimate triumph of good.[19] What this construal does not on the face of it tolerate is moral and spiritual ambiguity on the part of the Creator. In the immediacy of human suffering, both experienced and witnessed, particularly when we perceive this suffering to be unjust, there is little solace to be taken from the knowledge that good will triumph, regardless of which view of evil it entails.

Both Buddhism and Christianity share concern with the significance of human suffering. The Buddha addressed this aspect of the human condition in non-theistic ways that tended initially at least to focus on psychologically therapeutic relief. The Four Noble Truths culminating in the Eightfold Path show extraordinary insight into the role of human craving or desire in the generation of suffering; these teachings also provide astute and effective strategies to alter both desire and the behavior it produces.

Most discussion and practice in response to suffering that have taken place in a Christian context have focused upon human sin as the primary cause for suffering and injustice as the result. Christian soteriology definitely entails a psychology that addresses the individual human condition as sinner; however, because of the role of the Kingdom of God as a social reality as well as an inner spiritual one, Christian soteriology focuses upon relieving the suffering of others as concomitant with individual salvation. Furthermore, from a Reformed Protestant perspective neither individual salvation nor activism on behalf of others can be credited to human effort. Rather human ego and its self-centered exertions serve as obstacles both to individual and to social transformation. Whatever transformation occurs, occurs solely by the grace of God, for which humans may be the media or the receptacles. Both Buddhist and Christian conceptions of suffering address the condition in terms of human responsibility and transformation in ways that are profound and effective, up to a point. To my mind, however, both views inadequately address unjust suffering that cannot be fixed.

It is not my purpose to dispute the centrality of God's grace in Christian life. I suggest, however, that Christians oversimplify grace and the contexts it characterizes. By and large they refuse to admit to ambiguity within what Edwards saw as divine exertions of power causing pockets of resistance to nothingness, or the continual creation *ex nihilo* of the material order in which we find ourselves and of which we are part and parcel.

This ambiguity is natural in that it manifests itself in natural events of great destruction from a human perspective, for example, hurricanes, earthquakes, tornadoes, floods, and the eruptions of volcanoes. It is natural insofar as ecological harmony depends on nature 'red in tooth and claw.' That is to say, within species and up and down the food chain, future life depends for its survival on present and past violence and death.

This ambiguity is likewise moral and spiritual. The best way I know to capture the moral and spiritual aspects of the ambiguity of divine creativity is to define them in terms of loss – loss for which nothing can compensate, for which responsibility is at best complex and at worst obscure, and from which there can be no return to innocence. The kind of loss about which I speak is loss that, though it may be survived or even ultimately transfigured, can never be undone – for example, the killing fields of Cambodia and the Jewish Holocaust under Nazi Germany, in both cases as seen from the perspective of the victims. From the perspective of the victims such losses are irrefutably tragic.[20] If there were literally a heaven and every human on earth were redeemed and transported there, it would not undo such losses. Only a complete, permanent, and cosmic failure of memory and therefore loss of human history and divine omniscience could begin to eradicate such losses. Unfortunately, many Christians and other students whom I teach tend to deny the irreversibility of such losses, even when they suffer them. I see this denial as symptomatic of a dangerous refusal to admit that history may not only end, but end badly for the human species, particularly if we continue on our present course.

As Scarry indicates biblical narrative can be read as a history of making, both human and divine; furthermore, making itself, though inherently laden with value, is ambiguous. Making can be destructive or creative. If we take biblical narrative at face value, that is, as unfiltered by subsequent doctrine as possible, we may go one step beyond Scarry and claim that within making, the line between creation and destruction blurs precisely at the point of irreversible loss. So, for example in the Exodus story, God hardens Pharaoh's heart, which in turn results in God's destroying all the first-born of Egypt, 'both man and beast,' except those within the Israelite community (Exodus 12:12). Indeed, according to biblical tradition, the life of Jesus in human history is itself framed by such loss. So, shortly after Jesus' birth, in an ironic reversal of the Exodus story, the holy family flees to Egypt as King Herod orders the deaths of all male children under the age of two years in Bethlehem and in the surrounding area (Matthew 2:16). So, according to the gospels of Mark and Matthew, Jesus dies accusing God of having forsaken him (Mark 15:34, Matthew 27:46). And if we end the story of Jesus' life with Mark 16:8,[21] we are left like the women who went to anoint Jesus' body, standing in fear before an empty tomb – an enigmatic, empty place – an open space surrounded by the pain of loss.[22]

If we now return to Christian doctrine as an extension of the history of making, we confront the doctrine of the Incarnation, the claim that God became fully human and dwelt among us. For Christians, the Incarnation links creation to redemption. Here a disembodied God turns upon Godself and in a reversal of the process described by Scarry extends through imagination to acquire sensation. God becomes a human artifact, taking on the vicissitudes of the human condition, only to suffer the hideous and cruel death of a common criminal, leaving those who followed in fear before an empty space. What kind of redemption is this? What kind of making is this? Surely this moment is not simply an occasion for unrelieved joy!

Divine and Human Wagers[23]

The Creator who creates continually from nothing, who liberates an entire people from bondage, who dies on a cross but cannot be bound by a tomb, wagers human life including God's own human life in an effort to create justice on earth – a justice that extends beyond the human arena to include an entire groaning creation (Romans 8:22). The costs of God's wagers are enormous, and the losses are irreversible in the sense that there is no way back to innocence, either human or divine. There is something very trustworthy about a God willing to suffer as humans suffer, both sorrow and joy. There is something very terrifying about a God willing to wipe out entire populations, whether through natural disaster or through the slaughter of innocent children.

If Scarry, with Feuerbach and Marx before her, is right that we create God in our own image, then God's making is largely a projection of our own. If Darwin is right that we are nature's children, then our making is an extension of natural generation, albeit one that we can reflect upon and modify. And if, by some great act of faith, we might wager that beyond the deities of our own making and the material order of which we are a product there lies a power causing our resistance to nothing, a power not reducible to our own imaginings, such a power is at best ambiguous, even if it be the power of love. What little God reveals to us in scripture and in nature includes God's own willingness to take great risks, willing to wager death that life might triumph. In the knowledge that God would make something out of nothing over and over again lies our hope. Nevertheless, the same God willingly suffers inconsolable loss. We as a species may be a divine venture in a covenant that fails.

We, in this time, stand, like the women before us who sought the body of Jesus, in hope and fear before an enigmatic, empty space. Can we resist annihilation of global life? Are we willing to risk the full implications of our sentience? Dare we imagine the pain of other creatures both human and non-human and work toward its relief and repair? And can we mourn the tragedy of what we have wasted? Will we imagine from our own pain and pleasure and work toward a future for generations on earth that we will not live to see? If God can wager on us, how can we afford not to wager on the future?

Notes

1 For a relatively optimistic account see, Al Gore, *Earth in the Balance: Ecology and the Human Spirit* (New York: Penguin Books, 1993).
2 For recent scholarship representing Jewish, Christian, and Muslim traditions, see respectively Eric Katz, 'Judaism and the Ecological Crisis,' Jay McDaniel, 'The Garden of Eden, the Fall, and the Life of Christ,' and Roger E. Timm, 'The Ecological Fallout of Islamic Creation Theology,' in *Worldviews and Ecology: Religion, Philosophy, and the Environment*, eds. Mary Evelyn Tucker and John A. Grim (Maryknoll: Orbis Books, 1994), 55–95.
3 See, for example, Brian Brown, 'Toward a Buddhist Ecological Cosmology,' in *Worldviews and Ecology*, ibid., 128–137.
4 See McDaniel. *op. cit.* and *With Roots and Wings: Christianity in an Age of Ecology and Dialogue* (Maryknoll: Orbis Books, 1995).
5 For one notable exception see Gordon D. Kaufman, *Theology in a Nuclear Age*, (Manchester: Manchester University Press, 1985).
6 Kathleen Sands, *Escape from Paradise* (Minneapolis: Fortress Press, 1994).
7 Frederick J. Streng, *Emptiness, a Study in Religious Meaning* (Nashville: Abingdon Press, 1967).

8 Elaine Scarry, *The Body in Pain: The Making and Unmaking of the World* (New York: Oxford, 1985).

9 There are many discussions of *śūnyatā* available to novices, among whom I count myself. What follows is my own interpretation, dependent most of all on Frederick J. Streng's *Emptiness, a Study in Religious Meaning, op. cit.* Other valuable resources include: William Theodore de Bary, *The Buddhist Tradition in India, China, and Japan* (New York: Random House, 1972); John B. Cobb, 'Buddhist Emptiness and the Christian God,' *Journal of the American Academy of Religion* 45/1:1997; Edward Conze, *Buddhism: Its Essence and Development* (New York: Harper & Row, 1975, Ösel Tendzin, *Buddha in the Palm of Your Hand* (Boston: Shambala, 1982).

10 For God as *totaliter aliter* see Christian theologian Karl Barth, *The Epistle to the Romans*, trans. Edwyn C. Hoskyns (Oxford: Oxford University Press, 1968). For God as Void see respectively philosopher Alfred North Whitehead, *Religion in the Making* (New York: World Publishing, 1960) and Christian theologian H. Richard Niebuhr, 'Faith in Gods and in God,' in *Radical Monotheism and Western Culture* (New York: Harper & Row, 1960), 114–126. For God as Holy Nothing see Jewish theologian Richard Rubenstein, 'Person and Myth in the Judaeo-Christian Encounter,' in *After Auschwitz: Radical Theology and Contemporary Judaism* (Indianapolis: Bobbs-Merrill, 1966), 61–81.

11 Benedict de Spinoza, *Ethics and On the Improvement of the Understanding*, ed. with intro. James Gutmann (New York: Hafner Publishing Company, 1966).

12 What follows is a brief summary of *The Body in Pain: The Making and Unmaking of the World, op. cit.* Scarry's argument is far more nuanced than I can possibly render in the space allotted here.

13 Though Scarry develops criteria to help distinguish making as destructive from making as creative, she leaves the questions of whether and how making can be simultaneously both creative and destructive unanswered. Rather, she argues that while the processes of making themselves can devolve quickly into destruction, making itself, rather than neutral in value, is inherently good. I agree that we make the world most often from the pain and sometimes from the pleasure of our bodies as projected through imagination. I further agree that the making of an artifact is a value-laden act. However, Scarry's view of making as inherently good, from which destruction devolves, parallels an Augustinian world view of evil as a privation of good and of sin as a turning away from the good, a point with which I strongly disagree.

14 *Dissertation concerning the End for which God Created the World*, vol. 2, *The Works of President Edwards*, 4 vols., Worcester Edition (reprint) (New York: Leavitt, 1844); see also Paula M. Cooey, *Jonathan Edwards on Nature and Destiny: A Systemic Analysis*, vol. 16, *Studies in American Religion* (Lewiston: Edwin Mellen Press, 1985).

15 Jean Calvin, *Calvin: Institutes of the Christian Religion*, 2 vols., ed. John T. McNeill, trans. Ford Lewis Battles (Philadelphia: Westminster, 1975) especially 'Book One: The Knowledge of God the Creator,' 33–237.

16 See, for example, Hal Lindsey with C. C. Carlson, *The Late Great Planet Earth* (Grand Rapids: Zondervan, 1970).

17 Jonathan Edwards, *Selected Writings of Jonathan Edwards*, ed. Harold P. Simonson. (New York: Frederick Ungar Publishing, 1970), 241–242.

18 Except for this quotation which reflects my own theological interpretation and my use of inclusive language, all scriptural references come from the *New Oxford Annotated Bible with the Apocryphal/Deuterocanonical Books*, eds. Bruce M. Metzger and Ronald E. Murray (New York: Oxford University Press, 1991).

19 *Op. cit.*, 17–36.

20 Theologian Wendy Farley notes that much of Christian talk about sin focuses upon responsibility from the perspective of the perpetrator, whereas focus on tragedy shifts the perspective to that of the victim; formal response to papers presented by Marjorie Suchockie and Kathleen Sands under the general title, 'Contemporary Interpretations of Evil and Sin: The Work of Marjorie Suchockie and Kathleen Sands, at the 1995 AAR meeting, Theology and Religious Reflection Section, Philadelphia: November 20, 1995.

21 Most New Testament scholars argue that verses 9 through 20 which narrate Jesus' post-resurrection appearances could not have been part of the original text. See also Matthew 28:1–8.

22 For some of the implications of the empty tomb as empty space see Milner S. Ball, *The Word and the Law* (Chicago: University of Chicago press, 1993), 124–128.

23 Ball, *ibid.*, 131, and Blaise Pascal, *Pensées and Other Writings*, trans. Honor Levi (New York: Oxford University Press, 1995), 152–158.

CHAPTER TWELVE

Creation, Redemption, and the Realization of the Material Order: A Buddhist Response

Alan Sponberg

In the chapter on 'Self, Nature and Ecology in Buddhism' I sought to articulate a comprehensive Buddhist perspective on the crisis of environmental degradation, a perspective informed primarily by my experience as a historian of the various traditions of Asian Buddhism and by my interests in Western philosophy and environmental ethics. In this response I shall I shall seek to bring to bear also my experience as a practicing Buddhist, as a Buddhist ordained in the Western Buddhist Order founded by Sangharakshita in 1968.[1]

As a preface to my response I would like first to note a feature of Buddhist-Christian dialogue that is easily overlooked, the fact that the two traditions bring quite different needs and objectives to the discussion, which means that the conversation is characterized by a fundamental asymmetry. Certainly there are a number of doctrinal differences that distinguish these two major religious traditions, but this is not what I have in mind. Similarly, the motivation that individual practitioners bring to inter-faith dialogue will differ, and even among those participating as Buddhists, there may be quite different personal needs and motivations. But again, this is not what I mean by a fundamental asymmetry. Over-riding these obvious differences I see a more basic dissimilarity characterizing the two sides of the dialogue, a dissimilarity arising from the fundamentally different relationship each of the two traditions has to modernity. We live, whether in Asia or in the West, in an increasingly modern world, which is to say in a world increasingly influenced by a complex set of social forces and institutions that are largely Western in origin. As religions with pre-modern origins, both Buddhism and Christianity

149

are struggling to come to terms with the challenge of modernity, yet the nature of that struggle is significantly different in each of the two cases.

Christianity is well embedded in the cultural context of modernity. Even when its values are challenged by modern notions of secularism and materialism, it nonetheless retains its preeminent position as the spiritual core of that broader Western tradition. The challenge faced by contemporary Christianity is thus to adapt the narrower perspective of its traditional theology and worldview to fit a more complex and multi-cultural world culture in order thereby to secure its position as the spiritual dimension of modernism. The task faced by contemporary Buddhists is quite different however – whether they be Asian or Western Buddhists. Even as Christianity makes significant in-roads into non-Western cultures, in large part precisely because of its association with modernism, Buddhism is struggling to retain its own basic identity, and it faces a dual threat. If it clings to its non-Western origins and fails to address the challenge of modernity it will inevitable become increasingly anachronistic, a cultural artifact of little but antiquarian interest in a world increasingly influenced if not dominated by modern ideas and institutions of largely Judeo-Christian and Greek origin. But this is not the only danger. To what ever degree Buddhism seeks, alternatively, to address the challenge of modernity by adapting itself to Western Culture, it runs the risk of becoming prematurely appropriated into the substrate of modernity before it succeeds in sufficiently establishing its own distinctive, non-Western assumptions and perspectives. Ironically it is the very fascination with Buddhist exoticness so evident in our own pop culture that constitutes the greatest danger to the integrity of this tradition in the modern world. To see the difficulty here, one has only to think of *Samsara*, the French perfume or of *Nirvana,* the grunge band – or even of Catholic nuns practicing *zazen* as a means of becoming more receptive to the word of God.

Hence the asymmetry: If Christian participants in Buddhist-Christian dialogue typically seek inspiration and stimulation from Buddhism in their effort to strengthen their well established, if vulnerable position within the tide of modernism, Buddhists in contrast benefit most, in my view, when the conversation seeks to clarify the differences between the two traditions, thereby helping Buddhism resist the tendency to become appropriated into a 'universalistic and inclusive religion' of modernism, one that will inevitably be constructed, consciously or not, on largely Western and

Christian assumptions. I should make clear that I mean this not as a call for Buddhist exclusivism, much less religious intolerance. I seek only to point out that the first task of contemporary Buddhists is to successfully secure the spiritual and philosophical integrity of their non-Western tradition within a world culture that is increasingly dominated by a basically Western and Christian worldview. Only in this way will Buddhists of the future have something to contribute to the inter-faith dialogue we initiate today. Otherwise the basic asymmetry of the relationship, however benign in appearance and intention, creates a situation reminiscent of the old South Asian story of the boa constrictor sliding up to the plump little piglet and whispering, 'Come, my dear, for the greater good, let us amalgamate.'

Given the nature of this basic asymmetry, how then might a Buddhist proceed in dialogue with Christianity? In the chapter accompanying this response I suggested that the first and most crucial task is to rigorously question any assumption of common ground between the two traditions, *especially* if the assumption seems so obvious that it is not even explicitly addressed. Let us pursue this approach by considering now a possible Buddhist response to two excellent questions raised by Paula Cooey in her chapter on 'Creation, Redemption, and the Realization of the Material Order.' She aptly identifies each of these two questions as fundamental to the attitude one adopts towards the natural environment, and both are useful for highlighting differences in the assumptions the two traditions bring to this discussion. One question focuses on our ability to envision the possibility of ecological disaster, and the other raises the importance of revalorizing the material realm. With respect to the first, Professor Cooey notes that the '[t]raditional Christian theological construction of good and evil simply does not easily admit the possibility that history may end badly for humans as a species, indeed may end permanently for the human species, ...' This observation underscores the fact that Christianity is as much a tradition of hope as of faith – a hope based in the Christian's faith in a loving, as well as omnipotent and omniscient God. It is a hope based, moreover, on the central doctrine of the covenant, God's promise of salvation for those who are righteous in the eyes of the Lord. The danger here is a naive optimism that assumes, indeed insists, that all will turn out for the good, whether unconditionally and for all, or at least minimally for the righteous. Cooey's point might seem to overlook the more apocalyptic and eschatological strains of Christianity, but even those Christians who have understood the covenant to be conditional and who stress that God has destroyed the sinful in the past and is likely to do so again, still have the hope that they will be among the Elect, among those who will be spared the cataclysm of the final days. Either understanding of Christian hope can and arguably often does subtly undermine any effort to see environmental degradation as a problem requiring human attention and action at an unprecedented level of global cooperation.

Are traditional Buddhists more likely to acknowledge the possibility of human self-destruction? I have noted already the optimistic (or at least melioristic) notion of human nature in traditional Buddhism, and we might thus expect, even assume, a doctrine of hope similar to what we find in Christianity. There are significant differences between Buddhism and Christianity in this respect however. And contemporary Buddhists, both Asian and Western, must be especially careful here not to unconsciously read Western cultural assumptions back on to Buddhism. While traditional Buddhism is quite hopeful in asserting that all beings, not *just* human beings, share the potential for liberation, this hope is quite conditional in that in arises not through the redemptive agency of a savior, but only through the personal practice of the individual being. Certainly the inspirational, even charismatic role of Shakyamuni Buddha, and of all the other archetypal Buddhas and bodhisattvas prominent in later Buddhism, is not to be minimized, but it is not the messianic role of a savior figure, rather the intermediary role of the teacher or the guide – of the physician who can prescribe the proper medicine and even provide it, but who cannot take it on behalf of the patient.[2] The locus of the hope or optimism in the Buddhist tradition thus remains always the individual being who must progress to liberation by actively following the practice of the Dharma. Simple belief, however sincere, is not soteriologically sufficient and is as likely to be seen as a spiritual liability as an asset.[3]

The significance of this point to Paula Cooey's first question becomes more clear when we consider the perspective of Buddhist cosmology. Birth as a human being has always been seen as spiritually advantageous, yet Buddhism has never seen the human species as particularly privileged, nor has it ever adopted a geocentric notion of the cosmos. Quite the contrary, the prospect that this particular world-system might suffer catastrophic decline, even destruction, is quite plausible. Indeed many traditional Buddhists may even see it as likely, given the fundamentally unsatisfactory nature of samsaric existence. The danger here is not that Buddhists are doctrinally incapable of imagining the degradation or even the destruction of this world, but rather that we might too readily accept the prospect of a 'local' decline – destruction of this particular environment – even while assuming the continuation of samsaric life in other, parallel world-systems. Similarly the destruction of the human species would indeed constitute a drastic degree of 'local' decline, but it would not in itself be unthinkable, since sentient existence and progress towards enlightenment is quite capable of proceeding through the medium of other life-forms.

Expressing a view encountered more often among Western critics of Buddhism, Cooey suggests that 'Buddhists often seek liberation from suffering by withdrawing from the world.' Perhaps some Buddhists have expressed a lack of concern about environmental degradation, but I doubt that it arises from such a sentiment. It is more likely to stem from a Buddhist misunderstanding of Buddhist cosmological and soteriological assumptions than from a devalorization of 'the material' in favor of 'the spiritual' of a sort that would parallel the problem Cooey and other environmentally sensitive theologians see in Christianity.[4] The Theravada tradition in Southeast Asia has shown some tendency towards asserting a dichotomy between nirvana and samsara in ontologically dualistic terms. Yet I question whether this betrays the same 'devaluation of the material realm' that Cooey and others have seen at the heart of Christian ambivalence towards environmental degradation. This is a crucial point for Buddhists to resolve, because if I am correct the strategies proposed by ecologically sensitive Christians for 'fixing' their own tradition may not work, indeed may not even be appropriate for those seeking to work on the same issues from within a Buddhist context.

This problem of an assumed commensurability between Buddhism and Christianity becomes more evident if we turn to the Mahayana tradition within Buddhism which explicitly rejects any ultimately dualist conception of samsara vs. nirvana, even as it recognizes a hierarchical continuum of matter, form, and spirit (or consciousness). In this context, active disregard for the natural environment is not, in the Buddhist analysis, a problem of devaluing the material so much as a failing to act sufficiently on the program of ethical and spiritual transformation that will take us, as Buddhists, beyond the constraints of present human tendencies towards greed, hatred and delusion. Hence the importance of considering Cooey's second question in revealing interesting differences between the two traditions.

Mahayana Buddhism is quite emphatic in rejecting any perspective that would allow, much less sanction, environmental degradation.

First, the possibility of any dualism that disregards 'the material realm' in favor of some ontologically distinct and separate 'spiritual realm' is explicitly rejected in the assertion that the realm of nirvana is none other than the realm of samsara. Enlightenment is located not *beyond* this immediate reality, but fully within it. Similarly any tendency towards an individual enlightenment arising in disregard of others is explicitly rejected as well. The individual becomes enlightened only through gaining insight into the fundamental interrelatedness of all aspects of existence. And that insight, truly realized, can express itself only as compassionate activity on behalf of all beings. The harmful and destructive effect of remaining ignorant of this insight – an ignorance manifesting as greed, hatred, and delusion – is neither reified nor denied, nor does it have to be reconciled with the existence of an ostensibly benevolent God. This ignorance is simply seen to be the nature of existence until wisdom manifests itself as compassionate activity.

In a Buddhist analysis, our current disregard for the environment arises thus not from de-valuing the material, but rather more from a lack of insight into our potential to change – to radically transform – how we relate to each other and to the environment. Rather than revalorizing Nature as a reified entity distinct from (and now *more* privileged than) humanity, the solution must lie in a radical revalorization of our very sense of 'self,' in a sense of self that relocates our 'nature' not in our distinctive 'humanity' but rather in our fundamental inter-connectedness with the rest of existence. This is the insight that has traditionally constituted Buddhist wisdom, especially in its Mahayana formulation. It is an insight into inter-relatedness, moreover, that can ultimately manifest itself only as active compassion, as the individual conscious choice to act in a way that supports the whole web of existence. This is the message of Shakyamuni's mission – of both his quest for insight into the nature of existence and the subsequent forty-five years of compassionate activity that followed from his realization.

Notes

1 For a comprehensive overview of the Buddhism of Sangharakshita and the international Buddhist movement he has founded, see in particular two books by Dharmachari Subhuti (Alex Kennedy): *Sangharakshita: a New Voice in the Buddhist Tradition* (Birmingham: Windhorse Pub., 1994) and *Buddhism for Today: a Portrait of a New Buddhist Movement* (Glasgow: Windhorse Pub., 1988).

2 This is one key point made in the well-know parable of the 'Good Physician' in the *Lotus Sutra* of Mahayana Buddhism; see *Scripture of the Lotus Blossom of the Fine Dharma*, trans. by Leon Hurvitz (New York: Columbia UP, 1976), 240–241.

3 Buddhist-Christian dialogue often focuses on the doctrine of faith (*shin*) in Japanese schools of Pure Land Buddhism, especially those deriving from Shinran. Setting aside the question of whether this late and seemingly exclusive focus on the soteriology of *shin* practice is representative of Buddhism as a whole, we must at least recognize the significantly different cosmological context of this Buddhist notion of faith. In the various forms of Pure Land practice, reliance on Amitabha Buddha gains the practitioner not the final goal, but rather rebirth in Sukhavati, a Pure Land in which the standard and traditional forms of Buddhism cultivation (ethics, meditation, and wisdom) are more readily completed than under the less advantageous circumstances of the Sukhavati world in which we live.

4 Western Buddhists may well manifest both problems to the extent that they have, however unconsciously, taken on the mistakes of both traditions. But this is all the more reason for Buddhists in the West to clarify the various sources of our own environmental insensitivity, even as we strive to articulate a solution to those problems based in our understanding of the Buddha-dharma. Just because some of us in the West have become Buddhists does not mean that we are thereby relieved of the same mistaken insensitivity endemic to the rest of the culture in which we were raised. But it does mean that we should undertake to address that insensitivity in ways that are more congruent with Buddhist rather than with Christian assumptions about the ultimate nature of reality.

PART FOUR

Social and Political Issues of Liberation

CHAPTER THIRTEEN

Buddhism and Social Engagement

Sallie B. King

Introduction

Mutual influence between spiritual social activists is already well under way. Mahatma Gandhi, the great pioneer of an East-West synthesis of spiritual social activism, has inspired and influenced almost everyone who has entered this arena since his time.[1] Surveying the mutual influence on spiritual social activism between Buddhism and Christianity, we may note that a Christian organization, the Fellowship of Reconciliation, was heavily involved in supporting the Buddhist anti-war movement during the war in Vietnam. Western influence has come into Asian Buddhist countries through such leaders as Dr. Bhimrao Ambedkar, Thich Nhat Hanh, Sulak Sivaraksa, and Aung San Suu Kyi, all of whom have spent considerable time in the West and received some of their education here. Even leaders such as the Dalai Lama and Daisaku Ikeda, who did not spend any of their formative years in the West, are in almost constant dialogue with Western leaders, both religious and secular. Thich Nhat Hanh convinced Martin Luther King, Jr. to speak out for the first time against the war in Vietnam. Martin Luther King returned the favor by nominating Thich Nhat Hanh for the Nobel Peace Prize. The Quaker activist organization, the American Friends Service Committee, recently nominated Sulak Sivaraksa for the same prize. Countless Christian (and semi-Christian Western) social activists read books by the Dalai Lama and Thich Nhat Hanh, and many attend workshops led by the latter. Thich Nhat Hanh has had profound, mutually influential, one-on-one exchanges with Daniel Berrigan and Thomas

159

Merton.[2] And, in probably the most complex case of mutual influence, the Friends of the Western Buddhist Order today heavily supports ex-untouchable Ambedkarite groups in India.

In my use of the term 'spiritual social activist,' I do not include everyone who engages in social and political affairs on the basis of a religious motivation. I specifically do not include in the term those who use their adherence to a religion as justification for hatred, aggression or violence. Such persons are to be found in all major religions; Buddhism is not immune. In the case of Buddhism, I agree with those who say that such persons, though they speak of loyalty to Buddhism, violate the spirit and the letter of the teachings of the Buddha and therefore represent secularism, not Buddhism.[3]

I shall briefly survey those whom I include among Buddhist social activists in the modern world, the Engaged Buddhists: In India, Dr. B. Ambedkar led millions of ex-untouchables in conversion to Buddhism for reasons of social equality and justice; his followers continue to strive for the same. In Sri Lanka, Dr. Ariyaratne founded the Sarvodaya Sramadana movement, in which countless monks and laypersons have participated, in order to 'develop' impoverished Sri Lankan villages on the basis of a Buddhist model that cherishes spiritual, psychological, moral, and cultural development along with economic development and protection of the environment. In Tibet, the Dalai Lama and uncountable monks, nuns and laypersons have participated in the Tibetan Liberation Movement, and have been supported by many Western Buddhists. The Dalai Lama has emerged as one of the best known, most revered and respected leaders internationally among Buddhist social activists. In Burma, Aung San Suu Kyi has led thousands of monks and laypersons in a struggle to establish a humane and democratic form of government there. Both the Dalai Lama and Aung San Suu Kyi have been awarded the Nobel Peace Prize. In Thailand, Sulak Sivaraksa, a self-proclaimed 'gadfly', attempts to make the Thai government accountable to humanistic and democratic norms and stimulates and organizes numerous grassroots action groups to respond to Thailand's cultural, ecological and political crises. The late Thai monk Buddhadāsa was a great leader with a broad vision applying Buddhist teachings to modern social and spiritual issues in a creative and compelling way. There are also in Thailand many individual monks working independently to protect the environment and to help villagers trapped by poverty and ignorance between traditional life and modernity. In Cambodia, on the heels of its Holocaust, the monk Maha Ghosananda emerged as a leader with words and actions contributing to healing the vast wounds suffered by the Cambodian people. In Vietnam during the war, the Buddhist Struggle Movement led a highly popular anti-war effort with broad-based support and participation. Since the war, Thich Nhat Hanh, one of the ideological leaders of the anti-war effort, has emerged as an international leader of spiritual social activists. In Korea, Won Buddhism applies Buddhist teachings to both the spiritual and social needs of its adherents, as do members of the Fo Kuang Shan in Taiwan and the Nichirenite movements Risshō Kōseikai and Soka Gakkai in Japan. Soka Gakkai has the unique distinction among Buddhist social activists of producing an actual political party, the Kōmeitō, which engages in partisan politics. Also in Japan and throughout the world, the Nipponzan Myohoji advocates for world peace through its Peace Pagodas, marches and vigils. Throughout Asia and the West, Buddhist nuns and quasi-nuns have organized and are pressing, gently, for improvement in their education, training, living conditions, and opportunities. Finally, in the West, numerous teachers, individuals and grassroot groups are inspired by their Buddhist values to engage in every kind of progressive social activism imaginable: work on behalf of the environment, work with those who have AIDS, work with the homeless, work on behalf of animals, work with Buddhist refugee groups and in support of Buddhist causes in Asia, and all kinds of creative attempts to apply Buddhism to their work as teachers, parents, psychologists, artists, social workers, etc.

All of the above I conceive as constituting the body of Buddhist social activists. The list is by no means complete; this is merely an illustrative selection. But even within these limitations, each movement should be seen as the unique response to the particular conditions facing each people; each came into being independent of the others, though networking has since ensued. And though each is unique, certain qualities hold for them all. All are movements of principled nonviolence; some, indeed, explore the possibilities of nonviolence in new and creative ways. All understand themselves to be expressions of such core Buddhist values as benevolence, compassion and selflessness. They all point to foundational Buddhist teachings, texts, and practices of their own tradition to justify and guide their activism – such teachings as the Four Noble Truths, interdependence, and the bodhisattva ideal; such texts as the *Dhammapada*, Śāntideva's *Bodhicaryāvatāra*, and the *Lotus Sutra*; such practices as the five lay precepts, mindfulness, the four Sublime

Abodes (*Brahmavihāra*), and the exchange of self for other. All, in short, are reformist movements attempting to identify the essence of their tradition and apply it to the challenges and crises of the modern world that demand, in their view, an active Buddhist response.

Buddhist Contributions

Let me now speak of contributions made by Engaged Buddhists to the global community of spiritual social activists. I will suggest what I think would be widely acknowledged to be six peculiarly Buddhist contributions that are making a significant, positive impact upon the way spiritual social activists of whatever stripe conceive and attempt to carry out their activism. In what follows, I will attempt to articulate what I see in the words and actions of the activists listed above; among them, I am most influenced by the Dalai Lama and Thich Nhat Hanh.

1. Thich Nhat Hanh's classic *Being Peace* suggests in its title what may be the single most important Buddhist contribution to spiritual social activism in general and peace making in particular: the affirmation that one must 'be peace' in order to make peace.[4] Likewise, the Dalai Lama says, 'Everybody loves to talk about calm and peace whether in a family, national, or international context, but without *inner* peace how can we make real peace?'[5] In other words, Buddhist social activists point out that there is an extremely close link between the spiritual/psychological condition of the activist, the nature of the action in which she engages, and the quality of the outcome that will ensue. There is a world of Buddhist experience in this simple suggestion.

Some of the most influential theory of Buddhist activism was forged in the midst of the most tragic, frightening and excruciating conditions imaginable: the war in Vietnam, the invasion and occupation of Tibet. There are good reasons for this. As Thich Nhat Hanh has pointed out, in an emergency the single most important thing is that one avoid panicking and keep one's head. But how *can* one keep one's head when the bombs are falling and the dead and injured are all around one, or when the enemy is advancing and one is on the brink of losing everything? If one's gut level reaction is 'save me!' it will be impossible. If, on the other hand, one's psychological/spiritual condition is such that fear and self-protection are not one's overriding responses, then one will be in a much better position to deal effectively with the crisis. Buddhist spiritual practice, of course, is intended to make the practitioner less ego-centric. If it works, it should reduce the strength of the 'save me!' reaction.

The same point holds for non-crisis situations as well. One who has cultivated mindfulness is much more likely to be capable of seeing reality as it is, surely a basic requirement for any form of social engagement. One who has cultivated equanimity will be in a better condition to deal with discouragement and burnout, probably the most common forms of self-limitation among social activists. One who has cultivated selflessness will not only be troubled less by fear, such a person will be more capable of getting herself out of the picture and dealing with the situation at hand.

In short, the most traditional kinds of Buddhist meditation practices may have extremely practical side-effects. The general term for Buddhist practice is *bhāvanā*, 'cultivation.' One cultivates in oneself certain psycho-spiritual qualities, dynamic propensities to behave in particular ways. Although they were certainly not designed with this purpose in mind, it seems that the qualities that are cultivated by certain forms of Buddhist meditation and discipline can be appropriate and helpful for one engaged in social action.

2. Related to this point is a second Buddhist contribution, the Buddhist conception and cultivation of selflessness. This, of course, is a fundamental aspect of Buddhist thought, practice and spirituality, going back to its origins, and continuing as a core theme in whatever form Buddhism takes. This theme reaches a peak in the *prajñā-pāramitā* literature, as expressed in the following passage from the *Diamond Sutra*.

> The Lord said: Here, Subhuti, someone who has set out in the vehicle of a Bodhisattva should produce a thought in this manner: 'As many beings as there are in the universe of beings, ... all these I must lead to Nirvana.
> ... And yet, although innumerable beings have thus been led to Nirvana, no being at all has been led to Nirvana.' And why? If in a Bodhisattva the notion of a 'being' should take place, he could not be called a 'Bodhi-being.' 'And why? He is not to be called a Bodhi-being, in whom the notion of a self or of a being should take place, or the notion of a living soul or of a person.' Moreover, Subhuti, a Bodhisattva who gives a gift ... should not be supported by sight-objects, nor by sounds, smells, tastes, touchables, or mind-objects.[6]

If we may interpret this as Engaged Buddhist activists are wont to do, here we are shown that the *bodhisattva* who engages in activities on behalf of others will ideally be oblivious of any notion of the persons involved, for example, of any notion of a 'giver,' and of 'one to whom something is given.' In such a case, there would be no sense of oneself as the strong one, the one with something to give, the one in the position of power, the one who may feel good about doing the right or generous thing; there would be no sense of the other as the weak one, the needy one, the subordinate one; there would be no feeling of pity, which incorporates a kind of condescension. I think everyone would agree in recognizing these kinds of attitudes and feelings as problematic. Buddhism has developed a conceptual language and a set of practices that can be used to address this constellation of problematic attitudes.

The import of Buddhist selflessness for social action may also be seen in clear Mahayana and Vajrayana statements that selflessness and compassionate action are two sides of a single coin; that is, to the extent that one can get oneself out of the center of the picture, one will be capable of being- and feeling-with the other in such a way that the focus is on the other, his situation, his needs, etc. Ultimately, and at the most ideal level, this takes the form in Buddhism of an experiential merging with the other in a strong form of empathy in which one ceases to be simply 'oneself,' and becomes, to an extent, the 'other.' Understanding and action are both deeply modified as a result. This is expressed in the Dalai Lama's advocacy of the practice of the equalization, or exchange, of self and other and in a poem and commentary by Thich Nhat Hanh.

The Dalai Lama writes:

> *Equalizing oneself and others* means to develop the attitude and understanding of, 'Just as I desire happiness and wish to avoid suffering, the same is true of all other living beings, who are infinite as space; they too desire happiness and wish to avoid suffering.' Santideva explains that, just as we work for our own benefit in order to gain happiness and protect ourselves from suffering, we should also work for the benefit of others, to help them attain happiness and freedom from suffering.[7]

In other words, through meditative practice, one should reduce one's preoccupation with oneself and develop an experiential recognition of the objective sameness of one's own and others' value and one's own wishes for well-being and those of others. On the heels of such a transformation of the way one feels, it should follow naturally that one would work for the well-being of another as readily as for one's own.

Thich Nhat Hanh takes this kind of thinking a step further by applying it to villains, as well as to neutral persons and victims, as follows.

> One day [during the crisis of the Vietnamese boat people] we received a letter telling us about a young girl on a small boat who was raped by a Thai pirate. She was only twelve, and she jumped into the ocean and drowned herself.
>
> When you first learn of something like that, you get angry at the pirate. You naturally take the side of the girl. As you look more deeply you will see it differently. If you take the side of the little girl, then it is easy. You only have to take a gun and shoot the pirate. But we cannot do that. In my meditation I saw that if I had been born in the village of the pirate and raised in the same conditions as he was, I am now the pirate. There is a great likelihood that I would become a pirate. I cannot condemn myself so easily.

The poem reads, in part:

> I am the 12-year-old girl, refugee on a small boat,
> who throws herself into the ocean after being raped by a
>   sea pirate,
> and I am the pirate, my heart not yet capable of seeing and
>   loving.
> My joy is like spring, so warm it makes flowers bloom in all
>   walks of life.
> My pain is like a river of tears, so full it fills up the four
>   oceans.
> Please call me by my true names,
> so I can hear all my cries and my laughs at once,
> so I can see that my joy and pain are one.
> Please call me by my true names,
> so I can wake up,
> and so the door of my heart can be left open,
> the door of compassion.[8]

'I' am the girl and 'I' am the pirate. Some might think that such a merging of identity with 'both sides,' victim and villain, would render impossible any and all action to respond to this suffering, to heal it,

165

cure it, prevent it. On the contrary, for Nhat Hanh, empathic suffering along with both victim and villain make imperative that one take action to relieve 'one's own' suffering. At the same time, this empathy prevents one from comfortably distancing oneself from the villain, condemning him, while leaving oneself superior and untouched. This is one component of Buddhism's 'nonadversarial' ethic, which we will explore further toward the end of this chapter.

Of course, Christianity has a notion similar to some degree to Buddhist selflessness: to the extent that one can put oneself aside, one will be capable of more fully loving God and loving others. The strength of Buddhism in this context is that it has had centuries of practical experience in which the focus has been upon concrete practices to cultivate selflessness.

The negative side of Buddhist insistence upon selflessness is a notion that appears fairly often that one is in no position to begin any form of social engagement until one is 'enlightened' or free of self. The following story from the Meiji period (1868–1911) in Japan illustrates this.

> A Zen master by the name of Kasan was on his way back to his temple with his monks after a begging tour. The party had reached the slope leading to the temple when they encountered an old man trying to draw a heavy cart up the hill. One of the monks, a young man who had recently joined the temple, ran and helped him. When they were back inside the temple, Kasan called the monk to his chambers. He gave him a severe scolding and then threw him out of the gate. But the monk did not leave. He stayed before the gate for three full nights, begging the master to accept him again as a disciple. Seeing how earnest he was to continue his Zen study, the master finally relented and allowed him to return. That young man later went on to become a great master himself.[9]

The narrator also mentions that if the monk in question had been advanced in his studies, he would have been punished if he had not helped the old man. Clearly, the idea is that a person early in his studies should not attempt to help others because such efforts will reinforce ego structures that conceive the self as important and the other as subordinate.

Of course, this notion is in tension within Buddhism with the straightforward and deep belief that it is always good to be kind, always good to respond to a need that comes before one, always good to give. Nonetheless, the concern to avoid aggrandizement of the ego through charitable actions that fill my ego with thoughts of how fine I am has tended, especially in some sects like Zen, to retard the development of an attitude that more energetically embraces social activism as a good thing.

Buddhist social activists today have creatively addressed this issue by drawing on Buddhist notions that erase the line between means (Buddhist practice) and end ('enlightenment'). Enlightenment, self-lessness, compassion, they say, are not things 'out there' to be gained at the end of a long path. They are qualities to be expressed here and now to the best of one's ability. Social engagment may present very useful opportunities for the cultivation and testing of these qualities. For those who use Buddha nature language, it is thus that one progressively expresses/realizes the Buddha who one already is. For others, this is *bodhisattva* action. In other words, one progressively becomes the being one is striving to be by behaving like that being in the present. Thus social engagment need not be regarded as a distraction from the 'higher' goal of enlightenment, but may be incorporated within the parameters of the latter. Nor is such thinking limited to Mahayana and Vajrayana circles. As a slogan of the Theravada movement Sarvodaya Sramadana puts it, 'We build the road and the road builds us.'[10]

3. A third area of Buddhist contribution is its theory and practice of nonviolence. Buddhists and Christians have begun to have some fine exchanges on this subject and there is surely room for much more. Consider: both Buddhism and Christianity are deeply nonviolent in their roots, the founders of each being two of the greatest exemplars of nonviolence the world has ever seen. On the other hand, the historical records of neither are without blemish; both have been used by secular power to justify and incite violence and there have been times when each has willingly participated in this. Both, of course, have resources for adressing this problem, but I will limit myself to discussing the Buddhist resources.

I have become impressed by the importance of the role played by the concept of *karma* in reinforcing Buddhist attitudes about nonviolence. Karma, the law of cause and effect, affects the ideology and practice of nonviolence in two ways, both apparent in the early text, the *Dhammapāda*. First is the role karma plays in one's construction of one's own future: 'Whatever harm a foe may do to a foe, or a hater to another hater, a wrongly-directed mind may do one harm far exceeding these.'[11] Here it is plainly stated that no 'other' person can do one as much harm as one can do oneself. To hate and to act violently are acts which, if I engage in them, earn me negative karma which will construct for me unpleasant consequences some-time in the future, either in this lifetime or in a future life. I alone control how I react to what happens to me. Enlightened self-interest plainly shows me I should refrain from all violent acts and even refrain from indulging hateful thoughts in order to avoid painful consequences in the future.

Second, if a foe harms me and I react with violence, what will be the results for my future relations with my foe and the future of our conflict? The *Dhammapāda* states, 'Hatred is never appeased by hatred in this world; it is appeased by love. This is an eternal Law.'[12] Karma is the law of cause and effect. Every action I perform sows karmic seeds which guarantee certain future consequences. I should think of the consequences before I act. If I harm another, the other will be hurt and angered and (unless he is a principled pacifist!) will look for an opportunity to harm me in return. I then, being harmed, will look for an opportunity to retaliate in kind. As long as the situation is played out on this level, it will never end. The only way to stop this cycle of harm-causing and harm-suffering is to react in an entirely different manner to an act of hatred or harm coming at me from another; this the *Dhammapāda* calls 'love.' Note that it will take an act of love of comparable magnitude and strength to counter the effects of an act of hatred. The cycle of violence in the Middle East as well as the process of its gradual cessation illustrate the *Dhamma-pāda's* point.

Thus on both counts, if I harm another, I am harming myself: first, by planting a negative karmic seed which will inevitably ripen into negative consequences for myself in the future; and second, by creating a situation in which the other will look for an opportunity to harm me back.

I recently had the opportunity to speak with Dith Pran, Cambodian Buddhist and subject of the film 'The Killing Fields.' After his talk in which he stressed the importance of peace and reconciliation in Cambodia, I asked him whether the Cambodian people don't want to take revenge on the people who caused them so much suffering. He said that the average Cambodian does not want to retaliate or to take revenge. I, surprised, pressed him on this point, asking him if this is really the dominant attitude of the average Cambodian. He assured me that it was, explaining: 'They don't want to suffer any more. They know that if they try to take revenge they are only going to suffer more, in the future. They don't want to suffer any more.' I was stunned to think that this rather lofty ideal was so real and viable on the level of the ordinary person and pressed him again, asking how this could be possible, after all that they have suffered, how could they have such self-restraint, such self-control; it didn't seem humanly possible. He simply repeated, 'They don't want to suffer any more.'[13]

In other words, we don't have to assume that all Buddhists are superhumanly selfless in order to understand how they might be able to embrace and practice nonviolence to a degree that a Westerner finds remarkable if we realize how deeply the notion of karma pervades Cambodian thought and how important karma is for showing that it is in one's own self-interest to restrain oneself from acts of violence. Self-interest is the common coin of human nature in every time and place. It seems that Buddhism may have found a way to enlighten that self-interest so that we may act in the light of our real, long-term self-interest, rather than indulging an apparent short-term interest by struggling to overcome the other.

The Dalai Lama makes this point for his own situation. Why does he not advocate a violent response to the Chinese invasion of Tibet (aside from the fact that he is the incarnation of Avalokiteśvara!)? He explains:

> Anger, jealousy, impatience, and hatred are the real trouble-makers; with them problems cannot be solved. Though one may have temporary success, ultimately one's hatred or anger will create further difficulties. With anger, all actions are swift. When we face problems with compassion, sincerely and with good motivation, it may take longer, but ultimately the solution is better, for there is far less chance of creating a new problem through the temporary 'solution' of the present one.[14]

Violence is simply inefficacious. Again, with the awareness of karma and the ability to take the long-term perspective, the Dalai Lama indicates that the Buddhist way is in principle not interested in a win-lose outcome of a conflict; Buddhists should seek a win-win outcome, in order to find a peace that will last and not simply be an interim before the renewal of violence and suffering.

Another element frequently appearing in Buddhist theory of nonviolence is the non-recognition of the 'enemy' as an enemy. Christians may see in this something close to Jesus' teaching to 'love your enemies,' but the Buddhist and Christian versions will each have their own peculiarities.

In a Buddhist version, one might think first of the role played by karma in making the 'enemy.' In the poem cited above, Nhat Hanh arrived at his perspective on the basis of both spiritual practice and Buddhist philosophy. According to the law of karma, certain causes and conditions produced a pirate capable of raping a twelve-year-old girl. Thus the best response becomes obvious: remove those causes and conditions.

> In my meditation, I saw that many babies are born along the Gulf of Siam, hundreds every day, and if we educators, social workers, politicians, and others do not do something about the situation, in 25 years a number of them will become sea pirates. That is certain.[15]

Second is the recognition that when the 'enemy' does one harm, he is harming himself even more than he is harming the other. Thus the *Dhammapāda* states:

> All (mental) states have mind as their forerunner, mind is their chief, and they are mind-made. If one speaks or acts, with a defiled mind, then suffering follows one even as the wheel follows the hoof of the draught-ox.[16]

The Dalai Lama, drawing on his experience in working with the Chinese, similarly declares, 'The poor enemy ... because of the negative action of inflicting harm on someone out of anger and hatred, must eventually face the consequences of his or her own actions.[17]

Third is the Dalai Lama's frequent assertion that one should feel gratitude towards the enemy since he provides one with the only opportunity one has to really test one's character.

> Now, as a genuine practitioner of compassion and bodhicitta, you must develop tolerance. And in order to practice sincerely and to develop patience, you need someone who willfully hurts you. Thus, these people give us real opportunities to practice these things. They are testing our inner strength in a way that even our guru cannot. Even the Buddha possesses no such potential. Therefore, the enemy is *the only one* who gives us this golden opportunity. That is a remarkable conclusion, isn't it?[18]

Thus on all these grounds, it is a mistake to regard the 'enemy' as the enemy. This directly reinforces the Buddhist desire to seek a win-win outcome to a conflict.

In the Vietnamese Buddhist response to the war in their country we see the conjunction of principled nonviolence, nonrecognition of the 'enemy' as an enemy, and seeking of a win-win outcome.[19] Surely one of the great examples in history of principled nonviolence sustained under conditions of high-tech military attack, state persecution, imprisonment, torture and death, the Buddhist 'Third Way' or 'Struggle Movement' refused to side with either the North or South, refused to recognize either side as an enemy, and tried only to protect the people, to bring the war to an end, to reconcile enmity, and to heal wounds. Of course there were quite a few who left the Buddhist order to join one army or the other. There were also those in the order who advocated noninvolvement, retreat from the war and its misery. The dominant Buddhist response, however, of both ordained and laity, remained active nonviolent engagement. The story of these millions of Vietnamese Buddhists who remained faithful to the ideal and who were active participants in the nonviolent 'struggle' under conditions of acute violence is worthy of far greater study than it has received. There is a self-restraint here – and also in the cases of the Tibetan and the Cambodian responses to the disasters that befell them – that we need to understand.

4. Another point which Buddhist social activists could contribute to global discussions and practice of spiritual social activism is its non-adversarial approach to social ethics. This non-adversarial approach is by no means fully articulated in Buddhism, but I believe it represents a perspective which, as it becomes more fully articulated, may be helpful. Indeed, I suspect that Christian ethics may also fundamentally be non-adversarial, though the articulation, again, would be different.

We have seen above in the discussion of nonviolence that Buddhists ideally recognize that it is in both one's own interest and the interest of the other that one practice nonviolence: the consequence to the other is that he is left unharmed; the consequence to oneself is that one avoids accruing negative karma. Thus our true interests are not fundamentally opposed. Though we may be in a situation of conflict, it is not correct to understand our relationship as adversarial. It is in both of our interests to strive to resolve the conflict and to do so nonviolently.

This analysis indicates the correct interpretation of the Buddhist five lay precepts as well. The five lay precepts, the foundation of the Buddhist personal ethical code, may thus be seen to have important implications for social ethics as well. A Buddhist undertakes to

171

observe the first precept – to abstain from the taking of life – for his own sake as well as the sake of the other; similarly, she undertakes to observe the other four precepts – not to take that which is not given; to abstain from misconduct in sensual actions; to abstain from false speech; to abstain from liquor that causes intoxication and indolence[20] – for her own sake as well as the sake of others. Thus what is good for you and what is good for me are fundamentally the same and it is an error to see our deep interests as opposed. Thus does Buddhism embody a non-adversarial ethic.

This notion is reinforced by the Buddhist concept of a human being as not-a-self, not a separate and autonomous indivdual, but a being produced through the developmental process of his own past and the conditioning of all forces in his environment. Thus, what is called 'I' includes much that is called 'not-I,' my family and friends, the ideas I have encountered, the music I have listened to, the Zeitgeist of my era, any opponents or 'enemies' with whom I may have struggled; in short, every person, idea, event, and phenomenon that 'I' have ever encountered has constructed 'me' and thus partially constitutes 'me' at this moment. 'I,' likewise, have constructed 'them.' Thus, the 'not-me' is the 'me' and the 'me' is the 'not-me.' Since, for a Buddhist, in truth 'you' are 'me' and 'I' am 'you,' how can our relationship be adversarial? We are not sufficiently separate to have an adversarial relationship. Thus, your good must be my good and vice versa.

I will mention one important implication and one important limitation of this approach. The implication: in Buddhist ethics the end does not justify the means. In a non-adversarial situation, I can never see harm to you as even a qualified good. I cannot harm or kill you for the sake of some alleged 'higher good.' Thus there can be no 'just war,' no violent revolution, no sacrifice of a small group for the sake of a larger group justified on Buddhist principles.

The limitation: if no more were said, this talk of 'my good is your good; your good is my good' could easily create a situation in which the one(s) in power might define for the other what their good is, in a manner either unhealthily paternalistic or straightforwardly self-gratifying and other-denying. Clearly, persons must be able to define their own good and others must respect this, within limits. Given the doctrine, universally accepted by Buddhists, that a human birth is a precious one since it is only as a human that conditions are right to practice Buddhism and attain liberation, Buddhists cannot condone (or, if courage and means permit, leave unchallenged) actions inimical to the physical, mental, or spiritual well-being of any human being.

172

This, it seems to me, is the line which marks the limits of Buddhist tolerance. Of course, there will always be debate over what constitutes mental or spiritual harm. However, when physical harm is being done, or when the mental or spiritual harm is severe and obvious, then, from a Buddhist point of view, there is no need to debate. This, I believe, is the foundation of much of the Buddhist human rights and human welfare work which has sprung up in many Buddhist countries in this century in response to situations of war (Vietnam), state tyranny (Burma), genocide (Cambodia), extreme social injustice (ex-untouchables in India), and suppression of religious freedom (Tibet and Vietnam).

5. Many Buddhists feel the same way about harm done to animals or the environment and considerable Buddhist activism is devoted to their protection. I believe that the most important source of Buddhist concern for animals and the environment is the strong Buddhist emphasis upon cultivating non-harmfulness (*ahiṃsā*). The first precept encourages Buddhists to avoid taking the life of any sentient being, a category which embraces human and non-human animal life without distinction. In this respect, humans and nonhuman animals are regarded as being fundamentally the same kind of being: sentient. Insofar as humans and non-human animals are fundamentally the same kind of being, fundamentally the same kind of behavior, non-harmful, is appropriate for both.

This notion that we are fundamentally the same kind of being as non-human animals, is, of course, tempered by the notion discussed above, that a human birth is a uniquely precious birth insofar as it allows for Buddhist practice. Thus, it might be fair to say, while we are fundamentally the same kind of being as nonhuman animals, we have certain abilities and potentials which distinguish us from other animals in a very important way. However, it is precisely this element of difference which opens us to the hearing of exhortations to practice non-harmfulness. Thus we come round to the same point: both because of our sameness with animals (our shared sentience and entrapment in samsara) and because of our difference (our ability to transform ourselves – which, in an important way, is manifest in our developing our ability to practice ever more complete non-harmfulness) as Buddhists we are directed towards practicing non-harmfulness towards non-human animals. It is an extension of the same point – the habit of practicing ever more complete non-harmfulness, plus the practical knowledge that the lives of human and non-human animals are utterly dependent upon it – that leads Buddhists to engage

173

in efforts to protect the well-being of the environment which supports all the sentient life we know, the planet Earth.

The concept of 'human being' as part of the larger category of 'sentient being' places humans in closer kinship with non-human animals than does Christian philosophy with which I am familiar. However, I suspect the habit of practicing non-harmfulness draws the two together.

6. Finally, I would like to suggest that one of the strengths that Buddhists bring to spiritual social activism in the global community is their fundamentally pragmatic, rather than ideological, stance. This is probably best articulated in the early tradition in the well-known 'Parable of the Raft.' The following is a synopsis. A man on a journey comes to a body of water. In order to cross it, he constructs a raft and then paddles himself across. The Buddha states that, rather than carrying that raft with him, he will act properly if he leaves it by the side of the water. He concludes:

> In the same manner, O bhikkhus, I have taught a doctrine similar to a raft-it is for crossing over, and not for carrying (lit. getting hold of). You, o bhikkhus, who understand that the teaching is similar to a raft, should give up even good things *(dhamma)*; how much more then should you give up evil things *(adhamma)*.[21]

This means, among other things, that Buddhist teachings are not absolutes; they do not embody the final Truth; they are not something that one can 'get' and then have done all that one needs to do. They are tools, means which should be skillfully used to reach a goal. Mind you, they are very useful tools, and Buddhists by and large believe they are most likely the most useful tools available for the purpose. Still, they are not the goal itself, and they do not themselves possess absolute truth or value.

Why is this important? One of the points stressed by both the Dalai Lama and Thich Nhat Hanh is the danger of ideology. Ideology kills. It kills by dividing people, who in truth are fundamentally interdependent, rendering them 'other' and 'not-me.' Buddhists were deeply aware, long before Sartre, that the ego-self is fundamentally threatened by the 'other,' and that the more alien that 'other' appears to be, the greater the perceived threat. A sense of threat, of course, produces fear, and from fear derive a host of 'unskillful' defensive and aggressive behaviors. In its more pernicious forms, ideology may proceed to label the 'other' as inferior, less deserving of our regard, and, at its worst, demonic.

174

Buddhism, of course, is no more free of ideology than is any other 'ism.' However, Buddhist ideology itself bears the seeds of its own destruction. This was shown in the Parable of the Raft, above. In modern times it can be seen as well in the following precepts, composed by Thich Nhat Hanh for the Order of Interbeing, which he founded during the war in Vietnam.

First: Do not be idolatrous about or bound to any doctrine, theory, or ideology, even Buddhist ones. All systems of thought are guiding means; they are not absolute truth.

Second: Do not think the knowledge you presently possess is changeless, absolute truth. Avoid being narrow-minded and bound to present views. Learn and practice non-attachment from views in order to be open to receive others' viewpoints. Truth is found in life and not merely in conceptual knowledge. Be ready to learn throughout your entire life and to observe reality in yourself and in the world at all times.

Third: Do not force others, including children, by any means whatsoever, to adopt your views, whether by authority, threat, money, propaganda, or even education. However, through compassionate dialogue, help others renounce fanaticism and narrowness.[22]

In a similar vein, the Thai activist Sulak Sivaraksa advocates what he calls 'small b buddhism' in preference to capital B Buddhism, which is acculturated Buddhism, Buddhism as an 'ism' which may be identified with nation or culture.

Anybody who wishes to be a buddhist with a small b is welcome. You don't have to profess your faith, you don't have to worship the Buddha, you don't have to join in any ceremonies. What is important is that you grow in mindfulness, your awareness, and you try to restructure your consciousness, to become more selfless, to be able to relate to other people more meaningfully, so that friendship will be possible and exploitation impossible. To me, the essence of Buddhism is this. But when Buddhism becomes a church linked with certain cultures and nations, then it can easily become negative. So I feel that small b buddhism is much more essential.[23]

No one is so foolish as to suggest that Buddhism is free of ideology. But from a Buddhist point of view, the ideology itself is not the measure of value. The measure of value in Buddhism is pragmatic results. Does the ideology lead to peace, nonviolence, compassion, the reconciliation of enmity, the healing of wounds? Then embrace it. Does it lead to division, enmity, hatred, violence? Reject it, whatever its name. This pragmatic attitude derives from the Buddha, who called himself a physician and Buddhism a medicine (again, a tool), to cure the suffering of humankind. If an ideology, a belief, a practice, an action, or a thought of any kind promotes peace and an end to *duḥkha*, said the Buddha, embrace it, follow it. If it causes pain, disease and promotes the continuation of *duḥkha*, he said, abandon it. Santikaro Bhikkhu expresses the heart of the teachings of the great modern Buddhist reformer, Buddhadāsa Bhikkhu, in exactly this way.

> Having understood what the Buddha had discovered, Buddhadasa Bhikkhu pursued the same course and objective; all that matters to him is *dukkha* [Pali for *duḥkha*] and liberation from *dukkha*. For Buddhadasa Bhikkhu, something is Buddhist solely because it quenches *dukkha*. When asked if something is 'good' or 'correct,' Ajarn Buddhadasa asked in return, 'Does it quench *dukkha*?' *Dukkha* provides the existential test to all ideas and experiences. Is there *dukkha*? Then, something is not yet right. If no *dukkha* can be found, then things are correct, at least for a while....
>
> Here it would be good to remember that the Dhamma [Pali for Dharma] we are discussing is not primarily the Buddha's 'teachings,' although the word 'Dhamma' is commonly understood in this limited way. Rather, Dhamma is the Truth, Reality, Law, or that to which the teachings point. Or, as Ajarn Buddhadasa liked to remind us, Dhamma is Nature.[24]

Christianity has resources in this domain as well, notably injunctions against idolatry. Injunctions against idolatry have, of course, been applied to social activism with great benefit by way of the Protestant Principle which holds that the only thing that is holy and above challenge is God; all secular and religious institutions, persons and actions are less than God and thus subject to challenge. On the basis of this principle, articulated or not, Martin Luther could challenge the Catholic Church and Martin Luther King, Jr. could challenge American racism. From a Buddhist point of view, I often wonder why more is not made of this principle (both the Protestant Principle specifically and Biblical injunctions against idolatry more generally) in such a way that it would cause Christians to hold their theology more loosely, while striving to embody the spirit of Christ's teachings.

Buddhist Openings

Having concentrated in this essay upon points which Buddhism has to offer the global community on the basis of its spirituality and social activism, I turn to briefly mention a few points on which Buddhists might particularly invite and benefit from dialogical contributions from Christians.

1   Buddhists have yet to seriously confront the tension within their own tradition between structures of spiritual and institutional hierarchy, on the one hand, and, on the other, egalitarian notions and structures. There is no doubt that engagement with the West in general, and Christianity in particular, eventually will challenge Buddhism to grapple with its own power structures and a host of associated issues.

2   Buddhist theorists have already begun rethinking the role and meaning of karma, but there is much more to be done here. Traditionally, Buddhism seemed to teach that if one was poor, of a low social class, etc., one deserved to be – one's karma had earned one this status. Modern Buddhist activists, however, are much more apt to speak of righting such 'social injustices.' How can the notion of karma be reconciled with the notion of social injustice? Furthermore, given karma, what are the respective responsibilities of the individual and of society? Nhat Hanh's poem and commentary seem, through karma, to put all the responsibility on society – yet surely most Buddhist schools (and Nhat Hanh himself) have tended to emphasize self-reliance and self-responsibility. There is much yet for Buddhists to work out in these matters; Western and Christian social theory will have much to contribute to this process.

3   Buddhist spiritual social activism has come of age only in the modern world. Modernity, however, has been particularly unkind to the Buddhist world, with the near extinction of Buddhism in the People's Republic of China, the invasion of Tibet, the holocaust in Cambodia, and the prolonged war in Vietnam and South East Asia. Consequently, most Buddhist spiritual social activism has come into being in the throes of crisis. It is no wonder that Buddhist leaders have had little time to articulate the theory underlying their activism. As crises are resolved, or reduced to a simmer, it is to be hoped that Buddhist leaders will find the opportunity to articulate, in particular, their vision of the ideal society in a modern world. We

have as yet very little of this sort of thing from the Buddhist world, yet it is crucial to the continuation of a socially engaged Buddhism and could constitute a valuable contribution to the global community. There is no doubt that this will be an important point of Buddhist-Christian dialogue in the future.

Conclusion

Both Christianity and Buddhism have, in the past, embraced ideologies that turned its adherents away from engagement with the world. In the Christian case, at times, emphasis upon salvation and one's eternal destiny not only turned a Christian's attention from this world to the hereafter, it also was used by some to encourage Christian passivity, a meek acceptance of whatever life gave one, in the hope that such meekness and humility earned one a reward hereafter. This would not be regarded as a dominant Christian view today. Similarly, in the past, the strong negativity associated with samsara in some forms of Buddhism seemed to some to indicate that since the only cure for samsara was to leave it, one should simply turn one's back upon it and concentrate upon attaining nirvana. The uproar caused in some Buddhist countries when Pope John Paul II wrote in *Crossing the Threshold of Hope*[25] that Buddhists today hold this kind of view is sufficient evidence to establish that this is not a mainstream Buddhist view today. Suffice it to say, then, that while both Christianity and Buddhism have elements in them, which may manifest from time to time, that can effectively turn adherents away from serious engagement with this world and its problems, such views are not mainstream views endorsed by the respective institutions today. Buddhist-Christian dialogue on social activism, then, need waste no time worrying about their respective worldliness or otherworldliness.

At the same time, looking back at history, a Buddhist might be forgiven for thinking that while Buddhists, perhaps, have not done enough by way of living out their ideals in engagement with the needs of their societies, Christians have perhaps done much too much. I suspect that today Buddhists and Christians are converging on a Middle Path between these extremes, a Middle which may be more deeply based upon spiritual practice, more clearly limited by strict nonviolence, and more capable of striving in conflict situations in which fundamentally no enemy is recognized.

Notes

1 The one notable exception to this rule among Buddhists is the great leader of the Indian untouchables, Dr. B. Ambedkar, who broke with Gandhi over the latter's refusal to condemn the Indian caste system and led a mass conversion of untouchables to Buddhism.

2 Thich Nhat Hahn has carried on a lifetime of personal Buddhist-Christian dialogue, the fruits of which were recently published in his *Living Buddha, Living Christ*, Introduction by Elaine Pagels, Forward by Brother David Steindl-Rast, O.S.B. (New York: Riverhead Books, 1995).

3 Brian Victoria's important study, *Zen at War* (New York: Weatherhill, 1997), gives extensive documentation of Japanese Zen masters' extremely chauvinistic and bellicose language and behaviour during World War II. In this book, such important Zen masters as Shaku Sōen and Harada Sōgaku, along with many others, are shown eulogizing one-sided 'oneness' with country and emperor, urging their countrymen to go 'selflessly' into battle and to kill their country's enemies in the name of the Buddha. Their ability to twist and distort the teachings of the Buddha in this way makes it very clear that years of Buddhist meditation, or at least Japanese Zen Buddhist meditation, do not guarantee that one will develop the kinds of attitudes and behaviours that Engaged Buddhists advocate. Clearly, something additional – presumably ethical teaching – is required. The author recently had the opportunity to ask a well-known Engaged Buddhist leader about this matter. He was familiar with Victoria's study but nevertheless repeated that Buddhist meditation does support the cultivation of compassion and the breaking down of the barriers between self and other. When pressed on the matter of these bellicose Zen masters, he simply said, 'They gave in to circumstances.' This chapter is written from the point of view of Engaged Buddhism. It is not intended to negate the reality of what Brian Victoria describes. Neither, however, should the reality he describes be taken as negating the reality of Engaged Buddhism.

4 Thich Nhat Hahn, *Being Peace*, ed. Arnold Kotler (Berkeley, CA: Parallax Press, 1987).

5 Dalai Lama, *Kindness, Clarity, and Insight*, trans. and ed. Jeffery Hopkins, co-ed Elizabeth Napper (Ithaca NY: Snow Lion, 1984), 62.

6 Edward Conze, trans., 'The Diamond Sutra,' *Buddhism Wisdom Books* (New York: Harper and Row, 1958), 25, 26.

7 Dalai Lama, *The World of Tibetan Buddhism*, ed. Geshe Thupten Jinpa (Boston: Wisdom Publications, 1995), 85.

8 Thich Nhat Hahn, *Being Peace*, 61–64.

9 Nishimura Eshin, *Eastern Buddhist*, 1987: 143.

10 Joanna Macy, *Dharma and Development: Religion as Resource in the Sarvodaya Self-Help Movement*, Revised Edition (West Hartford, CT: Kumarian Press, 1985), 52.

11 *Dhammapada*, trans. by Walpola Rahula in his *What the Buddha Taught*, Revised Edition (New York: Grove Press, 1959), 126.

12 Ibid., 125.

13 Dith Pran, in a private conversation at James Madison University, Harrisonburg, VA in October 1995. Quotations are from the author's memory and are inexact.

14 Dalai Lama, *Kindness*, 62. This quotation and the other quotation from the same text are discussed in Jose Ignacio Cabezon, 'Buddhist Principles in the Tibetan Liberation Movement,' 273–298 in Christopher S. Queen and Sallie B. King, eds., *Engaged Buddhism: Buddhist Liberation Movements in Asia* (Albany, NY: State Univesity of New York Press, 1996).

15 Thich Nhat Hahn, *Being Peace*, 62.

16 *Dhammapada* in Rahula, 125.

17 Dalai Lama, *World*, 81.

18 Ibid., 82, italics in the original.

19 See Sallie B. King, 'Thich Nhat Hahn and the United Buddhist Church of Vietnam: Nondualism in Action,' Queen and King, 299–341.

20 Hammalawa Saddhatissa, *Buddhist Ethics: The Path to Nirvana* (London: George Allen and Unwin, 1970, Reprint Edition, London; Wisdom Publications, 1987), 73.

21 *Majjhima-Nikāya* (Pali Text Society Edition), cited in Rahula, 11–12.

22 Thich Nhat Hahn, 89, 90, 91.

23 Sulak Sivaraksa, *A Socially Engaged Buddhism* (Bangkok: Thai Inter-Religious Commission for Development, 1988), 186.

24 Santikaro Bhikkhu, 'Buddhadasa Bhikkhu: Life and Society Through the Natural Eyes of Voidness,' Queen and King, 157, 159.

25 His Holiness John Paul II, *Crossing the Threshold of Hope* (New York: Alfred A. Knopf).

CHAPTER FOURTEEN

Some Questions About the World

John P. Keenan

Religious traditions work within their narrative contexts. Constantly they reinterpret and reenvisage those narratives, gaining new insight and the will to tackle problems not foreseen in the ancient days. Reinterpretations sometimes are easily performed, simply by explicating ideas assumed by the ancients. Sometimes they are performed by selective memory, ignoring a part of a tradition deemed irrelevant. And sometimes a portion of an ancient narrative is simply rejected. In any event, one has to grapple with the foundational traditions and narratives.

And here I think Buddhism and Christianity diverge on the issues of social justice and engagement. Sallie King's paper presents in concise and incisive fashion the Buddhist attempts to develop a basis for engaged social action in the world. It becomes obvious that the modern Buddhist thinker-activists are reclaiming perhaps neglected aspects of Dharma in order to elaborate an ethics of social engagement, just as Christian thinker-activists have elaborated little-remembered aspects of the Bible to insist upon the social gospel of worldly engagement.

Perhaps the issue has been similar, for the thrust of both traditions has often propelled one not to engagement in the world but to disengagement, to a severing of worldly bonds to facilitate union with God or final awakening. Religion becomes a world-denying practice. The physical removal from the 'world' marks the more monastic traditions as decidedly other-worldly. But in a Mahayana perspective, that will not do at all, for the world is not a double-decker tier of realms. All is empty, and the only field for compassionate practice is the one world in which we all live. And so Thich Nhat Hanh, Sulak Sivaraksa, The Dalai Lama, Dr. B. Ambedkar, Aung San Suu Kyi, Buddhadāsa, Maha Ghosananda, and a host of modern Buddhist thinkers map out a doctrinal understanding that demands social engagement. Similarly, Noriaki Hakamaya's argument about 'critical Buddhism' or Shirō Matsumoto's about doctrinal essentialism has focused not on doctrine, but on its lived implications, on its practice. These Buddhist thinkers are struggling with their early narratives and traditions, mapping ways in which Dharma may be authentically lived in the world of today.

When Pope John Paul II in his *Crossing the Threshold of Hope* wrote that Buddhist soteriology is too other-worldly, he elicited a strong response from Sri Lankan monks. Perhaps the issue is particularly sensitive because reformers within the Sri Lankan tradition have charged the traditional samgha with precisely that same accusation of other-worldliness. What one might accept from a fellow-religionist, however, is difficult to accept from an outsider.

In traditional societies, whether Buddhist or Christian, the normative political and social structures were regarded as much a part of the naturally given world as the physical environment. The only question directed to kings and rajas was how well they fulfilled their appointed roles, not whether there should be kings or rajas. Social horizons were limited to the possible, and no one saw the ideals of participatory democracy or the social possibilities of structural change. It is then no wonder that the religious traditions have tended to be other-worldly. This world was taken care of by divinely appointed kings or *cakravartins*, whose duty it was to support the faith. But with the advent of social awareness and engagement, all that has changed. To be Christian means that one has to adopt orthopraxis, has to live out the faith in deed and not just in verbal profession. To do so, Christians mine the scriptures and develop a social ethic. And Buddhist deeds of compassion take on a form of social engagement and struggle. Buddhist compassionate engagement is grounded in the traditions by all of the thinkers mentioned above. But I want to suggest that it is more of a struggle to develop a strong ethics of engagement in Buddhist traditions than in the Christian.

Buddhists have many more stories than Christians. With no commonly accepted canon, the number of scriptures is immense and the parables many. Christians have only the one Bible, and most of the stories in that come from the Hebrew texts. Perhaps, as John Dominic Crossan suggests, Christianity has transmuted its parables into moral allegories while the original Christian teller of parables – Jesus – has himself become the parable of God.[1] Yet there does remain a basic Christian narrative about the world. Imbued with all manner of scriptural notions about eschatology, Christians see the world as moving along a narrative track, to a last age, to a final fulfillment, to an Omega point. It is going somewhere, even though no one is really sure just where that where might be. The value of the world in its brute materiality is further grounded upon the doctrine of Incarnation, for God became man, taking upon godself the very matter that Plato found so disgustingly barbarous.

The Buddhist vision of the world presents a starkly different picture. In the constant coming and going of world realms that characterizes Indian culture as a whole, Buddhist thinkers can perhaps espy a spiral action, but hardly a historical movement. Final awakening engages in compassionate action to elicit awakening in others, not in order to build the world. Indeed, Buddhism glories in the absence of teleological presumptions.

In Mahayana development, Nāgārjuna offered a reinterpretation of the earlier scriptures by equating emptiness with dependent co-arising. Things are not only empty of inner, self-enclosed being, and do not simply disappear from the purview of an awakened mind. Rather, they inter-are, they rise in mutual relationship and inter-dependency. While the ultimate truth of emptiness remains ineffably other, the conventional truth of worldly engagement has its own proper validity.[2] In the Nikāyas, the notion of dependent co-arising was confined to the arising of suffering, samsara. The twelvefold dependent co-arising begins with primal ignorance and leads to old age and death, only to commence once again in constant turnings of samsaric suffering. This affords little room for narrative history, for the same events take place over incalculable periods again and again. But, what is even more to the point, once the compassionate work of Buddhas and Bodhisattvas is completed, the world itself, lacking the propelling power of defiled karma, is apt simply to disappear. When the Buddha was asked whether or not the world is eternal, he refused to answer, for such questioning is not conducive to practice.[3] But later monks and thinkers did indeed raise the question.

The *locus classicus* on the issue, the *Buddhabhūmyupadeśa*, comments upon a phrase from the *Buddhabhūmisūtra* that says Buddha 'will never come to an end.' The obvious problem is that, if the compassionate engagement of Buddhas is indeed efficacious, then when all sentient beings are saved and their defiled karma eliminated, the world itself, lacking any propulsive force, will lapse into nothingness. And then the highly touted goal of Mahayana is itself reduced to an all consuming cessation (nirvana), just like the goal of those two 'deficient' vehicles. The main reason given is that the merits of Buddha cannot come to an end because there will always be some sentient beings in need of their help, for there are some without lineage (*gotra*) for awakening. Such persons practice until they reach the brink of insight into the emptiness of all things, and then, terrified, fall back in craven attachment to life in the world and have to be again and again rescued by Buddha, a process that never comes to an end.

Tsong-kha-pa has a more subtle discourse on the issue, for he sees emptiness as entailing the continued existence of that which is empty, of the world in which one practices. Thus for him, if not for his followers, practice is interminable and the world does not come to an end.[4]

In the Christian sphere there is, I think, a greater insistence upon social engagement because its narrative does come to some final conclusion. We begin with a story of creation and end with a final reckoning. It is our task to build a world of peace and justice within history, for here is the locus of the rule of God. Historicity becomes the counterpart of dependent co-arising, for it too denotes the particular cluster of causes and conditions that result in the conventional existence we all lead. In a western Mahayana context, the emptiness and historicity are convertible, the one entailing the other. Nothing is set and firm, because no one is privy to any determined course for the future. Yet the world in its plenteous interbeing is itself a field of narrative story.

The conflict is, I think, one of assumptions more than explicit doctrinal positions. Buddhists inherited the notion of samsara and its eternality from earlier Indian traditions at a time when the structures of social life were set and determined by the *varna* system. True, the Buddha renounced those metaphysical class divisions, yet in the discussions of an endtime it does insinuate itself.[5] No Indian then envisaged a narrative history of the world. By contrast Christians inherited various notions of history, often a vision of a sacred history, God's history, seen through human eyes. And they set themselves the task of fulfilling that history, with all of the pain and injustice that mutated visions of Christian western progress would inflict upon a world deemed ripe both for conversion and for colonization. Institutional bishops and leaders sent missionaries far and wide to convert the world before the end time, often in the assurance that they knew the signs of the times and could predict its sequences.

Christians often fail(ed) to see the emptiness of their ideas and boast of their ability to scope the future. Some fundamentalist Christian groups support the rebuilding of the third temple in Jerusalem, not out of any love of Israel, but because they see that event as the precursor of the end time when Jesus will return on the clouds. Yet, the most obvious thing about clouds is that they are themselves empty and can support nothing at all.

Can Buddhists interpret dependent co-arising not just as the complex of causes and conditions whereby we inter-are at a particular moment in the ongoing flow of samsara, but also as the concrete unfolding of our historicity?

Many Buddhists share modern, scientific visions of the beginning of the world, and are hardly aware of the old notions of the samsaric world as 'merely the environment created by the karma of the unenlightened' or that 'when the last sentient being has made port, the sea will suddenly evaporate and all conditioned existence will end.'[6]

The issue is of more than academic interest, for it nurtures one's orientation toward the world itself, whether that world is to be merely the field for other-worldly activity, or whether it is to be part of our destiny as awakened human beings.

Notes

1 John Dominic Crossan, *The Dark Interval: Toward a Theology of Story* (Sonoma: Polebridge Press, 1988), 101–107.
2 This is the main theme of Gadjin Nagao, *The Foundational Standpoint of Mādhyamika Philosophy*, (Albany, NY: State University of New York, 1989), especially 39–42 on the meanings of *saṃvṛti*, where Nagao insightfully reads *saṃvṛti* in a very positive sense, although he admits there is little textual support for his interpretation.
3 See *Majjhima-nikāya* I. 483. See Henry Clark Warren, *Buddhism in Translations* (New York: Atheneum, 1969), 123.
4 On Tsong-kha-pa and other thinkers, see Donald S. Lopez, Jr., 'Paths Terminable and Interminable.' *Paths to Liberation: The Mārga and its Transformations in Buddhist Thought* (Honolulu: Kuroda, 1992), 170–183.
5 Ibid., 158–170.
6 Ibid., 174.

CHAPTER FIFTEEN

The Mind of Wisdom and Justice in the Letter of James

John P. Keenan

The Letter of James is perhaps the most neglected text of the New Testament. Not only because Luther, disliking its emphasis on the inadequacy of faith without works, disparaged it as the straw epistle, but even more because it lacks most of the expected Christian message. There are only two references to Jesus in the text, and these without much doctrinal content. Indeed, some exegetes have argued that even these are later insertions into a purely Jewish text. Doctrinally bare-boned indeed!

Yet perhaps there are hidden riches in so meager a text, riches that can be mined by employing the philosophical tools of Mahayana thought, its themes of emptiness and its understanding of truth. This is the approach Fred Streng employed in his studies of religion in its sundry and rich phenonemology. I propose to employ it here as a lens for reading James. In this essay, however, Mahayana thought will not make its presence felt directly, for the theological exegesis that follows will make little direct appeal to Mahayana categories. Rather, it forms the mind-set of the interpreter, directing attention to passages in the text about wisdom and compassion and suggesting on how these might be read most accurately and faithfully.

I will select out the passages that seem most germane and offer an interpretation that stresses the organic unity between the wisdom that comes from the Lord and the practices of compassion thereby entailed. The relationship between wisdom and practice is organic rather than sequential. It is not that one first has wisdom and then applies it in practice, for both wisdom and practice are described by James as non-discriminative. They are united as different aspects of the non-discriminative mind freed from its religious pretentions and committed to the service of the poor.

The Mind of Wisdom 1:5–8

[5]If any of you is lacking in wisdom, ask God, who gives to all generously and ungrudgingly: and it will be given you. [6]But ask in faith, never doubting, for the one who doubts is like a wave of the sea, driven and tossed by the wind [7-8]for the doubter, being double-minded and unstable in every way, must not expect to receive anything from the Lord.

The letter of James, addressed enigmatically to the twelve tribes in the Diaspora, begins in 1:2–4 with an injunction for steadfastness in the face of trials. It then turns immediately to a brief treatment of wisdom, which is to be prayerfully received from God (1:5), who gives generously and ungrudgingly (*haplōs kai mē oneidizontes*). This notion of wisdom constitutes, I think, the leitmotif of the entire letter. The point is that wisdom is not a human accomplishment attained through effort expended, but a gift given simply and without weighing the merits of the case. One need not worry whether or not one is worthy, for God gives spontaneously and naturally.[1]

However, although human beings cannot earn wisdom, they can obstruct it, for one must ask in faith without doubting. Here the term used for 'doubting' is '*diakrinomenos*', from the verb *diakrinō*, which means to make distinctions, to differentiate, judge, deliberate, dispute, and thus, to be at odds with oneself, doubt, waver. This meaning of discrimination as doubt or wavering first appears in the New Testament (See Mark 11:23). The sense of doubting derives from the basic meaning of distinguishing or deliberating – in Mahayana, *vikalpa*, discrimination, which is the converse of and obstacle to wisdom (*prajñā*). Wisdom is not firmness of conceptual faith, but the absence of clinging to ideas as if a chosen alternative could bring the calm and peace of wisdom, for 'the one who doubts is like a wave of the sea, driven and tossed by the wind' (1:6). What is at issue is the hesitation and doubt of trying to adjudicate final things by reasoning them out in the absence of faith, for wisdom moves only 'in faith.' The terms 'driven' and 'tossed' are of James' coinage and there is no earlier usage.[2] The image of the confused mind as a troubled sea is also a rather common Mahayana image.[3] The point is that discrimination occupies the mind by eliciting images clung to as if they represented the way things actually are, an existential imagining that mistakes its own constructs for reality. One who supposes or thinks (*oiesthō*) that discrimination leads to wisdom will receive nothing from the Lord (1:8). The term *oiōmai*, thinking, here means thinking in the context of discrimination (*diakrinomenos*), i.e., taking imagined concepts as representing reality. Such a person is double-minded (*dipsuchos*), another term peculiar to James.[4] To be double-minded is not to be devious or to have a hidden agenda, but simply and importantly to be of two minds, weighing alternatives, wavering back and forth between contrasting options. It is this that renders one 'unstable in every way' (*akatastatos en pasais hodos autou*). Again the term 'unstable' (*akatastatos*), which is present in the Septuagint, is confined to James in the New Testament.[5] It denotes that discriminative thinking encloses a person within his or her set of images and ideas, thus precluding the gift of wisdom which, given by God, frees one from false views and enables one to be steadfast in the face of trials, 'perfect and complete, lacking in nothing' (1:4). Furthermore, the phrase 'in every way' (*en pasais hodois autou*) suggests that wisdom, being non-discriminative, allows and demands that one engage in practice, for one cannot abide in non-discriminative wisdom without abiding in just and compassionate practice in all one's journeyings (*hodois*). This brief discourse on wisdom could have become central to the early Christian discourse on the nature of wisdom.[6] That it did not leaves modern readers of the New Testament with the opportunity to develop an alternate understanding of the scriptural notion of wisdom.[7]

Boasting and Riches 1:9–11

[9]Let the believer who is lowly boast in being raised up, [10]and the rich in being brought low, because the rich will disappear like a flower in the field. [11]For the sun rises with its scorching heat and withers the field; its flower falls, and its beauty perishes. It is the same way with the rich; in the midst of a busy life, they will wither away.

Here, the poor person is to boast (*kauchasthō*) in being raised up through wisdom, in being freed from delusions, while the boasting of the rich is the negation of wisdom, for such boasting clings to appearances and ignores reality.[8] The rich boast of their accomplishments indeed, of their positions and identities. Yet they have nothing stable to support those boasts, for their 'busy lives' (*en tais poreiais*) are empty of stable and enduring meaning. The acquisitive way of life of the rich is empty of meaning, precisely because it is centered on a false notion of a stable self in control of one's possessions (*ātma-ātmya*). James returns to the theme of boasting and judgment in 4:1–2; 11–17:

> ¹Those conflicts and disputes among you, where do they come from? Do they not come from your cravings that are at war within you? ²You want something and do not have it; so you commit murder. And you covet something and cannot obtain it; so you engage in disputes and conflicts. You do not have, because you do not ask.... ¹¹Do not speak evil against one another, brothers and sisters. Whoever speaks evil against another or judges another, speaks evil against the law and judges the law; but if you judge the law, you are not a doer of the law but a judge. ¹²There is one lawgiver and judge who is able to save and to destroy. So who, then, are you to judge your neighbor? ¹³Come now, you who say, 'Today or tomorrow we will go to such and such a town and spend a year there, doing business and making money.' ¹⁴Yet you do not even know what tomorrow will bring. What is your life? For you are a mist that appears for a little while and then vanishes. ¹⁵Instead you ought to say, 'If the Lord wishes, we will live and do this or that.' ¹⁶As it is, you boast in your arrogance: all such boasting is evil. ¹⁷Anyone, then, who knows the right thing to do and fails to do it, commits sin.

Conflicts and disputes arise from cravings (*ek ton hēdonōn*), which are embodied in desire for what one does not have (*epithumeite kai ouk echete*). Rather, one should ask God, who gives wisdom willingly to all who free themselves from such craving and conflict. Some commentators find the reference to murder out of place.[9] The terms 'conflicts and disputes' in 4:1 (*pothen polemoi kai machai*) are translated minimally in the NRSV, but the RSV renders them 'wars and fighting,' for they certainly do carry the primary meaning of armed conflict, war, and fighting. They describe historical conditions of oppression not at all unusual in the ancient, or the modern, world. The results of occluding wisdom affect not only the mind of the covetous, but also the broader social world of other people – and that is why practice is organic to wisdom.

This murderous mind begins with speaking against (*katalaeite*) and setting oneself up as a judge (*krinōn*) of others, discriminating

189

(*diakrinomenos*) and practicing partiality toward others. The root cause for social injustice lies in this self-absorbed, discriminating mind that sets itself up as the judge of others.[10] To assume the guise of such a judge is to become a judge of the law which enjoins love of neighbor, rather than one who actualizes that law (*poiētēs nomou*) in practice. It is to misunderstand who one is and what life is, for it ignores the transience of human life, that we are but a mist (*atmis*) appearing but briefly in time. The covetous, closed in upon themselves, boast arrogantly in their delusion, rejecting wisdom and engaging in evil practice.

Mirroring Truth in Doing 1:22–25

[22]But be doers of the word, and not merely hearers who deceive themselves. [23]For if any are hearers of the word and not doers, they are like those who look at their natural face in a mirror; [24]for they look at themselves and, on going away, immediately forget what they were like. [25]But those who look into the perfect law, the law of liberty, and persevere, being not hearers who forget but doers who act – they will be blessed in their doing.

Merely to listen to the word of God is to deceive oneself.[11] Mere conceptual knowledge, however correct, misleads and deceives, because it engenders the discriminative wavering that leaves human thinking in charge and obviates the need to receive anything from the Lord. It leaves intact a boasting consciousness which is content in its attainments and aloof from engagement in merciful actions in the world. To discriminately judge the law (*nomon krieis*) and speak evil of another prevents one from being a 'doer of the law' (*poiētēs nomou*). This last phrase 'represents apparently a Jewish idiom: in ordinary Greek ... *poiētēs nomou* would be a "law-maker". Paul uses [this] phrase in the same way as James in Rom. ii.13, for one who observes and practices the law....'[12] The point is not simply to listen, but to actualize the law in practice. That is to say, don't just be hearers (*śrāvakas*), but be bodhisattvas, being filled with wisdom and compassion.

Sophie Laws remarks that 'James' own parable is of a mirror, an image rare in biblical literature (Job 37: 18; Ecclus 12:11; Wisd 7:26; cf. 1 Cor xiii.8; 2 Cor 3:18).'[13] But it is a frequent image in Mahayana texts. The *Scripture on Buddha Land* describes mirror wisdom as follows:

Just as a great round mirror would be suspended in some high place by a fortunate, rich man, where it would not be shaken, and in it the limitless sentient beings who pass by could see their virtues and their imperfections, and thus would come to desire to hold onto their virtues and discard their imperfections, just so the Tathagata has suspended his round mirror wisdom in the pure realm of reality, which, being uninterrupted, cannot be shaken, because he desires to lead immeasurable, innumerable sentient beings to gaze upon purity and to come to desire to hold onto that purity and discard all defilements.[14]

But the point of wisdom is not personal purification. Of its very nature it entails engagement in benefiting all other beings:

Again just as the lustrous surface of a round mirror could be the basic condition for the arising of all images in all places, just so the Tathagata's mirror wisdom does not cut off the lustre of all the innumerable practices, for it is the basic condition for the arising of all wisdom images, i.e., the wisdom images of the Hearers' vehicle, the Solitary Awakened vehicle, and the Great vehicle, because he desires to lead all those of the *śrāvaka* vehicle to attain deliverance by means of that *śrāvaka* vehicle, etc.[15]

The phrase in verse 1:23, 'those who look at their natural face in a mirror' (*katanoouti to prosōpon tēs geneseōs autou*) can be read in terms of seeing into one's original nature. Sophie Laws notes that '[F.J.A.] Hort draws attention to the oddity of the phrase *prosōpon tēs geneseōs*; had the intention been to give simply the metaphor of a man looking at his face, *prosōpon* alone would have been enough. Hort therefore argues that *genesis* should be taken to mean not "birth" but "nature"...[16] Perhaps a more literal rendering is preferable: the face of one's birth, just as it is, apart from the differentiating roles that lead people to lord it over one another. Hearers who forget (*akroatēs epilēpsmonēs*) are literally 'hearers of forgetfulness,' balancing with doers of the law.[17] The contrast is between remembering one's original face and forgetting who one is.

Martin Dibelius sees the perfect law, the law of liberty, as indicating the implanted word of verse 21: 'Receive with meekness the implanted word, which is able to save your souls.'[18] If so, then one can see this law within, by attending to immediate patterns of experience, beyond limiting images and role conceptions.

Wisdom then entails not only action, but specifically compassionate action in accordance with this implanted law of love of neighbor. James returns to the theme in chapter 3:13–18:

> [13]Who is wise and understanding among you? Show by your good life that your works are done with gentleness born of wisdom. [14]But if you have bitter envy and selfish ambition in your hearts, do not be boastful and false to the truth. [15]Such wisdom does not come down from above, but is earthly, unspiritual, devilish. [16]For where there is envy and selfish ambition, there will also be disorder and wickedness of every kind. [17]But the wisdom from above is first pure, then peaceable, gentle, willing to yield, full of mercy and good fruits, without a trace of partiality or hypocrisy. [18]And a harvest of righteousness is sown in peace for those who make peace.

The contrast here is between selfish, ambitious (*eritheian*) wisdom and gentle wisdom, filled with mercy and good fruits (*mestē eleous kai karpōn agathōn*), for there is no authentic wisdom apart from compassion. Thus wisdom is further described as 'willing to yield' (*eupeithēs*), also translated in the Revised Standard Version as 'open to reason,' because it does not cling to any fixed set of ideas, even creedal affirmations. The text of James is meager in its doctrinal import not because it is underdeveloped, but because its focus is upon non-discriminative wisdom, authenticated not in hearing and learning the word, but in embodying the word in active mercy and good fruits.

Language and Religion 1:26–27

> [26]If any think they are religious, and do not bridle their tongues but deceive their hearts, their religion is worthless. [27]Religion that is pure and undefiled before God, the Father, is this: to care for orphans and widows in their distress, and to keep oneself unstained by the world.

This is the only passage in the New Testament where there is mention of 'being religious.' Nowhere else is the adjective 'religious' used at all, and here it has a clear negative meaning. 'The term *thrēkos* ("religious"), attested only in this text, can nevertheless be understood by comparison with the noun form *thrēskeia* ("religion"): what is involved here is the pious person, in quotation marks, who is distinguished not by a pious attitude in general, but by the fulfillment of the religious (in the thought of antiquity, this means "cultic") obligations – this is the sense of "religion" *(thrēskeia)*.'[19] Even '(t)he noun *thrēskeia* is rare in biblical Greek,' and denotes cultic worship.[20] The only use of the adjectival form 'religious' describes worthless, deluding professions about religion. For James being religious in professions of faith is worthless, vain, and empty of meaning *(mataios)*.

One must then bridle one's tongue, focus on orthopraxis rather than verbal confessions of correct faith. The term 'to bridle one's tongue' *(chalinagōgōn glōssan)* is another term not found elsewhere in the New Testament or in the Septuagint, but taming is a common theme in Buddhism. The word *chalinagōgōn* means to guide with a bit and bridle, to hold in check, to tame. The emphasis on the tongue, which is taken up again in 3:5 ff, reminds one of the Mahayana notion in *The Summary of the Great Vehicle* of the permeations of language *(abhilāpa-vāsanā)*,[21] for the linguistic construction of alternative conceptual views is the source of the discrimination *(kalpana)* that deceives *(apathon)*. One engages in the world and practices a pure and undefiled *(aklista)* religion by not discriminating and not being caught in the net of a verbal delusion that mistakes ideas for reality. One attains what the Mahayanists call undefiled purification *(vaimalya-vyavadāna)*, i.e., one's mind is pure and undefiled *(kathara kai aminantos)*.

For James the world from which one must keep oneself unstained *(aspilos ... apo tou kosmou)* is 'mankind in its false values, self-seeking and self-assertion, and in that dividedness that is for him [i.e., James] the essence of sin (cf. iv.8)'.[22] It is such self-assertion *(ātmagrāha)* that is indicated by double-mindedness, the attempt to control affairs through weighing all the alternatives in service of one's own position and gain. All quite Mahayana themes indeed.

Discrimination and Partiality 2:1–5

[1]My brothers and sisters, do you with your acts of favoritism really believe in our glorious Lord Jesus Christ?

This sentence has occasioned much discussion, particularly in regard to the reference to Jesus Christ, for together with verse 1:1 ('James, a servant of God and of the Lord Jesus Christ') it is the only mention of Jesus Christ in the entire letter. Some exegetes delete the reference and regard the letter as a thoroughly Jewish document into which a

Christian hand has inserted these two surface references to Jesus.[23] But my present interest lies elsewhere, in the extension of the critique of discrimination as a mental obstacle to wisdom to a critique of discrimination as an injustice against other people. For the verse speaks about showing favoritism or partiality. Here the term 'to show favoritism or partiality' (*en prosōpolempsisais*), and again in verse 2:9 (*prosōpolempteite*), are both derivatives of the Septuagint expression *prosōpon lambanein*, 'to show partiality.' The Hebrew idiom *nasar panim* is rendered literally in the Septuagint as *prosōpon lambanō*, 'receive the face.'[24] Again the stress is on judging by appearances and thus being deceived. And James leaves no one in doubt as to what he means, for he follows up with a clear example of social discrimination.

> [2]For if a person with gold rings and in fine clothes comes into your assembly, and if a poor person in dirty clothes also comes in, [3]and if you take notice of the one wearing the fine clothes and say, 'Have a seat here, please,' while to the one who is poor you say, 'Stand there,' or 'Sit at my feet,' [4]have you not made distinctions among yourselves, and become judges with evil thoughts?

The phrase 'to make distinctions' (*diekrithete en heautois*) and to 'become judges with evil thoughts' (*kai egenesthe kritai dialogismōn*) means to separate people into categories and assume the role of social arbiters. And that in itself means that one is motivated by evil intent. James' point is enfleshed in the example of a man with golden rings on his fingers, who is favored in the assembly. James coins the adjective *chrusodaktulios*, 'with gold rings on his fingers,' to indicate social status, for a gold ring is an insignia of the equestrian order, the second rank of Roman aristocracy.[25] Leviticus 19:18 announces the norm of love of neighbor, 'and the word "neighbour" provides a link with another precept in which it occurs, Lev. 19:15: "Ye shall do no unrighteousness in judgment: thou shalt not respect the person of the poor, nor honor the person of the mighty: but in righteousness shalt thou judge thy neighbour." To love the neighbour is, then, to treat him without discrimination; to discriminate is to break that law of love.... Those who exercise discrimination, then, *make distinctions in your own minds*; *diekrithēte en heautois* should be taken as having a middle force, for it is the personal, internal dividedness that is the target of James's attack.'[26] There is a direct linkage between the mind that discriminates and thus renders iself immune to receiving the gift of wisdom and the practice of discriminating social classes of persons. False practice flows from the mind of discrimination, not from the gift of non-discriminative wisdom which makes no distinctions between persons. But James' world, as ours, is not a level playing field on which all have equal access to victory. It is a world of oppression in which the poor have little or no access to the great game of self-assertion.

The Chosen Poor 2:5–9

[5]Listen, my beloved brothers and sisters. Has not God chosen the poor in the world to be rich in faith and to be heirs of the kingdom that he has promised to those who love him? [6]But you have dishonored the poor. Is it not the rich who oppress you? Is it not they who drag you into court? [7]Is it not they who blaspheme the excellent name that was invoked over you? [8]You do well if you really fulfill the royal law according to the scripture, 'You shall love your neighbor as yourself.' [9]But if you show partiality, you commit sin and are convicted by the law as transgressors.

To make no discriminations between rich and poor is to undercut the basis for social stratification of classes – not in a Marxist sense, but by exposing the underlying double-minded sin of creating such a discriminated social world, for both rich and poor. James is indeed conscious of class society, i.e., of the divisions between the powerful oppressors and the powerless poor. And he is angry at the injustice of insititutional and legal violence that oppresses the weak and poor, over whom the name of God has been invoked. The term 'who oppress' (*katadunasteuousin*) comes from the Septuagint and is 'a term the prophets were famous for using in their denunciation of social injustice committed by the rich against the poor, widows, and orphans. The term is very strong and has violent, physical overtones, with the emphasis on exploitation and domination. It is also significant that in the only other place the word is used in the New Testament, the 'devil' is the subject (Acts 10:38).'[27] Any social history of the ancient world depicts the great masses of people as poor to the point of starvation, burdened with taxes, and without access to the courts of power. In James' view, that entire world is at enmity with God because it is constructed upon deluded and self-serving assumptions of discriminative thinking.

The royal law is the law of Moses in Leviticus 19:18 about loving your neighbor as yourself. And showing partiality 'discloses' (*elegchomenoi*) the structure of sin, for it lies at the root of the injustices afflicted on others in the service of a false and arrogant conception of self.

Woe to the Unjust Rich 5:1–6

[1]Come now, you rich people, weep and wail for the miseries that are coming to you. [2]Your riches have rotted, and your clothes are moth-eaten. [3]Your gold and silver have rusted, and their rust will be evidence against you, and it will eat your flesh like fire. You have laid up treasure for the last days. [4]Listen! The wages of the laborers who mowed your fields, which you kept back by fraud, cry out, and the cries of the harvesters have reached the ears of the Lord of hosts. [5]You have lived on the earth in luxury and in pleasure; you have fattened your hearts in a day of slaughter. [6]You have condemned and murdered the righteous one, who does not resist you.

James is angry and his charges are specific. They are directed not against an amorphous group of people with money, but against the rich who oppress and cheat the poor. I do not think one has to apologize for or downplay his anger or to note that there are indeed just and good rich people. James is being quite specific and takes aim at people who trust in their wealth as a bulwark against transience and who practice fraud and slaughter. He is talking about killing people.[28]

Patience 5:7–11

[7]Be patient, therefore, beloved, until the coming of the Lord. The farmer waits for the precious crop from the earth, being patient with it until it receives the early and the late rains. [8]You also must be patient. Strengthen your hearts, for the coming of the Lord is near. [9]Beloved, do not grumble against one another, so that you may not be judged. See, the Judge is standing at the doors! [10]As an example of suffering and patience, beloved, take the prophets who spoke in the name of the Lord. [11]Indeed we call blessed those who showed endurance. You have heard of the

endurance of Job, and you have seen the purpose of the Lord, how the Lord is compassionate and merciful.

What then are the poor to do? What does it matter that God has chosen the poor, if they are unable to free themselves from their oppressors? Pedrito Maynard-Reid writes that '[t]hroughout much of the scriptures, God's option for the poor is explicit. It is forcefully revealed when in James 5:1–6 God is shown to be attentive to the cry of the oppressed.'[29] Clearly the import of such an option is that, receiving wisdom, we engage in compassionate justice without discrimination.

Yet the issue faced by James' audience was different: how to live in a world in which justice is not practiced. And James' advice is to endure and be patient. In the very opening of the letter he speaks of being steadfast and enduring trials, and here toward its end he again counsels patience. This is hardly a Marxist-inspired liberation approach that would overthrow the rich and powerful.

What is the content of such patience? James compares the patience that waits upon the coming of the Lord (*heos tēs parousias tou kuriou*) to that of a farmer waiting for his crop to ripen, and promises that 'the coming of the Lord is near (*ēggiken*).' This is the same term used in Mark 1:15, in which Jesus announces that the time is fulfilled and the kingdom of God is at hand (*ēggiken*). Throughout the text James has been criticizing the discriminations that block wisdom and separate people. Here again he is, I think, rejecting the way humans discriminate time itself, for he, like Mark, says that the coming of the Lord is 'at hand,' has already come near, is available to those who do not prevent its actualization. In contrast to the rich who fatten their hearts in injustice, James' readers are to establish their hearts in wisdom, without grumbling, lest they be judged by the judge who stands even now at the doors (*pro tōn thurōn hestēken*). The verbs 'to be at hand or draw near,' and 'to be at the doors' are both in the perfect tense, denoting an action already completed, yet not actualized. The time frame is not the linear flow from past through present to future, but the wisdom insight into the available present. Thus James can draw his example of suffering and patience from the prophets and from Job, who lived in the linear past. They were steadfast, and showed that the Lord is compassionate and merciful. Indeed, the theme of suffering runs through the entire letter, from beginning to end. And it does not come to a final, happy conclusion. 'The proper reaction to suffering, then, is not to give in to the evil impulse and accuse God, but to endure patiently.... This is the call of the book both in its introduction and its thematic reprise.'[30]

Yet this seems meager fare in the face of oppression and injustice – just have patience that when the Lord comes all will be reversed. But James does not say that. He does warn the rich that their riches will disappear, as will indeed their very selves. And he does roundly condemn their unjust actions in no uncertain terms. But he does not promise that the poor will inherit the earth or replace the rich. Perhaps there is more to this patient endurance than just waiting for an uncertain day of reversal. The Mahayana thinkers speak of the patience that gains insight into the non-arising of all things (*anupattika-dharma-kṣānti*), i.e., to the emptiness of all things. Such patience flows from the wisdom of emptiness, eschewing appearances for insight into the authentic being of that which is and, being freed from clinging to false imaginings, liberates one for compassionate action in the world of suffering. Perhaps that insight signals the coming of the Lord, the Lord of true wisdom who even in the midst of suffering saves one from delusion. Apart from the abandonment of attachment to self and self-possessions, there is no avenue to justice and freedom except intelligent and compassionate engagement in the arena of the world in all its suffering and injustice. The coming of the Lord is already at hand and the judge is right now standing at the doors. Everything has been accomplished, and yet needs to be actualized in the present moment of our living.

Notes

1 See J. Danielou, *The Theology of Jewish Christianity* (London, 1964), 362–65 on the contrast between this spontaneity and doubleness of mind.
2 See Sophie Laws, *A Commentary on the Epistle of James* (San Francisco: Harper and Row, 1980), 57.
3 See, for example, Yoshito S. Hakeda, trans., *The Awakening of Faith: Attributed to Aśvaghosa* (New York: Columbia University, 1967), 41 and 119. For parallels in Greek literature, see Martin Dibelius, *James: A Commentary on the Epistle of James* (Philadelphia: Fortress Press, 1975), 56–89.
4 Laws, *The Epistle of James,* 60. 'James's adjective *dipsuchos, double-minded,* used here and again in iv.8, is unparalleled in the LXX, NT, or any other known earlier literature, though with the noun *dipsuchia* and verb *dipsucheo* it appears in other early Christian literature.'
5 Ibid., 61.

6 See John P. Keenan, *The Meaning of Christ: A Mahāyāna Theology* (Maryknoll, NY: Orbis Books, 1989) on the historical development of Christian thought within the available patterns of Greek metaphysics.

7 Laws, *The Epistle of James*, 59. She quotes the Gospel of Thomas, log 22: 'Jesus said to them, "When you make the two one, and when you make the inside like the outside, and the outside like the inside, and the above like the below, and when you make the male and the female one and the same, so that the male shall not be male nor the female female ... then you will enter (the kingdom)."'

8 See Dibelius, *James*, 84, and note 75 on prior use by Philo.

9 Ibid., 217.

10 Ibid., 229.

11 Ibid., 115.

12 Laws, *The Epistle of James*, 85.

13 Ibid., 85.

14 See John P. Keenan, *A Study of the Buddhabhūmyupadeśa: The Doctrinal Development of the Notion of Wisdom in Yogācāra Thought.* (Ph.D. diss., University of Wisconsin, 1980), 656.

15 Ibid., 676.

16 Laws, *The Epistle of James*, 86.

17 Ibid., 87.

18 Dibelius, *James*, 115ff.

19 Dibelius, *James*, 121.

20 Laws, *The Epistle of James*, 88.

21 Asanga, *The Summary of the Great Vehicle*, tr. John P. Keenan (Tokyo and Berkeley: Bukkyō Dendō Kyōkai, 1991), 28.

22 Laws, *The Epistle of James*, 91.

23 Ibid., 94

24 Ibid.

25 Ibid., 98.

26 Ibid., 102.

27 Pedrito U. Maynard-Reid *Poverty and Wealth in James* (Maryknoll, NY: Orbis Books, 1987), 63.

28 Ibid., 81–98.

29 Ibid., 98.

30 Peter Davids, *The Epistle of James: A Commentary on the Greek Text* (Grand Rapids: Eerdmans, 1982), 38.

CHAPTER SIXTEEN

Response to John Keenan

Sallie B. King

Justice is truth in action.
Benjamin Disraeli

It is often said that though Buddhism has at least the seeds of a social ethic (in its emphasis upon selflessness and compassion), it is entirely lacking in a concept of justice. Obviously, one's view on this matter will depend upon how one conceives justice; Buddhism does have a notion of justice inherent in the concept of karma. John Keenan's fascinating Buddhist reading of the Letter of James provides some perceptive suggestions for considering a Buddhist conception of social justice.

Keenan begins very helpfully by stating, 'the relationship between wisdom and practice is organic rather than sequential.... They are united as different aspects of the non-discriminative mind.' Thus, one expects certain kinds of behaviors from a certain state of mind – classically, in Buddhism, compassionate behaviors from an enlightened mind. Similarly, James writes, 'Who is wise and understanding among you? Show by your good life that your works are done with gentleness born of wisdom.' (3:13)

I am interested in Keenan's remark that James' letter is relatively neglected among Christians and even disparaged by Luther for its emphasis on the inadequacy of faith without works. In this regard, the Buddhist is much more in harmony with the spirit of James' letter than, evidently, a dominant stream of Protestant faith, insofar as a Buddhist expects as a matter of course selfless and compassionate behavior from one reputed to be wise or enlightened and would tend to turn away from one with such a reputation who failed to demonstrate it in his behavior. Still, I expect that most Christians would feel the same!

James goes on, 'But the wisdom from above is first pure, then peaceable, gentle, willing to yield, full of mercy and good fruits, without a trace of partiality or hypocrisy. And a harvest of right-eousness is sown in peace for those who make peace.' (3:17–18) I am not sure what 'pure' means here, but it is clear that the behavior to be expected from one with this pure wisdom is exactly the kind of behavior a Buddhist would expect: it should be peaceable, gentle, yielding, merciful, and full of good fruits, without a trace of partiality or hypocrisy.

Interestingly, for those interested in Buddhist social ethics, we see that we should expect a 'harvest of righteousness,' presumably in society, 'sown in peace for those who make peace.' This reminds me very much of Thich Nhat Hanh's expression that one must 'be peace' in order to 'make peace,' that, in other words, being peace is *already* making peace, as well as his idea (reminiscent of the thesis of the Confucian text, *The Great Learning*) that one creates a peaceful and harmonious world from the ground up, beginning with oneself, making oneself peaceable, then working with one's family, one's colleagues at work, one's neighbors to create peaceable micro-communities, then in progressively larger communities, working always with gentleness, always with peace as the goal, peace understood always as the peace that is the expression of the lack of conflict. With peace as the focus, this much is perhaps not surprising for Buddhism.

But are there also clues herein for a Buddhist conception of justice? The wise person's attitude, as Keenan emphasizes, is also 'without a trace of partiality.' James goes on to decry 'acts of favoritism,' giving as an example better treatment of a rich man than a poor man. (2:1–4) This opens up the classic conception of justice, which includes an idea of fairness that is specified precisely as impartiality.

> Distributive justice is a matter of the *comparative treatment* of individuals. The paradigm case of injustice is that in which there are two similar individuals in similar circumstances and one of them is treated better or worse than the other. In this case, the cry of injustice rightly goes up against the responsible agent or group.[1]

Keenan shows very well how impartiality, a.k.a. nondiscrimination, is an essential goal of Mahayana Buddhist practice and a mark of an enlightened mind. He is right; and, furthermore, the cultivation of such impartiality goes back much farther, all the way to the early days of Buddhism. Indeed, the very purpose of the well-known practice of the cultivation of the Four *Brahmavihāras* ('Sublime Abodes,' viz., loving kindness, compassion, sympathetic joy, and equanimity) is to cultivate such impartiality. The test of whether one has succeeded in this meditation is to observe, for example, whether one's feelings of loving kindness towards oneself, one's teacher, a very dear person, an indifferent person, and an enemy are all identical; whether one's compassion towards a pitiful person or evil-doer, a dear person, an indifferent person, and an enemy are all identical.[2] This practice is the classic place to find the cultivation of the social emotions approved in early Buddhism and is still very much used today by such Engaged Buddhist groups as Sarvodaya Sramadana.[3]

I take it as well established then, that impartiality is a long-held and fundamental aspect of the attitude and behavior of the wise, according to Buddhism. This impartiality, it seems to me, can be taken to establish in Buddhism the foundation of an affirmation of a principle of distributive justice. Perhaps Buddhists need not use the word 'justice,' inasmuch as it contains considerable Judeo-Christian-Muslim connotations. There is no question, however, of a strong commitment in Buddhism to fairness understood as impartiality.

The question remains of how to respond to injustice. For the most part Buddhists, including Engaged Buddhists, tend to be spurred into action by a compassionate response to suffering, or an urge to protect well-being and lives, whether the lives of humans or animals, or to protect vegetation or the environment. There are certainly examples, though, of Engaged Buddhists responding to injustice, unfairness, or discrimination among persons. One major example is the ex-Untouchable New Buddhists of India who converted to Buddhism expressly as a repudiation of an unjust social system that discriminated among persons by virtue of birth into caste. The Buddhists who have responded to their plight are also responding to injustice. In this case, clearly, there is a large element of response to the vast suffering these people have endured as well (as, indeed, there is in James' case of the laborers who were not paid and suffer to the point of starvation). A case of Buddhist response purely to injustice or discrimination may be seen in the incident which sparked massive Buddhist rebellion against the government of South Vietnam in 1963:

the state's forbidding the Buddhists to publicly celebrate a Buddhist holiday by flying the Buddhist flag, when the Catholics (whom the state favored) had been allowed to publicly fly their flag not long before.[4]

What is one to do when injustice and/or suffering is occurring? In what may be the most debatable part of his letter, James counsels patience: 'Be patient ..., beloved, until the coming of the Lord.' (5:7) I think Keenan is on to something in his interpretation, insofar as James goes on to expressly urge his readers to take up the example of the prophets (who by no means sat on their hands and did nothing) and insofar as he counsels endurance. I am reminded here most of the Dalai Lama who often expresses his patience in the face of the massive injustice suffered by his country and religion at the hands of the Chinese, a patience that allows him to acknowledge that he does not expect the full resolution of Tibet's crisis during his lifetime. Of what is his patience constructed? Of several things, I think: (1) his belief that as the global community sees ever more clearly the nobility of the Tibetans' largely non-violent, patient endurance and the justice of their cause, gradually a fair resolution will be reached; (2) his firm belief that the nonviolent approach is the only one that can truly resolve the conflict at its roots; (3) his equanimity.[5] At the same time that he displays this patient endurance a.k.a. equanimity, the Dalai Lama is the embodiment of constant active engagement, doing everything he can in a nonviolent way to bring about that eventual day of justice in which he seems to have unshakable faith. This is, for me, an example of the kind of response to injustice that Keenan's reading of James calls forth.

In closing, I think John Keenan's and my exchange is a good example of how dialogue with Buddhists can enrich Christianity (in opening up a text to a fresh, thought-provoking reading) and dialogue with Christianity can enrich Buddhism (in provoking Buddhistic thoughts about justice).

Notes

1 William K. Franken, *Ethics*, second edition (Englewood Cliffs, NJ: 1973), 49. Italics in the original.
2 See Edward Conze, *Buddhist Meditation* (New York: Harper and Row, 1969), 126–133.
3 See Joanna Macy, *Dharma and Development: Religion as Resource in the Sarvodaya Self-Help Movement*, revised edition (West Hartford, CT: Kumarian, Press), 38–40.

4   See Christopher S. Queen and Sallie B. King, eds., *Engaged Buddhism: Buddhist Liberation Movements in Asia* (Albany, NY: State University of New York Press, 1996) for accounts of both these cases.
5   See Jose Ignacio Cabezon, 'Buddhist Principles in the Tibetan Liberation Movement,' Ibid., 295–320.

PART FIVE

Ultimate Transformation or Liberation

CHAPTER SEVENTEEN

Under the Bodhi Tree: An Idealized Paradigm of Buddhist Transformation and Liberation

Thomas P. Kasulis

Twenty-five centuries ago in north India Siddartha Gautama continued to sit under thc tree in deep meditation. He had gone through an ordeal to get there: he had given up a life of luxury as a prince in an opulent, sequestered palace; he had relinquished the chance to fulfill a prophesy that he could become a monarch of all the known world; he had spent years wandering the forests futilely seeking a teacher to guide him to what he needed; he had undergone brutal ascetic austerities that had brought him time and again to the brink of death. All he had left was this spot under the tree and his resolve to sit there until there was a breakthrough. In his resolve he was alone with neither teacher nor text to guide him. It was just he himself and the ineluctable presence of things as they are.

His breathing and heartbeat were slow and steady, a sign he was devoid of distraction, anguish, or anxious anticipation. He waited. He let go. Images and memories flashed through his mind, but he let them go and pass away. His breathing and heartbeat remained steady. Supernormal powers to see, to hear, and even to remember past lives arose in his consciousness. They were noted and left aside. His breathing and heartbeat remained steady. Images that would usually generate distraction or desire, terror or trepidation, flashed by. They were noticed but not engaged. The breathing and heartbeat remained steady. Siddhartha Gautama continued to sit without distraction, without the desire to hold on to any particular image. Then he suddenly experienced and understood the things around him and their interrelationship. He encountered the world for what it is, not as we might want it to be. A sense of relief and well-being charged his awareness and Siddhartha Gautama opened his eyes to see the morning star shining on the horizon, the dawn's light filtering across the eastern sky. The night was over. When Siddhartha Gautama arose from his spot, he would no longer be known by his personal name, but by his title: the Buddha, the Awakened One.

One of Frederick Streng's central insights was that religion ultimately coalesces around a vision of self-transformation or spiritual liberation.[1] Since the beginning the story of Gautama's enlightenment has served for Buddhists as an idealized paradigm of religious liberation or transformation. It is an *idealized* paradigm because most Buddhists do not even try to emulate it. Perhaps for some select monastics, the story does function in that manner, but only a tiny portion of the Buddhists in the world could identify with the rigors and sacrifices of such a single-minded quest. Most Buddhists do not leave family or home to live alone in the forest, for example. There are, however, elements of the story that serve as a defining spiritual orientation for most Buddhists. In that way the story is an idealized *paradigm* that lends focus and meaning to how Buddhists hope to achieve transformation and liberation in their own lives, whether or not they have abandoned the secular world.

One idealized element of the model is that it presents liberation as an all-or-nothing affair. One either achieves perfect enlightenment or continues to live in delusion. The story has no room for transformative progress, except for the sequence of extraordinary powers developed in the very final phases of the path to enlightenment. If we were to apply that criterion to the lives of most ordinary Buddhists, Buddhism looks like a religion of failure. So few of the over 300 million Buddhists in the world have truly achieved perfect enlightenment (or will likely achieve it in this lifetime) that we would have to wonder what the religion could possibly mean for them. Sometimes this issue is addressed in light of the belief in rebirth: we may not make it in this life, but we are gradually getting there. The individual Buddhists may believe they are closer to the goal than they were a few hundred lifetimes ago and if they keep focused, they will be closer still in another few hundred lifetimes. This addendum only changes our view of Buddhism from being a religion of failure to a religion of patience – extreme patience. If this were all there was to it, it is hard to conceive why Buddhism would be one of the world's largest and most widespread religions.

When we think of Buddhism as a living religious tradition, therefore, we should not identify it with the goal of duplicating the experience of the Buddha under that tree twenty-five centuries ago. The unfolding of Buddhism in the West is illustrative. Precisely because Buddhism was introduced to the West in this century in terms of that all-or-nothing ideal, its growth peaked rather quickly. On one hand, the prospect of Buddhist liberation may have initially attracted many Westerners interested in alternatives to the spiritual options traditionally available to them. Thousands of Americans 'became' Zen Buddhists, for example, with the hope of achieving that blazing insight of *satori* that would change their lives forever. For most, of course, that did not happen and they lost interest. Yet, there are also many who continued to be involved with Zen and to engage at least irregularly in some form of practice. For them there seems to be something transformative in their Buddhist experience that continues to be a meaningful source of psychospiritual liberation, even without the all-or-nothing, once-and-for-all insight. I suspect Buddhism functions in this way for the vast majority of the hundreds of million Buddhists around the world. For them, the paradigm of the Buddha's enlightenment is not a *modus operandi,* but rather a spiritual heuristic. The Buddhist understands the meaning of whatever transformation and liberation they experience in terms of the paradigm, even though they may have little or no expectation they will fully duplicate the experience, at least in the foreseeable future.

If we need an analogy to this use of the idealized paradigm, we can look no further than our popular culture. When the kid in the playground makes a drive to the basket, shifts his direction while in midair, and scoops in the shot, the idealized paradigm of Michael Jordan may be there. When the girl runs like the wind and passes all the other kids in the race, the paradigm of Olympian Jackie Joyner-Kersee may flash through her mind. The same for the student cellist and Yo Yo Ma, the pianist and Vladimir Ashkenazy, the rock guitarist and Eric Clapton, the tennis player and Steffi Graf. Few practitioners honestly believe they will ever become the paradigm. Not only may they not have the talent, but they also may be in circumstances that would not allow them the time, resources, and energy to focus so restrictively on one thing. What is important for our analysis, however, is that for those brief moments, they 'know what it's all about,' they find a meaning in their experience that goes beyond the ordinary into the extraordinary. By knowing the idealized paradigm, they know what it was that was excellent and why, however briefly, they felt free. They know what counts as success.

If indeed the Buddha's enlightenment story is such an idealized paradigm of transformation and liberation, we must ask what the story tells us about 'what counts.' What major items in the story help us know what is excellent, what is worthwhile, and what constitutes true liberation. Looking back at the story from this perspective, we find the following themes worthy of our special attention.

We begin with the reason for the Buddha's embarking on the path in the first place. The Buddhist quest begins, according to the first of the Four Noble Truths, with the recognition of *duḥkha*. This term has often been rendered simply as 'suffering' or even 'pain,' but those English terms are too broad. For example, physical pain itself is not *duḥkha,* but there is *duḥkha* in the anxiety about its onslaught or the anguish that might accompany it. In other words, *duḥkha* is not in the pain itself, but in the response to that pain. The *Parinirvāṇa Sūtra* depicts the story of the death of the Buddha. It was a painful death (according to many interpretations, one caused by food poisoning). The Buddha even had to interrupt his last sermon in order to enter a meditative trance (in Pali called *nirodhasamāpatti,* a state in which ordinary sensory input is shut down)[2] until the pain was no longer disruptive. If the Buddha had worried about the onslaught of the pain at that critical time or if he had let the pain generate feelings of anguish or despair, that would have been *duḥkha*. To accept the pain without turmoil is to be liberated from *duḥkha*.

When the nature of *duḥkha* is clear, the rationale behind the second Noble Truth is also clear: the cause of *duḥkha* is '*tṛṣṇā*,' that is, 'craving' or 'attachment.' If one becomes fixated on a phenomenon (e.g., physical pain), its role in one's life will be out of proportion to its own natural presence. For example, if I worry about the pain before I have the pain, I have made the pain present when it is not yet there of its own accord. That is delusion, the opposite of enlightenment. Delusion makes present what is not there. Similarly, when the pain is present, it is usually not the only phenomenon present. Only an extreme pain so completely fills the consciousness that there is room for nothing else. Fortunately, such pain is rare.

Again the story of the Buddha's death is illustrative. Most of the time during the sermon, the Buddha was probably in pain, but usually the pain did not so dominate his consciousness that he was unable to give his sermon. If he had fixated on the pain, it would have overwhelmed him. He would have cried out in anguish; he would have personalized the event ('why did this have to happen to me now?'); he would have been distracted in what he was saying. Instead he put the pain in its place; he neither denied nor focused exclusively on its presence. As he talked, he kept marginally aware of the pain. Not being obsessed with his sermon – 'how wonderful this is coming out!' – he had 'room' in his consciousness to be aware of more than one phenomenon at once. As the pain increased, it moved from the margins to the center of his awareness. When it demanded more attention than the sermon or his audience, the Buddha excused himself and dealt with the pain. Since he was not obsessed with that either, when the pain subsided, he let it go back to the margins of his awareness and he returned to the audience in front of him. He simply dealt with the pain as it was, not as he wished it would be nor as he feared it would be. It would be delusion to experience it other than as it is. To eliminate *tṛṣṇā* (craving, desire, or attachment) is to eradicate delusion. To eradicate delusion is to overcome *duḥkha*. To overcome *duḥkha* is to achieve enlightenment.

The term 'delusion' has a precise meaning and should not, for example, be conflated with 'illusion.' An illusion (e.g., a magician's trick or the sight of a puddle up ahead on a dry, very hot road in the daytime) is a false appearance. The appearance itself (the rabbit that came out of the empty hat; the puddle) is not what it seems. A delusion (e.g., of paranoia or of my believing I am Napoleon), on the other hand, is a false projection: I experience something that is not only not there, but also that does not even appear to be there except in my own hallucinatory projection. When we understand an illusion, therefore, the appearance itself does not change (we still see what looks like a puddle), but we will know it to be something else (the refraction of light caused by the heated air). When we shatter a delusion, however, the false appearance disappears (released from paranoia, for example, I stop hearing voices plotting against me).

Unlike Hinduism, which has a strong emphasis on *māyā*, Buddhism is not generally concerned much with illusion. For the most part, it emphasizes the idea that things show themselves 'as they are' (*tathatā*). Buddhism is, however, very much concerned with delusion. This emphasis on overcoming delusion suggests that Buddhism is fundamentally more like psychology than epistemology. Its approach to transformation is more like a therapy than an argument. This further suggests Buddhism is the treatment of a spiritual illness so as to bring us to a state of health. In fact, the Four Noble Truths follow the rhetorical structure of analysis in traditional Indian medicine: (1) symptomatology, (2) etiology, (3) prognosis, and (4) therapy. Viewed in this light, it might be helpful to introduce into our account of

Buddhst liberation some contemporary psychological terminology, in particular the concept of addiction.[3]

An addiction is a self-defeating obsession with one source of satisfaction. It is driven by desire; it is a form of fixation; it is insatiable (and therefore self-destructive); it culminates in anguish. In these respects it shares many characteristics with our Buddhist analysis of *duḥkha* and *tṛṣṇā*. If this is correct, what addiction can we say Buddhism addresses? What addiction must be overcome (transformation) if we are to achieve our cure (liberation)? The addiction, I believe, amounts to the desire for (and pursuit of) continuous self-gratification or self-centered pleasure. Addicts live with the paradox that what they fixate on as the supreme source of pleasure leads to an endless pursuit of insatiable desire culminating in a life of anguish. Buddhism suggests the delusion that drives an addiction is the hope that I can be in a perpetual state of happiness, pleasure, and bliss. That delusion taints virtually every aspect of my experience. Things stop being simply what they are in and for themselves, and instead become (through my delusional projections) things of and for me. The beautiful sunset becomes my experience of the sunset, which gives me pleasure and my desire to wish it would last longer. This example, from the Buddhist perspective, exemplifies the two misconceptions fueling delusion: the hope for permanence and the belief in an abiding self or ego that is the subject and sole possessor of experience. Let us consider each of these purported delusional misconceptions in turn.

Nothing lasts forever. Nothing is eternal. The first statement is a fact of common sense. Stated simply in that way, most people would accept it without question. We come face to face with its truth over and over again in our lives: at the death of a loved one, at the end of a 'perfect day,' on the occasion of a graduation ceremony, at the close of a career. It is a commonplace statement that is not only true, but it is a poignant truth arising from the reflection on existence so central to our humanity.

The second statement, 'nothing is eternal,' has a more metaphysical than commonsensical ring to it, however. As such, it would not receive such universal acceptance. Various counterexamples might be offered: God, the soul, Brahman, the truths of mathematical relationships, Plato's forms, and so forth. That is, most people believe that behind the veil of impermanence lies an eternal realm free of decay and death. In fact, if people really believe in the tenets of the religions to which the census takers say they belong, the vast majority of people on earth accept that basic metaphysical belief. Yet, according to Buddhism, in that very metaphysical assumption lies the seed of delusion, the ground of psychospiritual addictions. The Buddhist claims that if you accept the commonsensical statement, you should also accept the metaphysical one. The puzzle for Buddhism to address is why most people do not.

One approach to explaining how Buddhism confronts this issue is to reflect on how we might try to justify metaphysical claims. By their very nature metaphysical assertions are not empirically verifiable in any positivistic sense. Suppose, for example, that I claim that reality is really one and you claim that it consists of discrete entities in diverse relationships to each other. There is no empirical evidence that would definitively settle the issue. Unless I am quite mad, I would concede that reality *appears* as many, but that behind that mere appearance is the unity. Therefore, our actual disagreement boils down to this: does the world appear the way it really is or is its appearance some form of illusion? I may claim that like some mystics I have had a direct experience of that unity while I was in a special state of consciousness. In that case, of course, I am saying *that* appearance in *that* kind of experience is true, whereas you are more likely to say it was a delusion or hallucination. In short, no appeal to empirical experience will settle our fundamental metaphysical disagreement.

Another tactic for settling metaphysical disagreements is to resort to logic. Given what we agree to be the case, what must be true so that it can be the case? Logic can try to answer that question. The Western scholastic arguments for the existence of God took this form, for example: given that things have causes, it follows logically that there must be a single first cause. That first cause we call 'God.' Such an appeal to logically derived first principles of metaphysics are, as Kant pointed out however, very tricky business. In fact in his discussion of the antinomies in the *Critique of Pure Reason,* Kant maintained that such logical reasoning could derive totally contradictory first principles, including the existence/nonexistence of God. Buddhism takes the same view. In fact, once the Indian tradition developed its own scholastic type of logical arguments to establish metaphysical principles, Buddhism produced its own Kant some eighteen centuries ago – Nāgārjuna.[4] Like Kant, he demonstrated that logical arguments can deduce contradictory propositions about such basic concepts as time, causality, self, and even nirvana. At best we can say logic is capable of refuting metaphysical systems only if they are incoherent. However, logical reasoning does seem destined to accept the possibility of alternative, yet mutually exclusive, coherent metaphysical systems.

Where does that leave us? Under the bodhi tree two and a half millennia ago. The Buddha's vow was to know the world as it is, not as he wanted it to be. In his introspection, he penetrated the truth of the commonsensical view that nothing lasts forever. But what is there behind that flux of impermanence? Nothing. That was the Buddha's insight. He realized that through the relational principle of conditioned coproduction or dependent origination (*pratītya samutpāda*), he could understand how things are. Although like the rest of us, he originally tended to think of the world as full of enduring objects, he came to see that nothing stands alone, nothing exists in and of itself as an individual thing. Therefore, nothing can be permanent or eternal. Although the early teaching of the principle of dependent origination was rather sketchy, through the centuries Buddhist philosophers developed the details of the theory. Their hope was to demonstrate that it was not only coherent, but also complete. That is, they sought to show the principle applied to the relationship among all dharmas, all phenomena.

Perhaps, a critic might say, the Buddha just did not sit long enough or did not sit in the right way during his introspection under the bodhi tree. If he only had had the experience of oneness, he would know there was something behind the impermanence. Yet, in that previously mentioned state of sensory cessation (*nirodha*) the Buddha entered during his last sermon, he must have experienced an undifferentiated unity. The Buddha realized, however, that although he could shut out the world in trance, that does not mean that the world itself disappears. After coming out of his trance, there was a continuity with what had come before: his disciples sitting around him with a look of concern, the birds chirping in the trees, the vegetation blowing in the breeze. He had shut his door to the world, but the world was there all along waiting for him to reopen the door to his senses.

Still, this does not prove the Buddhist metaphysics of impermanence. It may be that the theory of dependent origination can yield a coherent metaphysics, but it does not (as we have seen in our discussion of the limitations of logic) necessarily disprove a metaphysics of the eternal. It is one coherent metaphysics alongside another. There is no rational reason for choosing one over the other. Perhaps. But there is, according to Buddhism, a good psychological reason for doing so. Faced with two options – a world of flux with nothing self-existent or enduring versus a world of flux backed up by a realm of eternal, unchanging, perfect being – which would we prefer? Presumably the latter. That, the Buddhist would say, is the best reason for rejecting the metaphysics of the eternal. It seems to include something more than what we actually experience (the truth of 'nothing lasts forever') and what is added to the experience is something we desire (permanence, eternity). That suggests the possibility of delusory projection. The metaphysics of the eternal draws on our addiction to enduring self-gratification, to continuous self-centered pleasure. The Buddha's praxis under the bodhi tree gave him the technique to overcome that addiction. It disengaged his former belief in an abiding self or ego (*ātman*). This brings us to the second delusory misconception Buddhism criticizes: the belief in an I that is the enduring subject and possessor of experience.

The Buddhist *anātman* doctrine denies the assumption that there is an 'I' behind the experiential process. The self is neither fully individuated nor enduring. On this count it distinguishes itself from many of the common ideas of self in India as well as the West. The common Western notion of the soul, for example, is both individual (a basis of my unique personal identity) and an eternal substance. The Indian *Upanishadic* and Vedantic view rejects the notion that the self (*ātman*) is ultimately individual: from the absolute standpoint *ātman* is identified with the unity of *brahman*. Once liberated from ignorance, the classical theory maintains, the individual self disappears into the monistic whole as a drop disappears into the ocean. Yet, that ocean of being is itself eternal so, by extension, the true self is also an eternal substance. That Indian view is the mirror image of the Western philosophy of the transcendental ego found in various Kantian and phenomenological theories. That is, the transcendental ego is individual (it is the 'unity of apperception' that makes experience mine) but not substantial (it is neither an object of any experience, nor a provable metaphysical entity). So the Buddhist theory of *anātman* is by no means obvious and we need to inquire into its rationale. This takes us back to the Buddha sitting under the bodhi tree.

In many ways, the denial of the enduring substantiality of the ego or self follows directly from the Buddha's realization of impermanence. Through his introspection he experienced no abiding soul or individual identity. He was himself the flux of experience and not something that *had* or *underwent* experience. His personal identity was basically no different in form from the identity of a river. The river is always flowing; its boundaries constantly shifting in relation to the surrounding conditions; the water is always renewed. That is, the water in the river is not the same today as yesterday; the rate of flow is different; even the boundaries demarcating the river have shifted. Why then is it the same river? Does it have some abiding, unchanging substantial essence? Is it a unified substance with a changing set of attributes? No, the Buddha saw that the river is a process, not a thing. The continuity of the process entitles us to say it is the same river. In his introspection, he saw nothing else to explain his personal identity. A significant difference between him and the river was simply his constituents include consciousness and volition. So he could think of himself as continuing and could wish that he could continue forever. That is, unlike the river he had the potential for either enlightenment or delusion.

Furthermore, as in the case of impermanence in general, logic cannot settle the issue of the nature of the self. The *Upanishads* argued that personal identity requires a layer of reality behind the self of sensory experience.[5] There is the seer that is not seen, the hearer that is not heard. This deeper layer of the self gives continuity through the flux of experience. How else could one know in the morning, the Hindu philosophers argued, that one is still the same person who went to sleep the night before? During the night one not only dreamed but also underwent a dreamless sleep without any conscious content at all. Therefore, there was a break in the continuity of ordinary consciousness ('consciousness' as consciousness of something, even a dreaming consciousness of something). How then does one connect one's personal identity unless there is some continuity, the continuity of a pure, monistic consciousness with no subject-object dichotomy? This is a good logical argument that goes from what we agree is the case (the continuation of personal identity across a period of dreamless sleep) to what must be (a monistic, enduring *ātman* identified with *brahman)* such that things are as they are.

Of course, the Buddhists had logical arguments of their own. One of the most repeated was that the relationship among things is not another thing separate from the relations. The *locus classicus* is from the *Questions of King Milinda* wherein we have the example of the chariot. If we have all the pieces of a chariot, we do not have a chariot. Yet, that does not mean a piece, some *thing*, is missing. The interrelations are part of the things themselves when the conditions are correct. That is, the pieces of a chariot *are* a chariot under the right conditions (*viz.*, their being placed in a certain interdependent configuration). The chariot does not exist independently. Its coming into being is a *dependent* origination, a *conditioned* coproduction.

Similarly, there is no 'I' that is a piece (like either Hinduism's *ātman*, or Kant's transcendental ego) of what I am. 'I' refers to the pieces under the right conditions, the piecing together in a specific interdependent way. What gives the process I call 'I' continuity is not simply a thing (such as some special consciousness or dimension of consciousness) but the interrelated configuration of continuing processes. When those processes (bodily, mental, perceptual, etc.) no longer interrelate, I am no longer I.

So, as before, the issue of the true nature of the self is settled neither by direct experience nor logic. In our discussion of impermanence we contrasted the commonsensical 'nothing lasts forever' with the more metaphysical sounding 'nothing is eternal.' In terms of the self, we could find similarly contrasting terms. For example, 'I'm not the same person I used to be' (or simply 'people change') versus 'I have no self.' Few people would deny the first, but the second is somehow disturbing. Why? Because, the Buddhist claims, if we accept the second, we have lost the motive for our addiction to self-gratification and continuous self-centered pleasure. Our direct experience of ourselves, what is most clear when we return to our direct sensory experience, is a flow, what William James called the 'stream of consciousness.' Why do we assume there is something more? The Buddha looked for something more and did not find it. His insight stemmed from seeing that there was no need to assume there was something more. Logic tells us there *could* be something, but it also tells us there could *not* be. Why should we prefer one logical argument for the other? Again, the Buddha sees us drawn into delusions, to seeing what is not there, because of our addictions.

This concludes our discussion of the elements in the idealized paradigm that are most relevant to Buddhist notions of transformation and liberation. On some level, perhaps every Buddhist ideally seeks such an enlightenment experience, but I doubt that most have any expectation at all that they will actually have such an experience at least in this world in this lifetime. Nevertheless, that idealized paradigm continues to inform their lives, helping them to understand what is the reality of the human situation and helping them to structure their own spiritual insights, however fleeting. Let us review, therefore, the basic points not in the context of the Buddha, but in the context of the daily life of a Buddhist.

First, we have an addiction to self-gratification, to self-centered pleasure. Indeed, for those Buddhist traditions that foreground the idea of rebirth, our very birth in this world is a sign that we could not let go of our individual life. We are reborn in this world because we could not accept the extinction of nirvana. As with any addiction, the first step to help is to recognize that we are in fact addicts. We delude ourselves into thinking we have no problems and that very denial enflames the prospects of anguish. Although we may usually ignore the problem, however, there are moments of crisis when we wonder why our turmoil is so intense. At those times, we have a glimmer of the Buddha's message. We understand why we are suffering in the way we do.

Once we face the reality of our addiction, we know we have to do something, but what? The overall goals are quite clear: we must recognize the facts of impermanence and *anātman*. On this there is virtually universal agreement among all Buddhists. That is why the idealized paradigm of the Buddha's enlightenment can be so widely effective. Yet, the procedure for gaining that recognition and integrating it into our daily lives varies from sect to sect. It might be through the 'just sitting' of *zazen,* through the fathoming of *nembutsu,* through participation in esoteric ritual, through a series of controlled psychophysical yogic exercises, and so forth. Most disagreement among Buddhists is not over the nature of reality, but over which praxis and which way of thinking about that praxis is most effective.[6] The debates – whether enlightenment is sudden or gradual, whether we are already enlightened or we do need to do something to become enlightened, whether our primary goal is the enlightenment of ourselves or of others, whether practice as a form of self-effort is appropriate at all – are fundamentally disagreements about what therapy is best and why. There is virtually no disagreement about the state of health to be attained.

It is not surprising to find, therefore, that different traditions of Buddhism have developed different models of reality, of self, and of practice. Indeed the range of differences can be quite astounding.[7] Yet, once we fathom any of the different systems, we inevitably come back to the same insights about addiction, its causes and effects. In other words we come back to the idealized paradigm of what Buddhism is all about. We come back to the man sitting under the bodhi tree twenty-five centuries ago.

Notes

1 This is one of the main themes of Frederick J. Streng's flagship work in the *Religious Life of Man Series: Understanding Religious Life* (Belmont, CA: Wadsworth Publishing Company, 3rd ed., 1985).

2 For a discussion of this trance state and why it should not be confused with enlightenment, see David J. Kalupahana, *Casuality: The Central Philosophy of Buddhism* (Honolulu: University of Hawaii Press, 1975), 181–182.

3 One of the first scholars of Buddhism to make this fruitful connection with the modern psychological concept of addition was Roger Corless in his *The Vision of Buddhism* (New York: Paragon House, 1989), 81–83.

4 A classic work that explores many of the similarities (and some differences) between Kant and Nāgārjuna is T.R.V. Murti's *The Central Philosophy of Buddhism: A Study of the Madhyamika System* (London: George Allen and Unwin, Ltd., 1955, 1960 [2nd edition]. For a comparison of Nāgārjuna's enterprise and the antimetaphysical position of Jacques Derrida, see Part 3 of Robert Magliola, *Derrida on the Mend* (West Lafayette, IN: Purdue University Press, 1984). Nāgārjuna's use of an antimetaphysical position to ground a form of religious spirituality is best described in Frederick J. Streng, *Emptiness: A Study in Religious Meaning* (New York: Abingdon Press, 1967).

5 It is worth noting that Indian philosophy generally, both Hindu and Buddhist, understands us to have six, not five senses: the five typically recognized in the West as well as the inner perception that allows us to have sensory experience of our own inner states, both psychological and physical. In this respect, my awareness of my hunger or of my uneasiness, for example, is as much empirical data as what I see with my eyes or hear with my ears. This inner awareness is not, incidentally, identical with the mind. The mind interprets the sense data that are given by the six senses. Earlier in this essay, I noted that in some ways Buddhism is more psychological than epistemological. From the Indian perspective, however, some of what we consider psychological issues are really for them perceptual issues, that is, the problem of interpreting and misinterpreting data given by the sixth sense.

6 For an argument that religious differences are often over metapraxis rather than metaphysics, see my 'Philosophy as Metapraxis,' Frank Reynolds and David Tracy (eds.), *Discourse and Practice* (Albany, NY: State University of New York Press, 1992).

7 For a brief overview of these differences with an annotated bibliography, see my article '*Nirvāṇa*' in Mircea Eliade (ed.), *The Encyclopdia of Religion* (New York: Macmillan Publishing Company, 1987), 448–456.

CHAPTER EIGHTEEN

Nailed to a Tree: An Idealized Paradigm of Buddhist Transformation and Liberation

Ruben L. F. Habito

Addressing the theme of 'death' in one of the plenary sessions of the international Buddhist-Christian dialogue conference held in Berkeley, California in 1987, Taitetsu Unno, the Buddhist panelist, asked John Cobb, Jr., the question of how Christians understand the Resurrection of Christ, whether it is taken literally as an event in history, or whether it could be taken in a symbolic way. Cobb responded by posing a counter question as to how Buddhists understand the doctrine of transmigration.

The exchange that followed, which set the initial question about the doctrine of the resurrection in greater relief in comparison with parallel or resonating themes from Buddhist tradition, was more illuminating than what could have resulted from a straightforward theological answer from either of the participants. Instead of settling on one or the other theological position concerning the doctrines in question, the outcome was to throw the ball back, as it were, on the court of each Christian or Buddhist in the audience, inviting each to examine his or her own understanding of the particular doctrine, in the total context of one's faith understanding, now seen in a new light, that is, in contrast or comparison with a resonant theme from another religious tradition.

Reading Thomas Kasulis' 'Under the Bodhi Tree,' one is drawn to ask from a Christian perspective, how one may present an 'idealized paradigm of Christian transformation and liberation' that would cut through the different traditions and denominations, and bring all those who identify themselves as Christians under the shadow of the same tree. In other words, the question is about what Christians inevitably come back to as the rock-bottom core of their identity as Christians in a way analogous to how Buddhists come back to 'the man sitting under the Bo tree.' What immediately comes to light in this context for Christians is 'the man nailed to a tree.'

The Crucified One has always been the central image that expresses and sums up Christian identity throughout the ages. This is what we inevitably arrive at, borrowing Kasulis' words, 'once we fathom any of the different systems' of belief and practice professed by Christians throughout the various epochs of the Church's history. This, then, is what one could offer as 'an idealized paradigm of Christian transformation and liberation' – the Crucified One. But it is also a fundamental axiom of the believing community throughout the ages that the Crucified One is the same as the Risen One.

There has always been a number of influential 'theologies of the cross' throughout the history of Christianity, with their concomitant metaphysics and metapraxis. What is offered below is not meant to be another theology of the cross, but a tentative heuristic device for approaching this paradigm of the Crucified One as this has been inspired and illumined by our Buddhist-Christian dialogue. Our heuristic device is the schema of traditional Indian medicine: (1) symptomatology; (2) etiology; (3) prognosis; and (4) therapy, which also provides the underlying rhetorical structure of the Four Noble Truths.

The question, 'Why is the man on the tree?' leads us to the first and second themes in this four-fold structure: the examination of the human situation and the analysis of the roots and causes of this situation. Simply put, human beings in their existential situation find themselves in a distorted state which manifests itself in the various dysfunctions in our mode of existence: being at odds with our fellow human beings; alienation from the natural world; separation from our true and authentic self. What is the cause of this situation? In traditional Christian terminology, the cause of our situation is that we exist in a state of *sin*, understood as the state of separation from God, the ground and goal of our being. At the root of this situation is the inordinate attachment to *what is not God*, centered on a false self-image that gives undue importance to itself. Another name for this is *idolatry*, meaning the worship of that which is not God. Pride, greed, lust, envy, gluttony, anger, and sloth – the seven deadly sins – are but concrete manifestations of this inordinate attachment to that which is not God. To recognize our sinfulness and all its effects in our human society with all its conflict and violence and evil, is to look at the

Crucified One face-to-face. It is this recognition that enables one to proclaim, 'Christ died for our (*my*) sins.'

Having come to terms with one's sinfulness, that is, with one's dysfunctional and distorted state of existence, one is ready to receive the invitation to healing: *repent* (*metanoiete* or 'transformed in heart and mind') and accept the 'good news' (Gospel) of salvation (*salvus, salus, holos,* meaning 'whole' or 'healed'). This transformation of heart and mind (*metanoia*) involves a dislodging of the false self-image, the de-centering of the idolatrous self, and the acceptance of the Crucified One as one's savior. It is an opening of one's eyes to see that the Risen One *is* the Crucified One.

What, then, is the practice called for by the acceptance of the Good News of salvation? What does the path of ultimate transformation and liberation entail, in terms of our attitudes to ourselves, in terms of our concrete mode of life, our mode of relating to one another and to the natural world, now in a way no longer governed by sin nor based on separation and alienation, but in a way that *real*-izes the Reign of God?

Here again we turn to the story of the Last Judgment (Mt. 25:31–46) for illumination. And as we read this story not in the 'futuristic' mode that takes our human actions as merely *instrumental means* of piling up merit for the afterlife, but from a 'realized' perspective which regards this earthly life as the *very ground in which the Reign of God manifests itself* so that *we are called to manifest the Reign of God,* an important disclosure is waiting for us: 'For I was hungry and you gave me food, I was thirsty and you gave me drink. . .' – a flash of recognition that the Crucified One *is* the Risen One.

Following Kasulis, considering the different traditions of Buddhism, and noting the 'astounding' range of differences in models of reality, of self, and of practice, we still come back to the idealized paradigm of what Buddhism is all about: 'the man sitting under the Bo tree.' In an analogous way, considering the many different versions of Christianity, Christians too inevitably come back to the Crucified One, who is the Risen One. But here there is no mere *idealized* paradigm, that is, not like the kid playing basketball who 'does a Michael Jordan' and who may never come to equal Michael Jordan actually. One who, in all purity of heart, simply opens oneself to one's neighbor, be it someone who is hungry, thirsty, a stranger, or someone needing comfort, is assured: that very moment of opening oneself is a *real*-ization. The Risen One, who is the Crucified One, becomes manifest.

CHAPTER NINETEEN

The Resurrection of the Dead, and Life Everlasting: From a Futuristic to a Realized Christianity

Ruben L.F. Habito

The Christian doctrine relating to human ultimate destiny is given expression in the last two articles of the Apostles' Creed, as the community of faith proclaims: 'I believe ... the resurrection of the body, and life everlasting.' How each individual person who recites these words understands them, and how they impact that person's life, however, are open questions. This essay will focus on these two articles of Christian faith that relate to eschatology ('the doctrine of the last things') and consider their implications for Christian life and praxis. Its main thrust will be to set in comparison what we can call a 'futuristic' Christian outlook and a 'realized' Christian outlook, taking off from eschatological doctrine found in Christian tradition.

The first part will consider the scriptural background (in the Hebrew Bible and New Testament writings) of the two articles of the creed relating to eschatology. The second part will offer historical and theological considerations on developments of the doctrine of the 'last things' in Christian tradition, and describe the features of a 'futuristic Christianity' based on one reading of the doctrine. The third part will examine a New Testament account of the Last Judgment (Mt. 25:37–42), and consider two possible ways of reading the same passage, namely a 'futuristic' reading and a 'realized' reading, that reflect differing Christian views and consequent modes of life 'in the light of eternity.'

Scriptural Background

The proclamation of the early Church centered upon the good news of the resurrection of Jesus from the dead, and all that this implied (cf.

Acts 2:14–42). Preaching at Athens, Paul also conveyed a message that focused on Jesus' resurrection (Acts 17:18, 32). In a public confrontation before the Sanhendrin, Paul presents the gist of his message thus: 'Brethren, I am a Pharisee, a son of Pharisees; with respect to the hope and the resurrection of the dead I am on trial.' (Acts 23:6)

The connection between the proclamation of Jesus' resurrection and the ultimate destiny of humanity is emphasized by Paul in the fifteenth chapter of his first letter to the Corinthians:

> Now if Christ is preached as raised from the dead, how can some of you say that there is no resurrection of the dead? But if there is no resurrection of the dead, then Christ has not been raised; if Christ has not been raised, then our preaching is in vain, and your faith is in vain. (1 Cor 15:12–14)

Paul's epistles thus testify to the centrality of this teaching of the resurrection of Jesus Christ, and by consequence, the resurrection of (all) the dead. (Cf. Rom. 8:11; 1 Th 1:10, 4:14; I Cor 6:14, 15:12–22, among others.)

In the Synoptics, this connection between the resurrection of Jesus Christ and the ultimate destiny of all of humanity is more implied than clearly spelled out. However, that Jesus' teaching included this belief in the resurrection of the dead is evident, as indicated in his answer to the question proffered by the Sadducees (Mt. 22:23–33). Jesus' miracles involving the resuscitation of certain individuals from death, such as Jairus' daughter (Mk. 5:21–23, 35–43), or the widow's son (Lk. 7:11–15) are taken as signs of God's power over life and death. Incidentally, this theme of God's power over life and death is a prominent one throughout the Hebrew scriptures:

> The Lord kills and brings to life; … brings down to Sheol and raises up. (1 Sam 2:6)
>
> See now that I, even I, am the one, and there is no god beside me; I kill and make alive, I wound and I heal, and there is none that can deliver out of my hand. (Dt. 32:39)
>
> If I ascend to heaven, thou art there; if I make my bed in Sheol, thou art there! (Ps. 139:8)
>
> Thy dead shall live, their bodies shall rise, O dwellers in the dust, awake and sing for joy! (Is. 26:19)

(See also Isaiah 25:8, Wis. 16:3, Hosea 13:14, Amos 9:2, Ps. 16:10, Ps. 30:3, Ps. 41:3, Ps. 80:19, as well as the accounts of the resurrection miracles of Elijah and Elisha, 1 Kings 17: 17–23, 2 Kings 4:33ff, 13:21, and Ezekiel's prophecy about the raising of the dry bones from the graves, 37: 1–14, among others.)

Key passages in the Hebrew scriptures have served as the basis for Christian (re)interpretation of the phenomenon of the Empty Tomb, the reported historical fact upon which the Christian proclamation of Jesus' resurrection is grounded. The justification and the raising up of the Suffering Servant (Isaiah 53: 1–12) is one such classic example, as well as the others already cited above referring to God's power over life and death. (See Mt. 11: 2–6, Luke 7: 18–23, 24:2)

Christian rereadings of certain passages from Hebrew scriptures have connected these passages with prophecies about Jesus' resurrection and the concomitant resurrection of all the dead:

> For I know that my Redeemer lives, and at last he will stand upon the earth, and after my skin has been thus destroyed, then from my flesh I shall see God, whom I shall see on my side, and my eyes shall behold, and not another.' (Job 19:25–27)
>
> And many of those who sleep in the dust of the earth shall awake, some to everlasting life, and some to shame and everlasting contempt. And those who are wise shall shine like the brightness of the firmament and those who turn many to righteousness, like the stars forever and ever.' (Daniel 12:2–3)
>
> He will swallow up death forever, and the Lord will wipe away tears from all faces, and the reproach of his people he will take away from all the earth. For the Lord has spoken.' (Isaiah 25:8)

Some interpreters read such passages as signifying the restoration of Israel, rather than as attesting to belief in individual or collective immortality as such. (MacKenzie 1965, 731–32) There is evidence however, from the New Testament as well as other sources, that some groups, such as the Pharisees, did believe in the resurrection of the dead, and other groups, such as the Sadducees and the Samaritans, did not. However, such a belief is traceable only to a much later period of Jewish history, that is, around the Maccabean period or the second century BCE (See 2 Mac 7:9, 11, 23; 14:46). Daniel 12:2, as well as Isaiah 26:9 and 25:8, quoted above, are regarded as belonging to Apocalyptic literature, dated roughly from the early second century BCE on, during a period when there were many currents of thought and belief relating to the fulfillment of God's will and the establishment of God's eternal reign. (See MacKenzie 1965, pp. 41–42; 171–72; 397–98)

The New Testament Book of the Apocalypse (or the Book of Revelation) also belongs to such literature, and the passage from Isaiah (25:8) quoted above is echoed in one of its well-known apocalyptic sayings:

> (God) will wipe away every tear from their eyes, and death shall be no more, neither shall there be mourning nor crying nor pain any more, for the former things have passed away. (Rev. 21:4)

This is preceded by a vision of the ultimate destiny of humanity (and of the whole cosmos) in a realm that has overcome the passing things of this world:

> Then I saw a new heaven and a new earth; for the first earth had passed away, and the sea was no more. And I saw the holy city, new Jerusalem, coming down out of heaven from God, prepared as a bride adorned for her husband, and I heard a loud voice from the throne, saying 'Behold, the dwelling of God is with people. God will dwell with them, and they shall be (God's) people, and God(self) will be with them... (Rev. 21:1–3)

This book (of Revelation) is a work of Christian apocalypse that places the Risen Christ at its center and foundation-stone. Jesus Christ, Crucified and Risen, is the redeemer, the Son of Man (cf. Daniel 7:13) exalted in glory as the judge of the nations, the victor in the cosmic-eschatological struggle. (See Rev. 1:5; 2:26 ff.; 3:21; 5:6, 9; 7:14, 17; 12:5, 11; 13:8; 19:11, 15; 20:11–16; 21:1–4, 22; 22:1,3, 14)

Again in the Pauline epistles, the future day of Christ's full manifestation in glory (for example, 1 Cor 1:7–8; 5:5; 15:23–26; 2 Cor 1:14) is also the day when God's righteous judgment will be revealed to all (Rom 2:5, 16). Until then,

> ... creation waits with eager longing for the revealing of the children of God; for the creation was subjected to futility, not of its own will but by the will of the one who subjected it in hope; because the creation itself will be set free from its bondage to decay and obtain the glorious liberty of the children of God. (Rom. 8:19–21)

But during this intervening time, when believers are exhorted to continue in their hope, and to wait, 'with patience' (Rom. 8:25), they are also already assured in the promise that victory has been attained, and that the fullness of glory will indeed be manifested fully in its own due time. In other words, the power of the Risen Christ is already at work in those who believe, through the Spirit that they now have received, constituting them as true children of God and bearing witness to God's fidelity, as their assurance of the fulfillment of things to come. (Rom. 8:14–17)

This community of believers, the Church, is itself the very embodiment of 'the fullness of Christ' (See Ephesians 1:23, 3:19, 4:13), though still engaged in the ongoing historical task of bringing together in Christ 'things in heaven and things on earth.' (Eph. 1:10) The frequent appearance of the phrase 'in Christ' in the Pauline epistles indicates an understanding of the present mode of life and state of being of baptized Christians as already sharing in this cosmic fullness that is Christ's. In other words, in their participation in the death and resurrection of Jesus Christ through baptism, Christian believers are *now* already sharers in his glory, even as they continue to live in hope toward a future and final manifestation of this very same reality: 'For you have died, and your life is hid with Christ in God. When Christ who is our life appears, then you also will appear with him in glory.' (Col. 3:3–4) In short, although the theme of expectation of future glory remains a prominent theme in the Pauline corpus, this dimension of the Christian's (yet unmanifest) participation in that glory of the divine life is present even now, in and through the life in the Spirit (Rom. 5:1–5, 8:23, 2 Cor 3:17–18, etc.).[1]

The (Fourth) Gospel of John meanwhile calls attention to its presentation of the eschatological (and the eternal) dimension as *already realized* in encounter with the person of Jesus Christ. The Christ that speaks in this Gospel is not so much the flesh-and-blood Jesus of Matthew, Mark, and Luke, but the Eternal Word of God made flesh (cf. John's prologue, 1:1–18). Among the dominant themes that mark this gospel's character (including Baptism, Eucharist, Faith, Love, Light, etc.) the theme of Life is a prominent one. 'I came that they may have life, and have it abundantly (Jn 10:10b),' is a passage among so many other pronouncements affirming the message of Jesus as the good news of Eternal Life, the victory over death. (See John 1:4; 3:16; 5:21; 6:39–40, 44, 50, etc.)

'I am the resurrection and the life (11:25),' uttered in the context of the story of the raising of Lazarus from the dead (11:1–44), is a passage that resonates throughout the fourth Gospel. The acceptance of Jesus as the Word of God then is understood as the very reception of this eternal life itself: 'For this is the will of my Father, that every one who sees the Son and believes in him should have eternal life; and I will raise him up at the last day.' (6:40)

The life of the follower of Jesus then is one that already lives, having realized this promise of eternal life, with the Risen Christ in the fullness of glory. (See John 1:14) To such persons is given the assurance that 'even if they die, shall live (11:25),' repeated throughout the fourth Gospel in various forms.

> Truly, I say to you, one who believes has eternal life. (6:48)
>
> I am the living bread which came down from heaven; if anyone eats of this bread, that one will live forever; and the bread which I shall give for the life of the world is my flesh. (6:51)
>
> And this is eternal life, that they know thee the only true God, and Jesus Christ whom thou has sent. (17:3)

The same Gospel also alludes to a future resurrection on the 'last day' (as in 6:39–40, 44; 11:24, etc.) and exhorts the believers to fortitude during times of persecution, when they will 'weep and lament, but the world will rejoice' (16:20). This intervening time is likened to the birth pangs that are a prelude to the full glory of the Savior's coming.

> ... you will be sorrowful, but your sorrow will turn joy. When a woman is in travail she has sorrow, because her hour has come; but when she is delivered of the child, she no longer remembers the anguish, for joy that a child is born into the world. (16:20–21)

There is thus a seemingly deliberate interplay of the dimensions of the 'not yet' with the 'already there' in the fourth Gospel, as regards the destiny of the Christian. Nevertheless, here eternal life is not only a *promise* to be fully revealed in the future, but more significantly, *a present reality* that is opened to one who has accepted Christ in one's life.[2]

Historical and Theological Considerations

In Christian theology the term 'eschatology' has traditionally been understood to mean 'the study of the last things,' (based on the Greek *eschatos*, 'last,' or *eschaton*, 'the end time'). Two aspects of the study have traditionally been distinguished, namely, the individual dimension, referring to the fate of each individual human being after death, and the universal or cosmic dimension, referring to the final outcome of God's plan of creation, or 'economy of salvation.' The former would consider topics including death, God's judgment of the individual soul, heaven and hell, purgatory, and the like, while the latter would deal with issues involving the Second Coming of Christ or the 'Parousia,' apocalyptic prophecies (such as those in the Book of Revelations), universal judgment at the end of the world, and the resurrection of the body at this end-time.

In recent decades, with a renewed appreciation of the manifold nuances and plurality of perspectives in the Bible, as revealed by findings in Scripture studies and advances in Biblical theology, 'eschatology is now more integrated with the whole of theology and is no longer content merely with statements about a remote future.'[3] More than simply about 'the *last* things' in the sense of 'the ending' in a linear temporal series of events, Christian eschatology is better understood as the theological reflection on the dimension of 'the *ultimate*' in human existence as enlightened by the good news of Jesus Christ. In this context, theological considerations on 'the resurrection of the body, and life everlasting,' will not be mere speculation on what is to happen in the remote future based on what is given in scripture and tradition, but will necessarily address the question of how these doctrines shed light on Christian living and praxis *here and now*.

First, a rough historical sketch of some attitudes on 'the last things' taken by Christians throughout the ages may be of helpful reference for further theological reflection. There were those in the early Christian community who apparently believed in the imminent Second Coming of Jesus Christ, and hence disposed themselves accordingly, ceasing to work for their living and simply waiting for the hour to come. This Parousia (from the Greek, meaning 'presence' or 'arrival') incidentally was understood to be preceded by heavenly signs (the appearance of an archangel and the blast of a heavenly trumpet – 1 Th 4:13ff) and unusual phenomena (the departure of heavenly bodies from their courses – Mt. 24:29, etc.), an event that is to come like a flash of lightning (Mt. 24:27, Lk. 17:24), suddenly, like a 'thief in the night' (1 Th 5:2). This would be the hour of the resurrection of the dead, and those who had died who are judged among the righteous would join Jesus in glory in the clouds, while those still alive would be 'snatched up' into the same glorious state (1 Cor 15:23, 1 Th 4:13ff).

This belief in the imminence of the Second Coming among early Christians is suggested by many passages in New Testament writings (Mt. 10:23, 24:34, Mk. 13:30, Lk. 21:32, 1 Th 4:13ff, 1 Pt. 4:7, Rev 3:11, 22:20). In his second letter to the Thessalonians, Paul sees fit to rebuke those who, presuming the imminence of the Parousia, had abandoned their normal lives and were 'living in idleness and not doing any work' (2 Thes 3:11). But this attitude, which we can term 'futuristic' in the full sense of the term, meaning a relegation of everything to and total reliance on an expected future event (in this case the Second Coming of Christ) to the denigration of the present, was by no means the predominant one in the early Church. The community of believers in the good news of the Risen Christ continued to live their 'worldly' lives and fulfil their tasks in the temporal domain, and in so doing, forming the matrix of a dynamic movement that in due time came to transform the society of the period, even winning over the Roman empire.

During the early centuries of Church history, two elements stood out in particular in a way that served as markers for the Christian community's attitude vis-à-vis the world. One was the special veneration toward the martyrs, those who had laid down their lives in the imitation of Jesus Christ and in witness to the gospel. Another was the high esteem held for those who embraced the monastic life, understood as the abandonment of the world's values in order to witness with one's whole life to the values of the gospel. In other words, firm confidence in the coming future glory that awaits the righteous, expressed in the creedal formula 'I believe ... the resurrection of the body, and life everlasting,' continued to give Christians an acute sense of the impermanence and therefore the unsatisfactoriness of human existence in this world, inspiring them to 'seek the things that are above.'

The profession of belief in the resurrection of the body and the consequent everlasting life that this entails, has always been a keystone of the Christian tradition from its inception, defended and expounded on in early writings as the Didache, and by such authors as St. Polycarp, St. Athenagoras, Theophilus of Antioch, Tertullian, and others. In the fourth and fifth centuries, in reaction to Origen's (ca. 185–254) opinion that resurrected bodies consisted of some form of ethereal matter, other Christian writers found the need to emphasize that all will rise with the same bodies as they lived in their earthly lives.[4]

Official pronouncements of the Church have continued to affirm the resurrection of the body as a divinely revealed truth, in different conciliar and papal statements over the ages.[5] The Fourth Lateran Council (1215) formulated the basic structure of Christian belief regarding the resurrection of the body in a definitive way, specifying that a) there will be a resurrection, b) that it will be universal (that is, including both the just and the unjust), and c) that resurrected bodies will be the same as the ones lived in earthly existence.[6]

One important feature of the Christian doctrine concerning the ultimate destiny of humankind that defined the character of the Church from the early centuries on, proclaiming as it does that all are called to an eternal destiny, to the fullness of glory in the Risen Christ, is thus the placement of the *summum bonum* in an absolute, transcendent principle that is over and above anything of 'this world.' Thus, while living *in the world*, Christians continue to live grounded in the conviction that they are not *of it*, meant as they are toward a glorious and eternal destiny with God, a state of glory incomparable to any benefit or happiness attainable in this world.

On the down side, however, such an attitude can verge on and has actually led to a denial of any value at all to life in the world among some Christians (such as in the renowned case of Joachim of Fiore, 1132–1202) who harbor a radical dualistic outlook.

The dualistic tendency in the Christian mind-frame was further fueled by Platonic and Neo-Platonist elements that came to be influential in Christian theology from the early Middle Ages on. This point, of course, demands a much more detailed and careful account than can be presented here, but suffice it for us here to note that in place of the traditional (and orthodox) Christian profession of belief in the resurrection of the body, the belief in the *immortality of the soul* came to occupy the predominant position in Christian outlook on 'the last things.' Neo-Platonist philosophical underpinnings were influential in theological tracts as well as in popular views, making their definitive impact on Christian life and praxis.

Thus, death came to be conceived as the separation (liberation) of the immortal soul from the perishable body, and it was the individual soul (in contrast to the *whole person*) that faced judgment before God after death. Thus, a denigration, or positive disdain, for the body and all that pertains to it, became a widely held attitude. Needless to say, this outlook continues to be an influential one among many Christians today. The negative attitude toward sexuality inculcated among many Christians, for example, is one corollary of this dualistic mentality.

This body-soul dualism that has seeped into Christian thinking is not unrelated to what we can describe as a 'futuristic' understanding of the Christian message. Its extreme form can be seen in those in the early Christian community who simply abandoned their earthly tasks and sat around waiting for the Parousia, and who thus became a subject for reproach by the Apostle Paul (2 Thes 3:6ff). But there are varying shades of this kind of outlook that manifests itself in life and practice.

Simply stated, a futuristic Christianity can be described as one that lays emphasis on the fulfillment of God's promises in the future (whether imminent or distant), and understands the gospel message mainly in terms of that future fulfillment. History is understood as a linear movement that is directed toward that future point, wherein everything will come to its 'end' (both in the sense of 'termination' as well as 'goal.') Everything that happens in time is oriented toward that 'end.' Thus, to profess belief in 'the resurrection of the body' is to manifest one's hope in a future event wherein one's soul, separated at one's biological death, will again be reunited with one's physical body (unless one happens to be still alive when that time comes, in which case one will simply be 'snatched up'), to face final judgment before God. 'Life everlasting' will be a linear continuation from thence to infinity, in heaven for the just, and hell for the unjust.

In this context, this earthly life is taken as a transient state or process whose whole meaning and goal depends on that future event. Ethical behavior, 'obeying the commandments,' is geared toward the attainment of this goal. Individual prayer and communal worship ('attending church') are acts that are considered 'religious obliga-tions,' providing 'merit' that would help one attain that future goal. Those who, in Christ's name, so believe in the future resurrection of the body, who thereby obey the commandments and fulfill their religious obligations, are inclined to consider themselves the ones to be numbered among 'the just,' and woe unto those who believe and live otherwise.

The question at issue here is whether the above depiction exhausts the possibilities of reading the gospel in the light of its eschatological doctrine, or whether there is another way of understanding the Christian message, which, while affirming belief in 'the resurrection of the body, and life everlasting,' does so in a way significantly different from the futuristic kind as described above. The suggestion offered in this essay is this: right at the heart of Christian scripture and tradition we can find a way of understanding and living the gospel of Jesus Christ, including its eschatological message, not in futuristic terms as depicted above, but in a way that can be described as 'realized.'[7]

The Last Judgment: Toward a Realized Christianity

In order to highlight the features of a 'realized' way of understanding and living the Christian message as different from a 'futuristic' one, we will first explore two possible readings of a key passage depicting an eschatological vision: the Last Judgment scene in the Gospel of Matthew (25:31–46).

> When the Son of Man comes in glory with all the angels, then he will sit on his glorious throne. Before him will be gathered all the nations, and he will separate them one from another as a shepherd separates the sheep from the goats, and he will place the sheep at his right hand, but the goats at the left. Then the King will say to those at his right hand, 'Come, O blessed of my Father, inherit the Kingdom prepared for you from the foundation of the world; for I was hungry and you gave me food, I was thirsty and you gave me drink, I was a stranger and you welcomed me, I was naked and you clothed me, I was sick and you visited me, I was in prison and you came to me.'
>
> Then the righteous will answer him, 'Lord, when did we see thee hungry and feed thee, or thirsty and give thee drink? And when did we see thee a stranger and welcome thee, or naked and clothe thee?
>
> And the King will answer them, 'Truly, I say to you, as you did it to one of the least of these my brethren, you did it to me.'
>
> And he will say to those at his left hand, 'Depart from me, you cursed, into the eternal fire prepared for the devil and his angels. Truly I say to you, as you did it not to one of the least of these, you did it not to me.'
>
> And they will go away into eternal punishment, and the righteous into eternal life.

A futuristic reading will take the passage to mean that, indeed, as proclaimed in another article of Christian faith (formulated in the Nicene Creed), at some future time, Jesus Christ 'will come again in glory, to judge the living and the dead,' and that the judgment will be based on how each individual believer responded to the needs of 'the least of my brethren.' Those judged 'righteous' will enter eternal life in glory with God, and 'the unrighteous' will be taken by the devil down to hell, where they will burn forever in everlasting fire.

Christian life and praxis is thus seen as geared toward this ultimate goal, namely, the attainment of eternal life in heaven. And in order to attain this ultimate goal, one must live and act in the manner prescribed, that is, attending to the needs of 'the least of my brethren,' by feeding the hungry, etc., for Christ is present 'in' them. To perform charitable acts that benefit 'the less fortunate' is to do these things on behalf of Christ, who will be our judge on that last day.

It goes without saying that the history of Christianity is replete with examples of the good deeds and the charitable institutions that have flowed out of this vision of Christ in 'the least of the brethren.' If Christianity is to be judged by its results in human history, this is something that is not at all to be belittled.

However, seen in such terms, the message of Christianity would appear to be reducible to this framework: human life on earth is no more than a temporary testing place toward our permanent destination. To 'pass' (the test) is to merit heaven, and to 'fail' is of course to fall into hell. In crass terms, 'believe and behave, and you will get your carrot; otherwise, you'll get the stick.' This may verge on caricature, but this is what a futuristic kind of Christianity amounts to.

Under this conception, it would not make a significant difference whether the Gospel teaching is about 'the resurrection of the body' or 'the immortality of the soul.' In fact, the latter would fit the futuristic scheme more neatly and coherently: the doctrine of the resurrection of the body in such a framework would continue to present apparently insurmountable philosophical-scientific problems.[8]

However, and this is our central contention in this essay, there is an entirely different way of reading the Last Judgment passage, which would accordingly transform one's understanding (and consequent way of living) the message of Christianity.

Let us take a hint from the question raised by the 'righteous' (v. 37–39): 'when did we see thee hungry and feed thee ...?' This could be read of course as a mere dramatic ploy to accentuate the key point and climactic pronouncement in 25:40 – 'truly, I say to you, as you did it to one of the least of these my brethren, *you did it to me.*' To take it however at face value would give us an important clue: those who 'fed the hungry, gave drink to the thirsty, etc.,' *were not aware* that they were doing it 'on behalf of Christ,' nor did they seem to have done those things with the aim of meriting heaven at all, or with any religious motivation for that matter. *They simply responded to the needs of those persons, as the situations presented themselves before them.* In other words, they are those who were living their lives in a way that is totally open to one's neighbor, fully open to situations that called for their appropriate response.

The key point of the whole passage, then, the presentation of the coming of Jesus Christ in glory, announcing that 'as you did it to the least of my brethren, *you did it to me,*' *is* the Good News as such. In other words, the gospel message is the proclamation that a way of life open to one's neighbor and responsive to the needs of the situation, and acting accordingly, *is the gate to eternal life itself.* In short, the good news is that our life here on earth has infinite consequences, and eternal life is to be discovered *right here* in our midst as we go about our earthly tasks and lay ourselves open to our neighbor.

At the same time, this is also the bad news: those who live in a way opposite to that described, that is, in a way that closes them off from their neighbor and from the call of the situations around them pertaining to the needs of their fellow beings, in other words, those who live in a selfish, self-centered, and self-enclosed kind of way, do just that, that is, close themselves off from this invitation to eternal life in the Risen Christ, and thus, consign themselves to hell.

A realized Christianity thus sees this life is not merely a 'testing place' for a future destiny in eternity, but as *the very ground in which eternal life manifests itself.* The Lord of Judgment is not just to appear at some future time, but (as Mt. 25:31–46 suggests) is *present right at the heart of earthly realities and events.* History is not just a linear series of earthly or human events that will eventually come to a conclusion at some end point to give in to timeless eternity, but is the very field of the Eternal God's compassionate and salvific action (see John 3:16).

The 'realized eschatology' that permeates throughout John's Gospel can be taken as 'corroborating evidence' for the above reading.[9] In our first section above, we have looked at the fourth Gospel's emphasis on the *present realization* of God's eschatological promise, in the very coming of Jesus Christ, the Word-made-flesh. The judgment of God is imminent, *here and now,* inviting each one to accept Jesus Christ, God's Eternal Word, in one's life. The Matthean passage read above (25:31–46) gives us the clue as to where we can find Him, right in our very midst.

We have also noted in the first section how the Pauline epistles manifest the manifold dimensions of the fullness of life 'in Christ' in which the Christian is invited to participate in the here and now, in a way that maintains the interplay and the tension of the 'already-there' and the 'not-yet' – it is the life *in the Spirit* that bridges the two poles of the tension, placing the Christian right in the midst of the Trinitarian life, enabling us in Christ to cry from the depths of our being, 'Abba, Father' (Rom 8:15, Gal. 4:6), even as we groan with the whole of creation in its birth pangs (Rom 8:22).

We can find further corroborations of our reading of the Last Judgment passage from a perspective of a realized (as opposed to a futuristic) Christianity in other New Testament writings as well.[10] For example, the proclamation that God's reign has arrived (see Mt. 3:2; 4:17; 10:7; 12:28; Mk. 1:15; 11:10, Lk. 10:9, 11; 11:20, 17:20; 19:11, 21:31), and is already 'in your midst' (Lk. 17:21) is a pervading theme in the Synoptics. The announcement of this good news (i.e. of its arrival) is the central theme of Jesus' whole earthly mission, and his death-resurrection as his passage into glory is proclaimed by the believing community (i.e. those who accepted his message) as intimately connected with that mission, which is the realization of God's reign in history. That believing community, the Church, is thus understood as the agent entrusted with carrying out this same earthly mission of Jesus Christ – that is, the *realization* of God's reign in history.

The *content* of the proclamation, that God's reign is 'in our midst,' and its *intent*, namely the realization of this reign in the field of history until all things have come to their fullness in Christ (Eph. 1:3–10), constitute the two poles in tension, the 'already there' and the 'not yet' of the Christian eschatological vision. As we survey the history of the Church through the ages, we would be able to discern further evidence for a realized Christianity especially in the lives of numerous mystics and saints, who present themselves to us as models of Christian life, that is life 'in Christ,' and in whose very lives the presence of God was a transparent reality. (This is a task we can relegate to a future project.)

From the perspective of a realized Christianity, the doctrines of the resurrection of the body and life everlasting, are seen in full significance as the affirmation of the transformative power of the Spirit of the Risen Christ *in this very body*. It is this body that 'I live' and 'I am' (as opposed to 'I have') that is affirmed by scriptures and tradition as that same one that is the subject of resurrection (see sections 1 and 2, above). It is this very body that constitutes me in the totality of my human personhood, that is the subject of 'life everlasting' in a vision of God face-to-face, that is called to its ultimate destiny in heaven, in communion with all the saints.[11] And again, it is this very body wherein the polar dimensions of 'already there' and 'not yet,' always in mutual tension and interplay in Christian eschatological doctrine, come to converge at one point; in this very body (i.e., the subject of the resurrection), one is able to proclaim, with Paul, that 'I live, not I, but Christ in me.' (Gal. 2:20)

The suggestion made in this essay is that the core message of Christianity is not about something that will happen in a remote future, but an invitation to consider the ultimate implications of our life on this earth here and now. The acceptance of this message, of the good news of Jesus Christ, of the reality of God-with-us, is itself a transformative event that can unleash the creative and healing power of God's presence in this very body, on this very earth. As the Christian allows this power to work in her whole being, s/he is enabled to participate in that divine creative and healing work, toward a 'new heaven and a new earth.' (Rev. 21: 1).

Concluding Reflections

The further elaboration of the features of a realized Christianity and its implications for Christian life and praxis remains a continuing theological task. This essay has only presented the bare outline of what it involves in terms of understanding and living the eschatological doctrine proclaimed by the Christian community since the start. The continuation of such a theological task would contribute to the overcoming of stereotyped notions of Christianity (that is, those based on the futuristic kind) as earth-negating, body-denying, future-oriented, moralistic and judgmental of others, exclusivistic in its view of final salvation, etc. It would contribute significantly in the presentation of a radically different view of Christianity, as one that affirms the earth and history as the field of God's action and the locus of the manifestation of God's presence; as one that treasures this earthly body as the temple of God and as the subject of the resurrection; as one that celebrates our life together in the here and now; as one convinced that it is the Lord of history, and not frail human beings, who is the ultimate source of salvation.

Such a Christianity then is able to open itself in dialogue with members of other religious traditions, to discern common tasks toward ultimate transformation and liberation, in the light of the concrete socio-ecological and political realities of our time. A realized Christianity will enable its adherents to embrace peoples of other faith traditions or of differing belief systems as fellow sojourners, and taking up common tasks of healing our wounded Earth, walk together toward a 'new heaven and a new earth.'

Notes

1 Here I am indebted to and heartily thank Prof. Victor Furnish for bibliographical suggestions and helpful hints in the reading of Paul's letters in preparation for this part of the essay.

2 Here I acknowledge my gratitude to Prof. Jouette Bassler for her helpful suggestions on 'realized eschatology' in the Gospel of John.
3 *New Catholic Encyclopedia*, 5 (Washington, D.C.: Catholic University of America, 1967), 536. Hereafter cited as NCE.
4 See NCE 12, 426.
5 See Denzinger, H and C. Rahner, *Enchiridion Symbolorum,* 31st Edition. Freiburg, 1960, Nos. 11, 30, 56, 150, 801, 859.
6 NCE 12, 426.
7 See John P. Keenan, *The Gospel of Mark: A Mahayana Reading* (Maryknoll: Orbis Books, 1995) as a corroborative example of a reading along these lines.
8 See NCE 12, 426–427. Also see Gregory of Nyssa (*On the Soul and the Resurrection*), 27–121. Critical Edition Ed. by G. Krabinger, Lezig 1837. De Anima Resurrectione.
9 See 'Beatific Vision,' NCE 2, 186–193; 'Heaven,' NCE 6, 968–975; 'Communion of Saints,' NCE 4, 41–43.

CHAPTER TWENTY

The Momentous and the Momentary

Thomas P. Kasulis

In his essay 'The Resurrection of the Dead and Life Everlasting,' Ruben Habito gives an insightful and provocative reading of Christianity, emphasizing the elements that would support what he calls a 'realized' rather than 'futuristic' Christianity. As he suggests at the very end of his piece, such a reading opens Christianity to deeper levels of dialogue with other traditions. In fact, throughout his discussion, he teases out possible points of dialogue by using terms often associated with Buddhism: salvation as 'right now,' 'participation in the here and now,' achieving salvation 'in this very body,' and so forth. Even the term 'realization' has a Buddhist, as much as Christian, ring to it. In short, by discussing Christianity in such a manner, Habito has consciously set parameters for Buddhist-Christian dialogue. In such a short essay, of course, Habito could only intimate what those issues might be. For my response, I will try to draw out more clearly issues I think he needs to address as he brings us into further interreligious dialogue.

Whose Christianity? Which Salvation?

'Christianity' and 'Buddhism' are obviously complex traditions and it is often useful to identify which kinds of Christianity or Buddism are involved in a particular dialogue. What kind of Christianity is Habito explicating? His exegesis of Matthew 25:31–46, for example, suggests that salvation may derive from how righteously one responds to the needs of others. In this case the primary principle of soteriology appears purely ethical: one need not have faith in either God or Jesus

Christ and one need not participate in sacraments or a church. Consider a Marxist materialist who renounces all religion and the very reality of spiritual transcendence, but who feels a humnanistic urge to eradicate poverty and starvation, helping his fellow human beings whenever possible. According to Habito's realized Christianity and his exegesis of the passage from Matthew, such a person would presumably be saved. I suspect many other Christians, however, even many who would be sympathetic to the ideals of realized Christianity, would also expect to find some appeal either to a principle of justification by faith or to a principle of justification by (sacramental) works in the Church.

Of course, Habito is not excluding such theories of justification in his vision of realized Christianity. In fact the passage from Matthew suggests it is almost an addendum to the regular path to salvation. It can in this sense be the basis for a principle of anonymous Christianity, extending salvation to those who performed acts of compassion without realizing those acts were for Christ. It allows good non-Christians to be saved along with good Christians. If this is indeed a principle of anonymous Christianity, though, it is quite different from Rahner's, for example. In developing his theory, Karl Rahner maintained that the anonymous Christian must recognize one's connections with fellow human beings, but also some ontological commitments about the spiritual dimension of reality. As Habito rightly points out, it is not simply the act of helping others, but also the *responsiveness* to the plight of others that counts. I suspect that point will be critical as Habito develops a fuller version of his realized Christianity. To put the point pithily, it is not that caring for the needy makes one an anonymous Christian, but that by being an anonymous Christian (having the appropriate sense of spirituality and responsive-ness), one will naturally care for those who suffer. I do not think that most Christians who read Matthew 25:31–46 would understand it to mean that whoever takes a payroll deduction for the United Way will be saved. A spiritual component must be present in the act of charity.

This brings us to the spiritual nature of the responsiveness Habito outlines. In what respects is it similar to Buddhism and in what respects not?

Being Here Now – Christian and Buddhist

In developing a realized Christianity that emphasizes the 'here' and 'now,' Habito establishes a critical point for Buddhist-Christian dialogue. The similarities between the traditions on this point are plain enough: in realized Christianity and in most forms of Buddhism, the present is the arena of religious manifestation. This is in contrast with the futuristic Christianity that emphasizes a nonpresent time *(eschaton)* and place (heaven) as the focus of spiritual authentication. If we look more closely, however, at *why* the here and now is the focus of both realized Christianity and Buddhism, important differences between the two traditions begin to emerge. It amounts to differences in ontology and the view of time. We begin with the latter.

According to Buddhism, the 'now' is momentary, whereas for realized Christianity it is momentous. According to Buddhism no moment is ultimately more important than any other. Only the present, not the past or future, now exists. Even past-directed memories and future-directed aspirations are in the present. Therefore, the present has a priority. It is what-is as-it-is. In Christianity, on the other hand, not all moments are spiritually equal in value. Christianity is inextricably a historical tradition that has a deeply embedded teleology. There are special moments in the Christian history of humankind. In Buddhism the present is important because it is momentary and must be realized before it passes. In Christianity the present is important because it is momentous and its special spiritual significance must not be missed. This is sometimes expressed in Christianity as *kairos,* the time of fruition.

Because *kairos* assumes teleology, it might seem it is inherently affiliated with futuristic rather than realized Christianity. Not necessarily. When we follow Habito's analysis of realized Christianity, we realize that the present is transformed through the presence of Jesus Christ. That is, the Incarnation and life of Jesus in this historical world constituted a momentous event that transformed time for all realized Christians. From this perspective Matthew 25:31–6 is not focusing on ethics or even anonymous Christianity as much as it is focusing on the triumph of the suffering Christ and its relevance to life in this world. Because of God's incarnate suffering in this world as a human being, the entire context of human suffering has been transformed. Christ is in the sufferer and if we attend to that suffering, we attend to Christ. This is the Christian ontological transformation that accompanies the temporal transformation. It changes the significance of 'here' as much as it changes the significance of 'now.' The world is transformed here and now into the Kingdom of God.

Habito's realized Christianity focuses on the here and now because of that momentous event of Christ's life on earth when he dwelled among us. Unlike futuristic Christianity, realized Christianity emphasizes that the world has been temporally and ontologically transformed so that Christ's *parousia* is not an isolated future event in eschatological time, but the culmination of a presence from the time of the incarnation through the present up to the Last Days. For the realized Christian, Christ is still among us, especially in the suffering inherent to our humanity. We do not have to wait for the Last Days to encounter Christ face-to-face. The Christ is there in the pangs of the hungry, the despair of the imprisoned, the shackles of the poor, and the limitations of the handicapped.

Yet, however much Buddhists might respect this Christian view, they cannot accept it for themselves. The Buddhist view of temporality and being cannot be readily reconciled with that of Christianity, even realized Christianity. Buddhism generally rejects the notion of a momentous event that transforms ontology and temporality. The Buddha did not change the nature of reality; he discovered it.

In fact, I think Buddhists can find realized Christianity's views on the transformation of time and being as not only alien, but 'unskillful' or 'counterproductive.' For Buddhism it is a dangerous self-delusion to believe some events are more spiritually momentous than others, are tinged with a religious significance deriving from an eternal, transcendent source. Such a view, Buddhism argues, leads to questions such as: 'Why is God letting this happen? What is my (or my people's) special role in history? What reality is there behind what appears here and now? Given the reality of a transcendent source of creation, how should I act toward my fellow human beings, even my enemies?' and so forth. From the Buddhist perspective such questions, so central to the Christian's world view, are not conducive to our realization. They inhibit our fully fathoming our own responsibility for our anguish. In so doing, they distract us from understanding the conditionedness that links us together in this ephemeral world and that can be the basis for a spontaneous compassion based in this world as it is.

The Buddhist would find the realized Christian view to be anchored in a faith in what is not directly experienced through the six senses (sight, touch, taste, smell, sound, and internal awareness). Such a faith allows the Christian to believe the transcendent can imbue the immanent with momentous significance. The danger, the Buddhist would claim, is that such a faith in transcendence is both ungrounded and a distraction from coming to grips with the impermanent and momentary character of reality. It clouds the axiological neutrality of events when viewed without ego and without the desire for permanence. Such a faith is not only not essential for realization, but can be a profound obstruction to it. For the realized Christian, however, it is essential. Without the awareness of how Jesus Christ has altered both ontology and temporality – an awareness that can only be achieved through faith – the very nature of realized Christianity has no foundation. Therein lies a central difference between the Buddhist and Christian traditions.

PART SIX

Epilogues

CHAPTER TWENTY-ONE

A Buddhist Epilogue

Taitetsu Unno

Reflecting on all the major papers and their responses, I am impressed by how far the enterprise of Buddhist-Christian dialogue has evolved since its beginning in the present form in the early 1980s. This is evident in the rich contents of Winston King's summation of the variables in dialogue, the principal voices of both Buddhist and Christian representatives, and problematics of dialogical concerns. His reflections are based on a lifelong involvement with Buddhist-Christian issues, ranging from Southeast Asia to Japan and from Theravada to Zen, providing us with much food for thought. His counterpart, David Chappell, adds substance to the dialogical encounter by giving a sweeping overview of the Buddhist perspectives from the Buddha's own attitude to the views of Ta-hui Tsung-kao and Ch'ongho Hyujong concerning other traditions. He provides especially illuminating information concerning Buddhist-Christian interchanges in the past century since the World's Parliament of Religions in 1893. Both articles lay a firm foundation for all future dialogical encounters, an appropriate tribute to the pioneering work and leadership that Fred Streng provided as the founding president of the Society for Buddhist-Christian Studies.

My task is to comment on the Christian contributions by John Keenan, Ruben Habito, Paula Cooey, and Bonnie Thurston from a Shin Buddhist standpoint and suggest further topics for dialogue based on my reading of these papers. I believe that all the participants are in basic agreement with Cooey, when she states that 'Both Buddhist and Christian traditions thus clearly see egocentricity as the root of suffering and damage – an egocentricity that can be transformed, though the conditions for transformation rest on very different assumptions.'[1] Among the assumptions that require our attention are the different uses of language and the crucial role of religious praxis in religious life. Since the Buddhist path requires some form of praxis (*bhāvanā, prayoga, gyō*), involving psychosomatic transformation, much of its literature is characterized by performative language.[2] Thus, when key terms, such as emptiness (*śūnyatā*), are understood as descriptive language (a common tendency among academics), distortions and misinterpretations result and dialogue serves only to create further misunderstandings.

Fred Streng was clearly aware of the centrality of praxis when he made explicit the soteriological intention of emptiness. In fact, referring to the writings of Nāgārjuna, he states, 'Because of this soteriological context, the statements are not ends in themselves. Rather, they provide the means for "awakening" the truth of emptiness in a person.'[3] Again, he later states:

> Thus, the religious significance of religious statements is not so much the 'facts' (i.e., *a* truth) which they assert, but the means of apprehending (realizing) Ultimate Truth, which is coextensive with the dynamics of salvation.[4]

Inheriting this basic approach, David Eckel also appreciates performative language, when he writes, 'The function of the concept of emptiness was to transform a person's understanding of reality through a dialectical process, in which the false reifications that afflict a person's ordinary understanding of the world are stripped away and a person is able to see the world as it is.'[5]

When practice, however, has been the central concern among some Buddhists and Christians, serious questions have been raised concerning its validity. Winston King, for example, states in his paper under 'Shareable Spiritual Techniques':[6]

> Is a sharing of a meditative technique a genuine interreligious *dialogue*? The answer must be negative. The 'sticking points' of basic viewpoint and doctrine between the two religious faiths remain unaffected; the pristine purity of each remains unsullied.

I agree that a simple sharing of meditative technique does not constitute dialogue in its true sense. But it may be indispensable in dealing with the 'sticking points' that divide Buddhism and Christianity. The reason is that from the Buddhist perspective religious praxis is essential to any doctrinal discussion. Dialogue concerning 'sticking points,' completely disjunct from praxis, will result in nothing more than empty rhetoric.

Religious praxis in Buddhism is varied and complex, depending on the particular tradition and the cultural context. In fact the various schools of Mahayana Buddhism evolved frequently from disagreements concerning practice, rather than from doctrinal disputes. Nevertheless, all are based on morality (*śīla*), meditation (*dhyāna*) and wisdom (*prajñā*) in some combination. Thus, to reject the sharing of spiritual techniques as a form of interreligious dialogue is not only premature but deprives dialogue of real substance.

Before proceeding to clarify the contents of Buddhist praxis, we need to understand that it is an *idealized* paradigm, as Thomas Kasulis points out in his illuminating article, 'Under the Bodhi Tree: An Idealized Paradigm of Buddhist Transformation and Liberation.' Not all Buddhists engage in praxis, and not everyone who undertakes praxis achieves the intended goal. Nevertheless, it is an idealized *paradigm* that 'lends focus and meaning to how Buddhists hope to achieve transformation and liberation in their own lives, whether or not they have abandoned the secular world.'[7] The centrality of praxis secures a place for the body, feeling, and intuition in human affairs; and it forms the basis of self-cultivation in East Asian cultural and martial arts.

We can demonstrate the significance of religious praxis by citing examples from the pragmatic teachings of Sakyamuni Buddha,[8] but for our purposes we shall focus on praxis as developed in East Asia. The classic definition is given by Chih-i, the great T'ien-t'ai master from the sixth century:

> Although religious praxis involves forward movement, there is no progression without *prajñā*. The guidance of praxis by *prajñā* would not be authentic unless it is based on the true and real. The eyes of true wisdom together with the feet of true praxis guide a person to the realm of coolness and serenity.[9]

The essential components of Buddhist praxis include (1) progression towards a goal, (2) guided by *prajñā* or non-discriminative wisdom which is (3) based on the true and real.

This tripartite scheme may be illustrated by Yogācāra praxis aimed at cultivating non-discriminative wisdom. First, the person of discriminative mind has a goal in undertaking praxis, moving forward guided by the teaching of non-discriminative wisdom (*prayogika-nirvikalpa jñāna*). Eventually a breakthrough into nondiscriminative,

Epilogues

fundamental wisdom (*mūla jñāna*) is achieved, but this is only a transitional stage. The ultimate goal is the realization of wisdom subsequent to that which is fundamental (*tat-pṛiṣṭhalabdha-laukika-jñāna*); this resurrects the discriminative mind to work together with the highest embodied wisdom. This results in the consummated nature of reality (*pariniṣpanna-svabhāva*). The entire process is based on that which is true and real: *śūnyatā* (emptiness) and *tathatā* (suchness), ontologically speaking, and the working of the compassionate Buddha, religiously speaking. The relationship of the two receives a clear formulation in the Pure Land tradition as the dynamic interplay of *tathatā-dharmakāya* and *upāya-dharmakāya*.[10]

The teaching of emptiness is directed primarily to the practitioners on the Buddhist path. The scriptures of *Prajñāpāramitā*, for example, were never meant to be studied objectively by nonpractitioners, whether academics, lay people or outsiders. Thus, the *Heart Sutra*, chanted daily in various settings, opens with the pronouncement, 'When the Bodhisattva Avalokitesvara was engaged in the *deep practice* of Prajnaparamita, he perceived that there are five skandhas; and these he saw in their self-nature to be empty' (emphasis added).[11] The same holds true for the twofold truth of Nāgārjuna as formulated in *Madhyamaka-kārikā 24*. Contained within Verse 10 is the unspoken role of religious praxis which is crucial (inserted in my translation below in parenthesis):

Without relying on verbal expression,
The highest object cannot be taught;
Without reaching the highest object (through praxis)
Nirvana cannot be attained.

Paramārtha, synonymous with *dharma* and *tattva* in the preceding Verses 8 and 9,[12] is the object of the highest supreme wisdom (*prajñā*), hence, 'highest object.' The later commentaries on the Twofold Truth invariably lose sight of religious praxis and become increasingly conceptual, theoretical, and abstract.

Religious praxis culminates in the awareness that the final awakening or consummation comes from beyond the self. One of the implications of the Twofold Truth is that our samsaric world is linguistically structured. Normally we speak of 'truth' as if self-evident.[13] Such a conventional notion, conceptualized by the unenlightened, is 'onefold.' But when conceptuality is pushed to the very edge, then we realize reality as 'twofold.' That is, each authentic, living moment is constituted by the nonduality of time and

250

timelessness, samsara and nirvana, linguistic designations and the trans-linguistic. The true and real penetrates the entire process on the path, beginning with the initial aspiration for enlightenment (*bodhicittotpada*) and culminating in supreme enlightenment (*samyaksambodhi*). Shin Buddhists speak of the entire process as the praxis (*gyō*) or working of Other Power, the 'other' not in the dualistic sense but as the power that informs the seeker on the path of awakening from samsara to nirvana and back to samsara to aid in the salvation of all beings.[14]

One of the finest fruits of our common dialogical endeavor is John Keenan's exegesis, entitled 'The Mind of Wisdom and Justice in the Letter of John.' Keenan utilizes Buddhist vocabulary to analyze this little known work and makes it come alive in a new and meaningful way. One of his main points may be summed up in his words as follows:

> The text of James is meagre in its doctrinal import not because it is underdeveloped but because its focus is upon non-discriminative wisdom, authenticated not in hearing or learning the word, but in embodying the word in active mercy and good fruits (p. 8).

Several points struck me about this passage. Both non-discriminating wisdom and embodying the word resonate with the Buddhist emphasis on the practical. Doctrinal elaboration and verbal exposition play a secondary role, for they can easily fall prey to *prapañca* (word-play). As David Chappell points out, Buddhists are not interested in theological issues in interreligious dialogue as much as they are in practical matters that affect the spiritual life of a society.[15]

While Buddhist praxis basically refers to the systematic, psychosomatic development leading to the realization of non-discriminative wisdom, Keenan stresses the action in conjunction with this acquired wisdom: 'one cannot abide in non-discriminative wisdom without abiding in just and compassionate practice in all one's journeying' (p. 3). This difference may be a matter of emphasis, but, depending on how Keenan defines non-discriminative wisdom, it might suggest a future area of Buddhist-Christian exploration and cooperation.

Keenan's analysis of discriminating mind overlaps with Buddhist criticism of conventional, conceptualized thinking-feeling (*vikalpa*): it causes wavering and deliberation, it relies on imaginary constructs and conceptual knowledge, and it is characterized by verbal delusion. 'False practice flows from the mind of discrimination, not from the gift of non-discriminative wisdom which makes no distinctions between persons' (p. 11). Here non-discriminative wisdom is understood as a gift and not something gained through religious praxis as in Buddhism. Keenan elaborates,

> Wisdom is not a human accomplishment given in payment for effort expended but a gift given simply and without weighing the merits of the case. One need not worry whether or not one is worthy, for God gives spontaneously and naturally (p. 2).

From the Buddhist perspective we would want to ask several questions in order to get a better sense of what is meant by nondiscriminative wisdom as used by Keenan. First, if nondiscriminative wisdom is a gift from God, may we assume that this wisdom is also an essential quality inherent in God? If it is innate in God, how is nondiscriminative wisdom which 'makes no distinction between persons' manifested in reality characterized by all kinds of discriminations? Simply put, what is the relationship between a nondiscriminating God and the discrimination-filled world?

Second, how does God give spontaneously and naturally? Are there no conditions for receiving the gift? What does it mean to say that it is granted whether one is worthy or not? Is it then available to non-Christians – Jews, Moslems, Buddhists? How does the spontaneous and natural giving of wisdom reach those consigned to hell?

Third, non-discriminative wisdom is organic with practice, but how does it actually work in society? How does one apply it to those situations outside of the Christian context? Concrete illustrations will help us appreciate this unity of wisdom and practice. A few years ago at Smith College we were confronted with an insoluble dilemma. In November of that year the Hindu students put up posters with the swastika, announcing Divali, the Festival of Lights. The date happened to coincide with the Jewish observance of Kristallnacht, the infamous beginning in 1938 of the persecution of Jews in Germany and Austria. The Jewish students demanded that the posters be taken down; the Hindu students adamantly refused. To Jews the swastika is the ultimate symbol of evil; for Hindus it is the sacred symbol of their faith, dating from prehistoric times. How would non-discriminative wisdom resolve such a conflict?

In sum, Buddhist praxis focuses more on the means or process to the goal of non-discriminative wisdom, whereas Keenan's practice clearly stresses action subsequent to the attaining of such a wisdom. If we may loosely apply Cooey's distinction between justification and sanctification found in her reponse to Sponberg's article, Keenan's wisdom tends toward the latter and Buddhist wisdom to the former.[16] Can the two approaches be shared to complement each other? A positive answer would lead to mutual transformation which will be welcomed by all people concerned with the survival of our planet, far beyond the confines of either the Christian or Buddhist circles.

The Buddhists mentioned by Sallie King in her article, 'Buddhism and Social Engagement' – Thich Nhat Hanh, the Dalai Lama, Sulak Sivaraksa, Mahaghosananda, leaders of the Nipponzan Myohoji, and others – all manifest Buddhist wisdom and compassion in one form or another, but I would like to see them articulate the relationship between their actions and non-discriminative wisdom. When I ask, for example, the leaders of the Nipponzan Myohoji, known locally in Western Massachusetts as the Peace Pagoda, to clarify the philosophical basis of their movement, they are reluctant to answer. Instead, they point to some concrete activity, such as their interfaith peace march from Auschwitz to Hiroshima,[17] or their proposed walk to retrace the slave trade from New England to the Caribbean and West Africa, officially known as The Interfaith Pilgrimage of the Middle Passage. The march begins in Massachusetts in May 1998 and concludes in South Africa in June 1999. While their dedication is plausible, it would be helpful for the cause of peace, if the Buddhist philosophical basis can be clarified.

Another area for possible Buddhist-Christian cooperation is social action, applying non-discriminative wisdom especially to the problem of justice. Justice, as ordinarily implemented, is too often tainted by partiality, whether it be in terms of race, color, ethnicity, class, gender, sexual orientation, creed, military, or economic allegiance. Keenan alludes to this when he writes:

> The royal law is the law of Moses in *Leviticus* 19:18 about loving your neighbor as yourself. And showing partiality 'discloses' the structure of sin, for it lies at the root of the injustices afflicted in others in the service of a false and arrogant conception of self (p. 12).

More than ever the world needs impartial justice, and only religion can penetrate the structure of sin which causes rampant injustice. In the past Christians have been involved with social justice because of historical necessity, but if the assumption is that true justice can be realized only within the Christian world view, then it becomes a real problem, a critique made by Edwin Burtt concerning the social ethic of Reinhold Niebuhr.[18] Perhaps Buddhists might contribute to formulating a universal sense of justice applicable to all people, regardless of religious affiliation. Sallie King's proposal moves in such a direction with her six points for consideration: personal embodiment of peace, cultivation of selflessness, principled nonviolence, non-adversarial approach, practice of non-harmfulness (*ahiṃsā*), and pragmatic stance.[19]

Religious praxis also plays a major role in Ruben Habito's excellent piece, 'The Resurrection of the Dead and Life Everlasting.' He presents an informed discussion of two interpretations of Christianity, 'futuristic' and 'realized.'[20] Following a detailed and lengthy description of futuristic Christianity, he gives convincing arguments for realized Christianity. While realized Christianity has always been implicit in the tradition, Habito brings it out even more clearly without losing sight of the tension between the poles of 'not yet' and 'already there.' The focus on realized Christianity would seem to be the inevitable consequence of religious praxis. Could this be due partially to Habito's long and fruitful experience with Zen Buddhism?

Futuristic Christianity alone would be problematic for Buddhists, because of the traditional linear view, exclusion of the body, negation of this world, denigration of the present, and eternal damnation of the unjust. Realized Christianity provides a welcome balance by its emphasis on the here and now, the inclusion of the body, and the affirmation of this earth. Habito sums up realized Christianity simply and succinctly:

> Eternal life is to be discovered *right here* in our midst as we go about our earthly tasks and lay ourselves open to our neighbor (p. 20).

The essential point is that we live the Gospel of the Good News by responding to the plights of people, remaining fully open to one's neighbor, and answering to the needs of others.

Central to Habito's argument is the Last Judgment in Matthew 25:31–46. His reading, however, raises some basic questions. In his optimistic assessment of human potential is there any room for sin and evil? Is the ethical sufficient in the salvific scheme of Jesus Christ? What is the relationship between ethical acts and grace? How would Habito incorporate Thomas Kasulis' assertion that this passage is 'not focusing on ethics of even anonymous Christianity as much as it is focusing on the triumph of the suffering Christ and its relevance to life in this world'?[21]

In society there are many thoughtful, compassionate, and altruistic people who act selflessly on behalf of others without any religious motivation and without any reference to Christ or Heavenly reward. In fact, some so-called religious who are self-righteous, prideful of their acts, or smug in a particular belief system create more dissensions in the world than the non-religious. If a religious grounding is unnecessary for good works, why does one have to be a Christian, or a Buddhist, in order to be ethical?

But a further question arises. What happens to people who cannot live the life of serving humanity? Surely they are not left out of God's salvific design, but what is their destiny? More precisely, what is the fate of 'those who live in a selfish, self-centered, and self-enclosed way ... close themselves off from this invitation to eternal life in the Risen Christ, and thus, consign themselves to hell'? Do they end up with a conclusion identical with that of futuristic Christianity, whereby the unrighteous 'will be taken by the devil down to hell, where they will burn forever in everlasting fire'?

Here I am reminded of the two types of compassion that Shinran discusses in the *Tannisho*.[22] First is the compassion practiced by those on the Path of Sages 'expressed through pity, sympathy and care for all beings.' This ethical imperative is followed by immediate self-reflection: 'but rare is it that one can help another as one desires,' opening the door to the religious dimension. Summed up in the words of Shinran:

> In this life no matter how much pity and sympathy we may feel for others, it is impossible to help another as we truly wish; thus our compassion is inconsistent and limited. Only the saying of nembutsu manifests the complete and never ending compassion which is true, real, and sincere.

The last sentence on the nembutsu requires fuller exposition but suffice it to say that the source of love and compassion must come from beyond the limits of our linguistically structured world. The saying of nembutsu is the recognition of egocentricity, yet in that acknowledgement of limitedness one is made to entrust the self to a greater power and thus become a conduit for the boundless, unlimited compassion of Amida Buddha. I find a parallel structure in Matthew 22:37–40: 'You shall love the Lord your God with all your heart, and with all your soul, and with all your mind. This is the great and first commandment. And the second is like it, 'You shall love your neighbor as yourself.'

Paula Cooey in her article, 'Creation, Redemption, and the Realization of the Material Order,' utilizes the Buddhist concept of emptiness and Elaine Scarry's making as creation and destruction to review some assumptions in traditional Christian thought. She notes three problematic areas: 1) denial of change and reification of space, 2) avoidance of the ambiguity of life, and 3) assertion of absolute reality .

From the standpoint of religious praxis, reality is seen as part of a never ending process open to the unpredictable future. This emphasis on process accounts for the Buddhist understanding of self in the world. As Alan Sponberg states, 'The first thing to note about the Buddhist conception of ethical agency is that it posits a notion of the self that is both dynamic and developmental.'[23] Dynamic means that it is constantly undergoing change and evolution, and developmental means that the limited, karmic being ultimately realizes Buddhahood. This self-authenticating process is ongoing, as expressed in the East Asian definition of 'Buddha': 'self-awakening and awakening others; the praxis of awakening, endless and all encompassing (*jikaku kakuta kakugyō gūman*).'

If the 'person' of non-discriminative wisdom, as Keenan points out, is defined by compassionate action, it cannot be a reified self, for such a self is the greatest obstacle to the religious life. Again, as Sponberg points out, 'While substantialist views of the self are seen thus to be characteristic of all human culture, they represent in the Buddhist view the very problem itself, the obstacle that obstructs a life of liberated, compassionate activity' (p. 14). Thus, a radical transformation of self-delusion becomes crucial in order to truly abide in interdependence and interconnectedness which is the basis of any possible solution for the ecological crisis.

When self and world are seen as dynamically evolving, the focus is on the here and now. Absolute reality, divorced from this moment, is an arbitrary mental construct. This moment, however, is not an isolated moment but interrelates with all existence in both time and space, making life open to endless possibilities. When we cling to absolutes, whether human or divine, we are shut off from dynamic life. Cooey understands this from the perspective of praxis and states:

> *Śūnyatā*, existentially realized in the context of Buddhist practice, dramatizes to the adherent that her ego has no independent existence.... The realization of *śūnyatā* serves ultimately to derail a human craving for absoluteness.

256

This freedom from ego and absolutes of any kind is one with the awakening to 'interdependence and interconnectedness of whatever is – past, present. and future' (p. 5). This means that, first of all, we are the recipients of love and compassion that infuses all life and, second, in acknowledgement of this fact we respond by manifesting love to the best of our limited and imperfect abilities.

Cooey then proceeds to find in the central doctrine of *creatio ex nihilo* a source of liberation from absolutes: 'To realize the continual creation ex nihilo is to dissipate the desire for an absolute reality as a means of escaping the circumstances of our materiality.' In this universe of constant change, free of materiality and sustained by boundless interrelationships, the human agent becomes a creative force. This is where Scarry's fascinating notion of creation comes in, reminding us of karmic agency which produces the world of 'facts' as projections of subjectivity (retained in such words as arti*fact*, manu*fact*ure, *arte factum*, etc.).

While finding positive meaning in emptiness and giving us an enlightening interpretation of creation *ex nihilo*, Cooey's position is open to question from the standpoint of religious praxis. All the ideas that Cooey cites – denial of absolute, liberation of ego, life as interrelational, reality as flux – may be simply replacing an outdated set of words with a new set of words. If we accept the fact that our world is linguistically structured, then no matter the vocabulary used we remain caught up in samsara. The important thing is that we push to the limits of the linguistically structured world and live on the edge of samsara, where bodhisattvas engage in their play and the nirvana of no-abode (*apratishthita-nirvāṇa*) exists.

From the standpoint of religious praxis, we can also appreciate, as well as question, the main points made in Bonnie Thurston's paper, '"In the beginning ... God" A Christian's View of Ultimate Reality.' In understanding God's 'personhood' Thurston makes reference to many human qualities ascribed to Him in various sources. God is described as having a face, arms, and legs. God exhibits human emotions like jealousy, anger, and forgiveness. God acts like a warrior, king, judge, shepherd, or a woman nurturing a child. Thurston qualifies these descriptions by stating that 'The point is not to anthropomorphize God, and certainly not to suggest that Christian faith is anthropocentric, but to underscore that God is understood as a person' (p. 5).

Religious praxis is undertaken by a concrete human subject whether described as 'person' or understood as 'nonself,' and the encounter with that which is beyond linguistic constructs in both Buddhism and

Christianity can be expressed only in terms of concrete human experience. Especially is this true, if as Thurston points out, 'God cannot be comprehended by the finite minds of human beings' (p. 2). A human description of God may be fashionable or unfashionable, but if we do not confuse words for reality, signifier for signified, then there is no need to hesitate talking about God in the most familiar terms. In Shin Buddhism the most common understanding of Amida Buddha is *oya-sama*, a term consisting of the honorific (*sama*) and the word for father or mother or both (*oya*, literally means 'parent' and 'intimate.'). Scholars may discuss Amida Buddha as the embodiment of *śūnyatā*, or in terms of the two kinds of *dharmakāya*, but the average Shin devotee knows Amida only in very intimate terms, such as *oya-sama*, 'my dear, loving mother/father.' This is akin to the 'absolute tenderness and nurture' of *Abba*, mentioned by Thurston, but without the aspect of 'absolute authority' (p. 10).

Thurston also quotes Arnold Toynbee, who summarizes the essential characteristics of Christianity as God's sacrifice of himself for humanity's sake, the example set by His incarnation and crucifixion, and the mandate for humans to emulate him. Hidden within this, however, is a problematic in interreligious dialogue that Toynbee raises concerning Christianity (subsumed under the rubric 'Judaic' which includes Judaism and Islam): the deep-rooted self-centeredness at its core. Self-centeredness can appear in various guises. According to Toynbee,

> A sense of the greatness of God might be expected to be as effective a cure for the self-centredness of one of God's creatures as a sense of the inexorability of laws of Nature. But the Judaic societies have re-opened the door to self-centredness by casting themselves, in rivalry with one another and ignoring the rest of Mankind, for the privileged role of being God's 'Chosen People,' who, in virtue of God's choice of them, have a key part to play in History – in contrast to a heathen majority of Mankind who are worshippers of false gods.[24]

In contrast, Toynbee writes that the so-called Buddhaic religions liberate people from self-centeredness, because of its cyclic view of history and its stress on the impersonal. The cyclical stereotype is critically analyzed by Nishitani Keiji in his *Religion and Nothingness*, and, probing into the problem of self-centeredness, he concludes, 'Intolerance here is essentially bound up with the fact that faith comes into being here on a *personal* standpoint of a personal relationship with a personal God. This is so because, in the last analysis, in religion the personal contains some sort of self-centeredness.'[25]

If we follow Toynbee and Nishitani, then, love which is bound up with a 'person' involves some form of self-centeredness. Of course, Christian notions of love are complex and multi-dimensional, frequently impacted by prevailing Western cultural views, but it would be helpful to get a clearer definition of the religious meaning of love (*agape*), especially in relation to the instinctual passions.[26] The aim of psychosomatic praxis in Buddhism and self-cultivation in Asian cultural arts is to purge deep-rooted self-centeredness, such that it reduces immature, egoistic love and nurtures mature selfless love. The fact that the word 'love' is not found in abundance in Buddhist literature is because the term has been more closely associated with self-centered love, fueled by the three poisons of greed, anger, and ignorance, which must be overcome. When it does occur, such as in the Four *Brahma-vihāras*, it is in terms of religious praxis and attainment: love, compassion, sympathetic joy, and equanimity.

Praxis and attainment are also central to the Buddhist understanding of selfhood or personhood. When Lin-chi speaks of the 'true person of no rank,' or when Dogen aims at training 'one person, or even half a person,' they denote a person who has undergone religious praxis to bring out the highest potential of the individual. We find the same emphasis on the person also in Shinran, when he proclaims,

> When I ponder on the compassionate Vow of Amida, established through five kalpas of profound thought, it was for myself, Shinran, alone.[27]

In the case of Shin Buddhism, religious praxis is not a matter of outward form, such as sitting meditation, but the same intense grappling with the immature, egocentric self and a dialectical development of a true, real, and sincere person.[28]

When considering personhood or selfhood in other cultures from the Western vantage point, we have to be careful not to judge the other based on our prejudices. Social scientists frequently make this mistake. In a fascinating collection of seven essays by Western anthropologists published in the *Japanese Sense of Self*, the editor Nancy Rosenberger sums up the study of the Japanese self:

> Throughout the volume, each author presents self as multiple, moving, and changing. They show people grounded in meanings beyond themselves, meanings that shift in relation to other

people, close and far, to nature, wild and tamed, and to the political economy, past and future. People continually create themselves and are created in terms of the multiple pictures that people weave with others and their environment as they move through life.[29]

The series of articles demonstrate the changing views of Western scholars which undergo transformation from simplistic to complex not because of changes in the Japanese self but in shifting Western perspectives, always made from a position of superiority. Rosenberger puts this as follows:

> If, as scholars, we never examine the common sense presuppositions that guide our theories and interpretations, we will continue to ask either-or questions of individualism vs. collectivism, placing 'them,' the non-Western others, on the negative side of apparent dichotomies – or else making them like us.[30]

In the Asian context, what is more basic than self as conventionally understood is the interdependence and interconnectedness of life of which each person is a part. The self here is neither negated nor affirmed; rather it is seen contextually and relationally. This means that the self displays multiple dimensions, depending upon the situation. Such an understanding is current in various sectors of contemporary thought, as reflected in the following statement by Kenneth Gergen:

> Here the individual experiences a form of liberation from essence, and learns to derive joy from the many forms of self-expression now permitted. As the self as a serious reality is laid to rest and the self is constructed and reconstructed in multiple contexts, one enters finally the stage of the *relational self*.[31]

In this understanding of personhood, the autonomous self is characterized as follows: it is not a given but must be achieved through some form of discipline, effort, and transformation; such a realized self is dynamic and evolving, as part of the vast web of interconnectedness; and thus it can be multi-faceted, relating to all kinds of life situations and in turn impacted by them. This relational self constitutes personhood in East Asian cultures. The elemental fact of interdependence and interconnectedness, not the assertion of individual ego, is the basis of ethical life and the source of love and compassion. This is ingrained in the people's lives beyond any formal doctrine or philosophy. Thus, as Winston King observed, 'In practice one finds Buddhist people loving, gentle, and helpful in many cases, apparently because of and in spite of their religious beliefs.'[32]

Praxis is integral to another statement, ascribed to King, that Buddhist loving kindness is 'systematic and calculated, indirect and impersonal, and atomistically individualistic,'[33] quoted by both Thurston and Eckel. This is addressed to monastics who are expected to undertake systematic, disciplined training of the mind in order to overcome immature, self-centered impulses and manifest wisdom and compassion, just as athletes undergo strict training to develop their highest potential. Selfless love, compassion, sympathetic joy, and equanimity must be not only cultivated systematically but directed to all sentient beings equally, not just to one's kind and kin. Ultimately, it is extended to all forms of non-human life and the material world.

When one achieves enlightenment or awakening, one embodies the *dharma*, frequently rendered as 'truth' in English translation. This word has multiple meanings in South Asian religions, but its basic usage in Buddhism is twofold. According to the *Ratnagotravibhāga*, dharma can mean liberative *teaching* (*deśanadharma*), but its more basic denotation is *reality-as-it-is* (*adhigamadharma*)[34] which includes both that which realizes (*prajñā*) and that which is realized. The realization of *adhigama-dharma* results in a truly awakened self, the very opposite of the immature, egocentered self, steeped in the darkness of ignorance. Reference to this awakened self is made by Sakyamuni Buddha, when he proclaims: 'The self is the lord of self, who else could be the lord? With self well-subdued, a man finds a lord such as few can find.'[35]

The self as manifestation of *adhigama-dharma is* worthy of reliance. This is the self that the Buddha refers to in his Final Sermon:

Therefore, Ananda, be ye lamps unto yourselves. Rely on yourselves, and do not rely on external help. Hold fast to the truth as the lamp. Seek salvation alone in the truth. Look not for assistance to anyone besides yourself.[36]

At the conclusion of her paper Thurston states that, 'We Christians do not believe that, in the final analysis, we can be "lamps unto ourselves." It is just too dark.' Buddhists would agree completely with this statement if the reference is to the unenlightened, delusory self, but the Final Sermon points to the enlightened self who has embodied the dharma, 'who holds fast to the truth as a lamp.'

I believe that we are now at a stage in Buddhist-Christian dialogue whereby we can have Christians give exegeses on Buddhist scriptures to help plumb the latter's depth, and Buddhists might give their own reading of the Gospels to shed new light on them. Such an enterprise will help us avoid lifting phrases and sentences out of context and encourage dialogue on another level.

In concluding my reflections on all of the papers and the valuable exchanges, I should like to propose some future areas for dialogue and cooperation. First, if non-discrminative wisdom is common to Buddhism and Christianity, a closer working relationship on social issues – justice, overpopulation, ecology, ethnic and religious violence – grounded in such a wisdom may make substantial contributions and be welcomed by all thinking people.[37] Second, since both Buddhism and Christianity cope with sin and evil, regardless of differing views, we might discuss and formulate a new ethic which takes into serious consideration the deep-rooted egocentricity in humankind that might appeal to all the peoples of the world. Third, a dialogue centered on religious praxis and transformation in relation to the linguistically structured world may contribute to furthering reflections on the philosophy of language and the sociology of knowledge. Finally, a more precise reading and commentaries on the scriptures of Buddhism and Christianity by representatives of the opposite tradition may be fruitful and raise Buddhist-Christian dialogue to a higher level of exchange.

Notes

1 'Response to Sponberg'.
2 See application of 'performative utterance' (J.L. Austin) to Confucianism in Herbert Fingarette, *Confucius – The Sacred as Secular* (New York: Harper, 1972).
3 Frederick J. Streng, *Emptiness: A Study in Religious Meaning* (Nashville: Abingdon, 1967), 171.
4 Ibid., 178.
5 Eckel, 'The Concept of the Ultimate in Madhyamaka Thought'.
6 King, 'Interreligious Dialogue'.
7 Kasulis, 'Under the Bodhi Tree'.
8 See my article, 'The Middle Path of Buddhism,' *Religious Humanist* 26 (Winter, 1992): 36–47.
9 *Taishō Daizōkyō* 33:751b, lines 17–18.
10 The relationship is discussed by Shinran in his *Notes on Essentials of Faith Alone* (Kyoto: Hongwanji International Center, 1980), 43. The English equivalents used in this translation are 'dharmakaya-as-suchness' and 'dharmkaya-as-compassion.'

11 From D.T. Suzuki, *Manual of Zen Buddhism* (New York: Grove Press, 1960), 26.
12 See my article, 'Philosophical Schools: San-lun, T'ien-t'ai, and Hua-yen,' *Buddhist Spirituality*, ed. Takeuchi Yoshinori (New York: Crossroad, 1995), especially 344–346.
13 Cf. Neitzsche in his *The Will to Power*, tr. W. Kaufman and R.J. Hollingdale (New York: Vintage Books, 1967), 334. And number 625: 'The concept of "truth" is nonsensical. The entire domain of "true-false" applies only to relations, not to an "in-itself." (It is only relations that constitute essence–), just as there can be no "knowledge-in-itself."'
14 In Shinran the process from samsara to nirvana is called ōsō-ekō and the return process to samsara is gensō-ekō. The paradigm is the ascent and descent on the bodisattva path.
15 Chappell, 'Buddhist Interreligious Dialogue: To Build a Global Community.'
16 Cooey's 'Response to Sponberg'.
17 Recorded in *Ashes and Light: From Auschwitz to Hiroshima – Interfaith Pilgrimage for Faith and Light* (Leverett, MA: Nipponzan Myohoji, 1966).
18 Burtt in *Reinhold Niebuhr: Social and Political Thought*, ed. C.W. Kegley and R.W. Bretall (New York: Macmillan, 1956), 356–366.
19 S. King, 'Buddhism and Social Engagement.'
20 This distinction reminds me of 'futuristic' Pure Land which was standard in Mahayana Buddhism until the time of Shinran in thiteenth century Japan. The hope for salvation was entrusted to a future birth in the Pure Land. Shinran stressed 'realized' Pure Land here and now in the transformative experience of true entrusting (*shinjin*), while maintaining complete enlightenment at the moment of death when birth in the Pure Land is attained.
21 Kasulis's response to Habito.
22 See my *Tannisho: A Shin Buddhist Classic* (Honolulu: Buddhist Study Center, 2nd Revised Edition, 1996), 7.
23 Sponberg, 'Self, Nature, and Ecology in Buddhism'.
24 Arnold Toynbee, *An Historian's Approach to Religion* (London: Oxford University Press, 1956), 12.
25 Nishitani Keiji, *Religion and Nothingness* (Berkeley, CA: University of California Press, 1981), 208.
26 See, for example, Morton M. Hunt, 'The Trouble with Word,' in *The Natural History of Love* (New York: Knopf, 1959), 3–7.
27 *Tannisho*, 33.
28 For further discussion, see my 'Interior Practice in Shin Buddhism,' *The Pacific World* 6 (1990): 41–49.
29 Nancy Rosenberger, *Japanese Sense of Self* (Cambridge: Cambridge University Press, 1992), 14.
30 Ibid., 16.
31 Kenneth Gergen, *The Saturated Self* (New York: Basic Books, 1992), 147.
32 Winston King, *Buddhism and Christianity: Some Bridges of Understanding* (London: George Allen and Unwin, 1962), 93.
33 Ibid., 91.

34 Takasaki Jikidō, *A Study of the Ratnagotravibhāga* (Roma: Istituto italiano per il medio ed estremo oreinte, 1996), 182.
35 Edwin Burtt (ed.), *The Teaching of the Compassionate Buddha* (New York: Mentor Books, 1982), 60.
36 Ibid., 49.
37 Such cooperative ventures have already begun in some areas, such as ecology. See, for example, ecology as the central topic of the 1998 International Buddhist Christian Theological Encounter held in Indianapolis, April 30–May 3, under the sponsorship of the Lilly Foundation. See also Mary Evelyn Tucker and Duncan Ryuken WIlliams, *Buddhism and Ecology* (Cambridge: Harvard University Center for the Study of World Religions, 1997).

CHAPTER TWENTY-TWO

A Christian Epilogue

John B. Cobb, Jr.

One thing that those who participate in dialogue learn early is that generalizations about Buddhism and Christianity, or about Buddhists and Christians, are difficult and dangerous. One can always find exceptions, sometimes so many exceptions that the generalizations turn out to be simply false. Furthermore, the generalizations are almost inevitably formulated in the categories of the generalizer and often seem misleading to the other party. Nevertheless, the need for some Christian generalization about the Buddhist and Christian contributions to this volume is suggested by my assignment to write one of a pair of epilogues.

One such generalization is that the Buddhist essays are more historical or descriptive and the Christian ones more personal statements of belief. Of course, both are both. But the difference is noticeable and fairly consistent. It is most striking in the essays of Winston King and David Chappell, and it is commented on by King himself in his response to Chappell. Although Chappell's own preferences come out in his essay, he writes primarily as an historian. Although one learns from King a little about the history of Christian approaches to other religious traditions, his focus is on what dialogue should be.

David Eckel provides us a close study about the treatment of the ultimate by a Tibetan Buddhist author. Bonnie Thurston presents us her own understanding of God. Of course, we gather that Eckel finds the work of his author highly illuminating of the question; and in making her statements Thurston is deeply and intentionally shaped by her understanding of how other Christians think. But in this pair, too, the difference is readily noticed.

My generalization works least well with Alan Sponberg and Paula Cooey. Sponberg is consciously making his own contribution to understanding Buddhism's approach to nature and ecology. He draws together several Buddhist teachings in a way that is intended to be normative as well as descriptive. Yet, when we read him alongside Cooey, a difference, at least of degree, appears. Whereas Sponberg is doing his own work in selecting and juxtaposing elements of traditional Buddhist teaching, Cooey is reflecting on the extent to which her Christian tradition is helpful at all.

With Sallie King we return to a primarily descriptive account of how Buddhists engage in social and political issues of liberation. This is a topic on which none is better informed than she. Her interest in it and her way of approaching it tell us much about her personal religious understanding. Nevertheless, her essay fits the generalization with which I began. John Keenan's also fits the generalization, but in its own unique way. He is continuing to pursue his very distinctive work of reading Christian canonical sources through glasses largely shaped by Mahayana Buddhism.

The contrast is not sharp between Tom Kasulis and Ruben Habito, yet it exists there too. Kasulis explains how the idealized image of Gautama coming to enlightenment functions for later Buddhists. His account is clearly normative, but it is formulated as description. Habito, in contrast, finds his way among alternative formulations of Christian faith, selecting and freshly developing the one that he finds most helpful.

I would not bother to make this generalization about the essays if I did not think that it expressed something about Buddhism and Christianity, or at least about the Buddhism and Christianity of contemporary Americans. At this point, however, generalization is even more dangerous! I hope for correction from both Buddhists and Christians.

Contemporary Christians inherit a long tradition of theology as a way of formulating Christian belief in light of the situation. During the early centuries the goal was to state the faith that had always and everywhere been held by Christians; that is, from our contemporary point of view, it was highly unhistorical. But today we understand the thinking in the early church as an historical development, adapting the understanding gained from the Biblical story to the Hellenistic context and engaging in the systematizing required by that context.

We then study the continuing history of theology, especially in the West, considering the strengths and weaknesses of successive formulations as the work of individual Christian thinkers more or less successful in gaining support from fellow Christians and even from the institutional church. We locate ourselves as heirs of that tradition, working in a time when the tradition as a whole has become problematic in terms both of credibility and relevance.

Our task, then, is to seek formulations that respond to these challenges. Our implementation of this task has become more and more fragmented. We all make our own personal moves, recognizing them as such. Of course, we want to persuade others, and we hope for enough consensus coming out of these personal journeys to be able to act together in relevant ways.

My own formulation of this situation is that Christianity is a socio-historical movement. The unity of such a movement does not consist in unchanging teachings but in a common origin that is celebrated in diverse ways. Reflection about the relation of the present to the common origin is essential for the continuation of the movement. If that ceases, or if it loses all credibility or felt relevance, the movement erodes. Hence the constructive theological task is necessary and unending.

To Christian eyes, the situation of Buddhist writers looks very different. Being a Buddhist is not nearly as problematic for thoughtful Buddhists as being a Christian is for thoughtful Christians. A generation ago Christians were inclined to think that this difference was because the cultures from which the leading Buddhists came did not have the historical self-consciousness that had become common-place for Christians as a result of secular developments in the West in the past two centuries. But this generalization has no relevance in the present situation in which American Christians are in exchange with American Buddhists.

It turns out that the historical relativity that forces Christians into ever changing formulations on even the most fundamental questions is not felt as having the same effect for historically self-conscious Buddhists. What they experience as core Buddhist teaching is not relativized in the same way. On the contrary, Buddhist teaching of the relativity of all things is confirmed. The nihilism that is so threatening to Christians is internalized and transformed into serenity. Because their tradition already contains and expresses a wisdom that is credible and relevant, Buddhists do not need to engage in 'constructive theology'.

I am not suggesting that the attitude of these Buddhist writers is arrogant or triumphalist. The sins and failures of Buddhists are freely and nondefensively acknowledged. The heterogeneity of Buddhist schools is recognized and studied in detail. Criticism of Christianity is far gentler than typical Christian self-criticism. The need of Buddhists for fresh reflection in a changing historical context is recognized, and contributions are made to that reflection. But this reflection is designed to bring to bear more effectively in the present historical context an understanding and realization that have been present in the tradition for millennia.

It may be possible to connect this difference with other, more personal, differences, highlighted in Buddhist responses to some of the Christian papers. I select three. Chappell notes that Winston King understands real dialogue as discourse about theoretical issues that distinguish Buddhism and Christianity. Chappell sees no need to focus so narrowly on this dimension of the religious life. For him many ways of being together and enriching one another should count as dialogue.

Although many Christians would agree with Chappell, King's position still reflects distinctively Christian concerns. Encounter with Buddhism poses fundamental new challenges to Christian self-understanding. It brings into being a new historical situation. That requires that Christians do fresh thinking, reevaluate our own heritage, and reestablish our relation to that heritage on new grounds. This is not an exclusively theoretical activity, but the theoretical component is large. Without it there is danger that changes resulting from Buddhist influence, in meditational practice, for example, would lead away from Christian faith altogether. The needed reflection can occur best in vigorous interchange through which the meaning of this new historical challenge can be refined and responses tried out.

Buddhists, on the other hand, do not experience Christian theology as a major threat to basic self-understanding. They are open to the possibility that interchange with Christians may enrich their meditational practice, provide ideas about social action, or deepen their understanding of their tradition. They are open to learning from the ways Christians have organized their institutions and adapted themselves to the modern world. They are interested in seeing where Christian thought has moved toward convergence with their own. But none of this *requires* dialogue in the narrow sense.

Near the end of Eckel's remarkably irenic response to Thurston's personalistic theism, he offers a vivid contrast of the two traditions. 'God once looked into nothingness and made something come to be ... Buddha ... saw that the world had always been, and he, in his wisdom, found a way to allow some of it to stop. His gift to us – his act of greatest compassion – was to teach us that way. Who is to say that this is finally any less loving than the Christian drive to mimic God's sublime generosity in a never-ending round of action and creativity?'

As I see the essays in this volume, they in some way reflect this difference. Christians are constantly engaged in action and creativity. The Christian essays in this volume are instances of such creativity and are all, in some way, explicit or implicit, calls to action. If we do not act creatively the world God loves may be destroyed.

Cooey speaks for many of us when she concludes her paper: 'We, in this time, stand ... in hope and fear before an enigmatic empty space. Can we resist annihilation of global life? Are we willing to risk the full implication of our sentience? Dare we imagine the pain of other creatures both human and nonhuman and work toward its relief and repair? And can we mourn the tragedy of what we have wasted? Will we imagine from our own pain and pleasure and work toward a future for generations on earth that we will not live to see? If God can wager on us, how can we afford not to wager on the future?'

The Buddhist papers are all accounts of 'the way', and although the way includes compassionate ministering to the needs of all sentient beings, it is a way of cessation. Sallie King's description of the desire of the Cambodian peasants, not for justice, but for a cessation of the round of suffering, illustrates this point. Of course, the Buddhist acts. But the goal of acting is to end the need for such acting.

This brings me to the third point I am selecting from the Buddhist papers. Sallie King raises the question of justice. The idea has played little role in Buddhism, but a central one in Christianity. This difference has not yet been sufficiently discussed in Buddhist-Christian dialogue. The account of the attitude of the Cambodian peasants raises the question for us in vivid form. Few Christians can avoid being moved by their repudiation of vengeance. But few Christians are fully satisfied by the outcome for which they hope.

Christian teaching about God stresses both love and justice. The relation of God to the world is characteristically viewed in terms of judgment as well as grace. In much of Christian history the theme of judgment has loomed very large indeed, even obscuring the priority of love in the scriptures. Much of Christian theology over the centuries has struggled with questions raised by this duality of God's character.

I am a follower of John Wesley who strongly emphasized the priority of love, and in my own constructive theology I see 'judgment' as an expression of love rather than a distinct characteristic of God. There is much in the way Christians speak of justice that reflects features of judgment that I find uncomfortable. I suspect that on the whole Christians who are drawn to dialogue with Buddhists share my emphasis. But we misrepresent our tradition if we do not emphasize how large a role judgment has played in the understanding of God's justice. Our mimicking of God in our quest for justice is rarely free of this element despite Jesus' explicit saying: 'Judge not that ye be not judged.'

Despite my minimizing of judgment and of the element of judgment in justice, I find myself not quite happy with the attitude of the Cambodian peasants. Christians generally, even those who most emphasize love and forgiveness, also want justice. When oppressive regimes are finally overthrown, we do not want revenge and retaliation, but we want those who have committed crimes to be legally prosecuted and punished. We do not think it good for them to 'get away with' their crimes and live in luxury abroad, even though we know that this is sometimes the best solution pragmatically, as recently in Haiti.

To take another current example, the great majority of Christians favor bringing those thought to be responsible for genocide in Bosnia to trial. But if this can be done only by plunging Bosnia back into war, we regretfully accept the lesser evil of letting them 'get away with' their crimes.

We distinguish this desire for justice from revenge. These crimes were not inflicted on us. If individual Christians decide to forego the quest for justice in relation to someone who has wronged them, we consider that admirable, even if ambiguous in its consequences. But to forego the quest for justice when it is others who have been wronged is not generally felt to be Christian. We can admire the Cambodians without agreeing that those who have caused all their suffering should 'get away with' their appalling crimes.

I put this on the table, not because I am asserting it as a superior position or because I think it is more faithful to Jesus. I put it on the table because I believe we Christians should reflect about our passion for retributive justice in the presence of Buddhists who do not share it. It may be that this is yet another area in which we must be creatively transformed as we learn from Buddhists. Or it may be that after such discussion we will retain our present commitments. It may even be that some Buddhists will come to share them. Until we have talked much more, we cannot know what the outcome will be. We need to talk.

This difference carries over to the issue of violence. In our tradition, and for most of us today, there is a tension between the ideal of nonviolence and the commitment to justice. As a result, the unqualified support of nonviolence that King finds in Buddhist tradition is rare in the Christian one. In standard Christian teaching, if not in that of Jesus, there are evils greater than violence or, perhaps better stated, there are occurrences of violence that, if they can only be stopped by violence, should be stopped in that way. Most Christians, probably even most of us engaged in dialogue with Buddhists, are not absolute pacifists. That, too, should be put on the table for discussion.

Perhaps Habito's response to Kasulis will offer the best place to bring these reflections to an end. For the vast majority of Christians the cross is the central symbol. Like any great symbol its meanings are diverse and inexhaustible. But for most it has something to do with the importance, even the supreme importance, of the willingness to suffer for others. Thus, it too is an expression of action and creativity.

It is quite possible for Christians to adopt Buddhist symbols. The image of the meditating and awakened One is attractive to us. But it is probably not possible for Buddhists to adopt the central Christian symbol even in a subordinate role. Especially in the more vivid form of the crucifix, it is my impression that most Buddhists find it discordant, even offensive. This illustrates my impression that, whereas Christianity should be, can be, and is being, transformed in a very deep way by its encounter with Buddhism, there are more drastic limitations to the extent to which Buddhism can be or, from a Buddhist point of view, should be, affected by its encounter with Christianity. But on this question it is for Buddhists to speak.

INDEX

Abe Masao, 13–15, 38–39, 54; and
  kenosis of God, 51–52, 73
Akṣayamatinirdeśa Sūtra, 96–97
Ambedkar, B., 160, 179 n.1
anātman (*anattā*), 109–112,
  215–218. *See also* selflessness
animals, Buddhist view of, 117–118,
  173–174
anti-foundationalism, xxii, 97–99
apocalypse, 139, 225–226
Apostles' Creed, 223
Ariyaratne, A. T., 24, 160
Augustine, Saint, 66

Bergson, Henri, 71
Berrigan, Daniel, 3, 20
Bhāvaviveka, 80, 88, 90, 91, 95–98
bodhisattva: and self-sacrifice, 82;
  and social engagement, 16, 55;
  compassion of, 82, 95, 164
body-soul dualism, 230–232, 237.
  See also resurrection of the body
Brahma-net Sutra, 6
Brahmavihāras, 124–125, 202, 259
Brendle, Franz, 36, 48
Buddha: and emptiness, 79–80; and
  God, 80
Buddha, Gautama: as idealized
  paradigm, 207–208; attitude
  toward other religions, 6–8
Buddha nature, 112

Buddhabhūmyupadeśa, 183
Buddhadāsa, Bhikkhu, 13–14, 20,
  160, 176
Buddhism: ahistoricism of, xxvi,
  182–185, 241; and modernity,
  xxv, 150; attitudes toward other
  religions, 4–16; devotion in, xxiii,
  53, 79–80, 258; relations with
  Confucianism and Taoism, 8–9,
  37; relations with Shinto, 10, 16,
  37; relations with *śramana*, 7–8
Buddhism, Engaged, 160–161
Buddhist-Christian Symposium, 58

Calvin, John, 139
Candrakīrti, 91, 93, 94
change, denial of, 140–142
Chih-i, 249
China, conditions for dialogue, 23
Christ: as foundation, xxiii, 103; as
  God, 68–69; as means of
  knowledge, 102; crucifiction of,
  xxviii, 72, 74, 221–222, 271;
  incarnation of, 69–70, 73–74,
  145, 241; resurrection of, 220,
  222, 223–228; risen, 221–222,
  226, 228, 236
Christianity: encounter with Zen
  Buddhism, 16, 17–18, 45–46,
  150; futuristic, 225–228,
  230–232, 232–237; realized,

272

Index

227–228, 232–237, 240–243;
understanding of human being,
53–54
Chrysostom, St. John, 66
Cobb, John, 15, 43, 47, 52
Cobb-Abe: collaboration of, 15
compassion, Buddhist: and Christian
love, 81–82, 261
concepts, functions of, xxii, 86, 102
Cook, Francis, 36, 49
cosmology, Buddhist, 114–116
creation, Christian view of, 138–140,
142
Creed: Apostles', 223; Nicene, 233

Dalai Lama: as political leader, 160,
203; attitude toward interreligious
dialogue, 14–16, 18–19, 22, 24;
teachings of, 164, 169–170
destruction of Earth, possible:
134–135, 137–138, 152–153
Dhammapāda, 167–168, 170
dialogue, Buddhist-Christian, xii,
xx–xxi, xxx–xxxii, 265–268;
asymmetry of, 149–151, 267–268;
non-negotiables in, xix, 50–51, 61
dialogue, interreligious, xii, xv, xviii,
xix–xxi; benefits for Buddhism of,
xxvi, 271; kinds of, 3–4, 36–39,
43–49, 57–60, 248–249; motives
for engaging in, 4, 22, 42–43;
non-negotiables in, xix, 51–55,
61, 271; social-historical factors
and, 4, 6, 17, 19, 22–25, 60,
267–268
Diamond Sutra, 163
differences, fundamental, between
Buddhism and Christianity: for
Cobb, 269–271; for W. King,
51–55; for Thurston, 65, 74
Dignāga, 90
duḥkha, 176, 210–211

East-West Spiritual Exchange, 18
Eckhart, Meister, 45–46
Edwards, Jonathan, 139, 141–142
egocentricity, xxiv, 130, 247–248,
255, 262. *See also* transformation,
personal; selflessness

emptiness, xiii, xxii, 79, 86; and
Buddha, 79–80; and God, 51–52,
79; as both goal and process, 92;
as empty place, 96–99; as path,
88; concept of, from Christian
perspective, 135–137, 142
enemy, non-recognition of, 169–170
enlightenment, 112, 251; in relation
to religious practice, 166–167;
seven factors of, 121
Enomiya-Lassalle, Hugo Makibi, 17,
46
eschatology, 225–229, 233
Exodus, 67, 68, 145

Ferré, Nels, 71
Fo Kuang Shan, 160

Gaṇḍavyūha Sūtra, 5, 85
Gandhi, Mahatma, 159
Genesis, 67, 72, 130, 142
Ghosananda, Maha, 160–161
Gilson, Etienne, 66, 73
Gimello, Robert, 8
God, xxi, 65–75; and Buddha, 80;
and Buddhist equivalents, 51, 61;
and emptiness, 51–52, 79; and
nondiscriminative wisdom, 252;
as creator, xxiv, 72, 81–82; as
Father, 70, 258; as personal,
66–71, 78–79; as stumbling block
in Buddhist-Christian dialogue,
45; as Void, 136; Buddhist
refutation of, xxiii, 79; reign of,
236, 241

Habito, Ruben, 17, 46
Hawaii, conditions for dialogue in,
60
Heart Sutra, 250
Hebrew Bible, 65, 67, 68, 72, 102,
130, 142, 145, 194, 224–226, 253
hierarchy, institutional, 177
hierarchy of life-forms, 115–116
Hirai Kinzō, 9–10
Hisamatsu Shin'ichi, 12–13, 37–38;
dialogues with Tillich, 10–11, 13
history, narrative, 182–183, 241
Honda Masaaki, 48–49

human being, Buddhist
understanding of, 53–54,
108–114, 172, 259–261. *See also*
identity, personal: trans-human;
self, Christian concept of
Hyujŏng, Ch'ŏnghŏ, 9

identity, personal: trans-human,
117–118, 130–131
identity, religious: and interreligious
dialogue, xviii; in Christianity, 103
ideology, 174–176
idolatry, 176, 221
Ikeda, Daisaku, 61
immeasurables, four. *See*
Brahmavihāras
immortality, 231–232, 236
Insight Meditation Society, 19

James, Letter of, 186–197, 251
Japan, conditions for dialogue, 11,
23
Jātaka tales, 122
Jesus Christ. *See* Christ
John, Gospel According to, 68–74,
102, 227–228
John Paul II, Pope, 12, 81, 178, 182.
See also Vatican
Johnson, Elizabeth, 71
justice, social: in Buddhism, xxvii,
xxxii, 177, 200–203, 253–254; in
Buddhism and Christianity, xxxii,
39, 54–55, 269–271; in *Letter of
James*, 189–190, 194–198

Kant, Immanuel, 213
karma: and justice, 39, 55, 177, 200;
and nonviolence, 167–171
Kennedy, Father Robert, 18
kenosis, 51–52, 73
King, Sallie, 48
King, Winston, 72, 78
Korea, conditions for dialogue, 23
Küng, Hans, 62
Kyoto School, 12–13, 14. *See also*
Nishitani Keiji

LaCugna, Catherine, 72
Last Judgment, 222, 233–235

Laws, Sophie, 190–191
liberation, ultimate, xvii–xxix,
208–209. *See also* transformation,
ultimate
Lotus Sutra, 16, 80
love: in Buddhism and Christianity,
xxiii, 81–82, 259, 261; in
Christianity, 71–75
Luke, Gospel According to, 225, 229

Madhyamaka school, xxii, 85; and
metaphor of vision, 94–96; and
reason, 89–90, 92; and two truths,
93–94, 95–96, 99; and Yogācāra,
97; anti-foundationalism in, xxii,
97–99; concept of "ultimate,"
90–94, 98–99
Mahāparinibbaṇa-sutta, 120–121,
210
Mark, Gospel According to,
102–103, 145, 229
materiality, xxiv, 137–138, 141–142,
256–257
Matthew, Gospel According to, 75,
102, 145, 222, 223, 225, 229,
233–235, 239–241, 254, 255
meditation: and worship, 52–53
Merton, Thomas, 103; dialogue with
Suzuki, 11, 16, 74
mettā, 124–125
modernity, challenges of, 150
Monastic Interreligious Dialogue, 18
morality, ambiguity in, 142–146

Nāgārjuna, xiii, 5, 93, 98, 183, 213,
250
Nara Yasuaki, 23–24
Naropa Institute, 19
New Testament, 68–74, 102–104,
145, 186–197, 222, 223–237,
239–241, 254
Nhat Chi Mai, 20
Nhat Hanh, Thich, 3, 19–20, 24,
161; teachings of, 162–163,
165–166, 170, 175, 201
Nicene Creed, 233
Nipponzan Myohoji, 161, 253
Nishitani Keiji, 12, 14–15, 98,
258–259. *See also* Kyoto School

Niwano Nikkyo, 11–12, 16
non-adversarial ethics, Buddhist, 171–173
nonviolence, in Buddhism, 167–171, 173, 271; in Christianity, 132, 271

Ohtani, Kosho, 21

Parable of the Raft, 174
Parinirvāṇa Sūtra. *See Mahāparinibbaṇa-sutta*
pilgrimage, 97
practice, religious: and realized Christianity, 254; as central, xxx, 248–262; as transformative, xxii, 113, 248–262; in relation to enlightenment, 166–167; in relation to environmental concern, 119–125, 154; in relation to social engagement, 162–167
pragmatism, Buddhist, 174–176, 251
Pran, Dith, 168–169
predestination, 139
Protestant Principle, 176
Psalms, 65, 67
Pure Land Buddhism, 53–54, 250, 251, 255, 258, 259

Quakers, 17, 44
Quang Duc, Thich, 19
Questions of King Milinda, 216–217

Rahner, Karl, 240
reality, ultimate, xxi–xxiii; Buddhist views of, 125, 250; Christian views of, 65, 68, 101, 103
reason: in Madhyamaka school, 89–90, 92
redemption, doctrine of, 139
resurrection of the body, 230–232, 236
rights, human: in Engaged Buddhism, 173
rights language: and Buddhism, 117–118
Risshō Kōseikai, 11, 16, 160
Rosenberger, Nancy, 259–260
Rupp, George, 47

salvation: in Christianity, 221–222, 228–229, 231–232, 239–240; outside Buddhism, 6–9; outside Christianity, 240
Saṃyutta Nikāya, 121
Sanbōkyōdan, 17
sanctification, 131
Sands, Kathleen, 143
Sangharakshita, 114
Śāntideva, 79, 118, 125
Scarry, Elaine, 137–138, 144, 256
Schreiter, Robert J., 48
Scripture on Buddha Land, 190–191
self: Christian concept of, 128–130. *See also* human being, Buddhist understanding of
selflessness, 163–167. *See also* egocentricity
sentience, 115–116, 118
Sharpe, Eric, 3–4
Shin Buddhism. *See* Pure Land Buddhism
Shinran, 255, 259
Shinshūren, 11
Simmer-Brown, Judith, 19
sin, 221–222, 253
Sivaraksa, Sulak, 20–21, 44, 160, 175
social engagement, xxv–xxvii, 269; and dialogue, 19–22, 54–55, 57–58, 262; and nondiscriminative wisdom, 253–254; and selflessness, 163–167; Buddhist-Christian mutual influence in, 159–160
Sōen Shaku, 10
Soka Gakkai, 61, 160
soteriology. *See* liberation, ultimate
Sri Lanka, conditions for dialogue, 24
Streng, Frederick J., xi–xvi, xvii; on emptiness, 84–86, 92, 98–99, 136, 248; on religion, 65, 103, 186, 208
śūnyatā. *See* emptiness
Suttanipāta, 7
Suu Kyi, Aung San, 160
Suzuki, D. T., 10–11, 37, 45–46, 52; dialogue with Merton, 11, 16
Swidler, Leonard, 4, 25 n.4

Ta-hui Tsung-kao, 8–9
Tertullian, 71
Thailand, conditions for dialogue, 20–21, 24
Theological Encounter with Buddhism Group, 15
theology, 266–268
Three Religions, 8–9
Thurman, Robert, 47
Tibet, conditions for dialogue, 24
Tillich, Paul, 42, 65; dialogues with Hisamatsu, 10–11, 13
Toynbee, Arnold, 74, 258
transformation, personal, 131, 222, 247–248, 256
transformation, ultimate, xiii, xiv, 84, 102, 222, 255. *See also* liberation, ultimate
Trinity, Christian, 70–71; and Buddhism, 80–81
Tsong-kha-pa, 86–89, 95–96, 97, 184
two truths: in Madhyamaka, 93–94, 95–96, 99, 250

Ucko, Hans, 58
"ultimate," concept of: in Christianity, 229; in Madhyamaka, 90–94, 98–99
Upanishads, 215–216

Vatican, 12. *See also* John Paul II, Pope
Vietnam, conditions for dialogue, 19–20, 24
violence and nonviolence: in Christianity, 132, 271
vision: as metaphor in Christianity, 103–104; as philosophy in Madhyamaka, 94–96
von Brück, Michael, 71

wisdom, non-discriminative, xxx, 187–195, 249–250, 251–253
Won Buddhism, 160
World Conference on Religion and Peace (WCRP), 11–12, 21
World Council of Churches, 58
World Parliament of Religions (1993), 22, 43
World's Parliament of Religions (1893), 9–10, 22, 43
worship: and meditation, 52–53

Yamada Kōun, 17–18, 46
Yasutani Roshi, 54
Yogācāra, 97

Zen Buddhism: encounter with Christianity, 16, 17–18, 45–46, 150
Zen-Christian Colloquium, 17, 23